"Barry Strauss has done it again: *M   * ieless
wisdom of the classical world with   rfare.
This is a stunning handbook on leadership—both on and off the battlefield."

—Nathaniel Fick, author of *One Bullet Away:*
The Making of a Marine Officer

"Barry Strauss has written a riveting, fast-paced, penetrating volume around three powerful war leaders—Alexander the Great, Hannibal, and Caesar. While other classicists draw on ancient philosophers for lessons on the life well lived, Professor Strauss looks to men of action and determination for lessons on leadership and strategy. It's a great read, packed with terrific insights."

—Karl Rove

"With *Masters of Command,* Barry Strauss further establishes himself as one of our premier historians of the classical world. . . . There are lessons here not only for budding military strategists but also for 'great captains' of the boardroom. And, most important, there is a crackling good read for anyone who delves into this insightful and entertaining new book."

—Max Boot, Jeane J. Kirkpatrick Senior Fellow for National Security Studies, The Council on Foreign Relations, and author of *War Made New: Technology, Warfare, and the Course of History: 1500 to Today*

"Alexander, Hannibal, and Caesar—this is a book on leadership like no other. A rare combination of stirring dialogue, masterful ancient scholarship, and sage advice—both lessons and warnings. Just as Asian corporate planners read Sun Tzu, Western entrepreneurs and strategic thinkers will want to read *Masters of Command.*"

—Robert L. O'Connell, author of *The Ghosts of Cannae: Hannibal and the Darkest Hour of the Roman Republic*

"Barry Strauss has no superior and few counterparts as a scholar of ancient military history and a student of war."

—Dennis Showalter, former president, Society for Military History

ALSO BY BARRY STRAUSS

The Spartacus War

The Trojan War: A New History

The Battle of Salamis: The Naval Encounter That
Saved Greece—and Western Civilization

What If?: The World's Foremost Military Historians
Imagine What Might Have Been *(contributor)*

Western Civilization: The Continuing Experiment
(with Thomas F. X. Noble and others)

War and Democracy: A Comparative Study of the Korean War
and the Peloponnesian War
(with David McCann, coeditor)

Rowing Against the Current: Learning to Scull at Forty

Fathers and Sons in Athens: Ideology and Society
in the Era of the Peloponnesian War

Hegemonic Rivalry: From Thucydides to the Nuclear Age
(with Richard Ned Lebow, coeditor)

The Anatomy of Error: Ancient Military Disasters
and Their Lessons for Modern Strategists *(with Josiah Ober)*

Athens After the Peloponnesian War: Class, Faction and Policy,
403–386 B.C.

MASTERS *of* COMMAND

ALEXANDER, HANNIBAL, CAESAR, *and the Genius of* LEADERSHIP

BARRY STRAUSS

SIMON & SCHUSTER PAPERBACKS

NEW YORK · LONDON · TORONTO · SYDNEY · NEW DELHI

Simon & Schuster Paperbacks
A Division of Simon & Schuster, Inc.
1230 Avenue of the Americas
New York, NY 10020

First Simon & Schuster trade paperback edition May 2013

SIMON & SCHUSTER PAPERBACKS and colophon are registered trademarks of
Simon & Schuster, Inc.

For information about special discounts for bulk purchases,
please contact Simon & Schuster Special Sales at
1-866-506-1949 or business@simonandschuster.com.

The Simon & Schuster Speakers Bureau can bring authors to your live event.
For more information or to book an event, contact the Simon & Schuster Speakers
Bureau at 1-866-248-3049 or visit our website at www.simonspeakers.com.

Designed by Akasha Archer

Manufactured in the United States of America

20 19 18 17 16 15 14 13
The Library of Congress has cataloged the hardcover edition as follows:

Strauss, Barry S.
    Masters of command : Alexander, Hannibal, Caesar, and the genius of leadership / Barry
Strauss.
        p. cm.
    Includes bibliographical references and index.
  1. Generals—History. 2. Command of troops—History. 3. Military history, Ancient.
  I. Title.
    UB200.S78 2012
    355.0092'237—dc23   2011036243

ISBN 978-1-4391-6448-8
ISBN 978-1-4391-6449-5 (pbk)
ISBN 978-1-4391-6907-0 (ebook)

To Donald Kagan, Walter LaFeber,
and in memory of Alvin Bernstein

CONTENTS

AUTHOR'S NOTE

Ancient names are spelled following the style of the standard reference work, *The Oxford Classical Dictionary*, 3rd ed. (Oxford: Oxford University Press, 1999).

Translations from the Greek or Latin are my own, unless otherwise noted.

CHRONOLOGY
(All dates are B.C.)

325	Alexander returns to Iran
324–323	Alexander prepares invasion of Arabia
Summer 324	Banquet at Opis
Autumn 324	Death of Hephaestion
June 10, 323	Death of Alexander
280–275	Pyrrhus's invasion of Italy and Sicily
264–241	First Punic War
247	Birth of Hannibal
237	Hamilcar Barca goes to Spain, taking Hannibal with him
228	Death of Hamilcar; Hasdrubal the Handsome, Hamilcar's son-in-law, now in command in Spain
226	Ebro treaty
221	Death of Hasdrubal the Handsome; Hannibal now in command in Spain
219	Hannibal captures Saguntum after eight-month siege; Rome issues ultimatum
218–201	Second Punic War
Autumn 218	Hannibal crosses the Alps; leaves his brother, Hasdrubal, in charge of Spain
November 218	Battle of the Ticinus River
December 218	Battle of the Trebia River
Spring 217	Romans defeat Carthaginian fleet off the Ebro River in Spain
June 21, 217*	Battle of Lake Trasimene

*All specific months and days in this list, from this point on, follow the Roman calendar in use at the time.

Summer–Fall 217   Fabius is appointed dictator and begins delaying strategy

August 2, 216   Battle of Cannae

Late 216   Capua joins Hannibal

215   Alliance between Hannibal and Macedonian king Philip V; Syracuse joins Hannibal

212   Hannibal takes Tarentum but Romans hold the citadel; Rome retakes Syracuse

211   Hannibal marches on Rome; Rome retakes Capua

210   Scipio takes New Carthage

209   Battle of Baecula; Rome retakes Tarentum

207   Battle of the Metaurus River; death of Hasdrubal, Hannibal's brother

206   Battle of Ilipa

205   Mago invades Italy; Hannibal places inscription in temple of Hera Lacinia

203   Hannibal returns to Africa; death of Mago

Autumn 202   Battle of Zama

201   Carthage agrees to treaty with Rome ending Second Punic War

196   Hannibal serves as chief magistrate of Carthage

195–183   Hannibal in the East

183   Death of Hannibal

149–146   Third Punic War

146   Carthage is destroyed

100   Birth of Caesar

82–81   Sulla is dictator

66–62	Pompey conquers the East
61–60	Caesar campaigns in western Spain
58–50	Caesar conquers Gaul
January 12, 49	Caesar crosses the Rubicon
February 49	Siege of Corfinium
March 17, 49	Pompey evacuates Brundisium
Spring–Autumn 49	Siege of Massilia
June–August 49	Battle of Ilerda
January 4, 48	Caesar crosses the Adriatic Sea
April–July 48	Dyrrachium campaign
August 9, 48	Battle of Pharsalus
September 28, 48	Death of Pompey
Autumn 48	Caesar meets Cleopatra
Winter 48–Spring 47	Caesar's war in Egypt
August 2, 47	Battle of Zela
December 25, 47	Caesar leaves Rome for Africa
46	Carthage refounded as a Roman colony
April 6, 46	Battle of Thapsus
Summer 46	Caesar celebrates four triumphs
March 17, 45	Battle of Munda
October 45	Caesar celebrates fifth triumph
February 44	Caesar named dictator for life
March 15, 44	Caesar assassinated

GLOSSARY OF KEY NAMES

Alexander the Great or Alexander III (356–323 B.C.) King of Macedon and conqueror of the Persian Empire.

Antipater (ca. 397–319 B.C.) Governor of Macedonia in Alexander's absence, Antipater organized the defense of the home front against a revolt by the Greek city-states.

Bessus (d. 329 B.C.) Satrap of Bactria, organizer of coup against Darius III and pretender to the Persian throne as Artaxerxes V, he was captured and executed by Alexander.

Craterus (d. 321 B.C.) Probably Alexander's best general after the death of Parmenio, he held important commands at Issus and Gaugamela and in Sogdiana and India.

Darius III (d. 330 B.C.) Ruled the Persian Empire beginning in 336 and organized resistance against Alexander, whom he faced in battle at Issus and Gaugamela.

Hephaestion (d. 324 B.C.) Alexander's closest friend and possibly his lover, Hephaestion had enormous influence with the king.

Memnon of Rhodes (d. 333 B.C.) Greek mercenary in the service of Persia, he commanded the Persian fleet and handed Alexander his worst defeats before his untimely death.

Parmenio (ca. 400–330 B.C.) Veteran general of Philip II, he played a key role as a commander in Alexander's pitched battles but was eventually executed as a rival.

Perdiccas (d. 321 B.C.) One of Alexander's best generals, both as an infantry and cavalry commander.

Philip of Macedon or Philip II, King of Macedon (382–336 B.C.) Father of Alexander, he founded the Macedonian empire and began the project of conquering Persia.

Porus, Indian king who fought Alexander bravely in the Macedonian's last pitched battle, at the Hydaspes (326 B.C.). He was rewarded by Alexander with additional land in spite of his defeat.

Ptolemy, Son of Lagus, or Ptolemy I (367–282 B.C.) One of Alexander's leading generals, he later became king of Egypt and established a dynasty; he also wrote an important history of Alexander.

Spitamenes (d. 328 B.C.) Warlord of Sogdiana and one of Alexander's toughest opponents for a while, but he faltered and his own men eventually killed him.

Gaius Flaminius (d. 217 B.C.) Prominent Roman politician and general who walked into Hannibal's trap at Lake Trasimene and was cut down with most of his army.

Gaius Terentius Varro (fl. 218–200 B.C.) Consul and commanding Roman general at Cannae (216 B.C.), Varro, along with the other consul and second-in-command, Lucius Aemilius Paullus, carried out tactics that led to disaster.

Hamilcar Barca (d. 228 B.C.) Father of Hannibal and Carthage's greatest general in his day, he began the conquest of southern Spain and may have conveyed a hatred of Rome to his sons.

Hannibal (247–183 B.C.) Carthage's greatest general, he was the driving force for war with Rome and the strategist behind the invasion of Italy.

Hasdrubal (d. 207 B.C.) Hannibal's younger brother, he was left in charge of Spain but lost it to the Romans. He marched his surviving troops overland to Italy, where he was defeated and killed at the Metaurus.

Mago (d. 203 B.C.) Hannibal's youngest brother, he invaded northwestern Italy by sea in 205, in support of Hannibal, but he was defeated and wounded and died at sea on the way home.

Maharbal, Son of Himilco (fl. 217–216 B.C.) One of Hannibal's main cavalry officers, he defeated a large Roman cavalry force after Trasimene and urged Hannibal to send his cavalry to Rome right after the victory at Cannae.

Masinissa (238–148 B.C.) King of Numidia whose defection from Carthage to Rome, with his excellent cavalry, sealed Hannibal's fate at Zama.

Polybius (ca. 200–ca. 118 B.C.) Historian who wrote the best surviving account of the Second Punic War, Polybius was a Greek statesman who was sent to Italy as a Roman hostage, and rose to a position of influence with the Scipio family.

Pyrrhus of Epirus (319–272 B.C.) He invaded Italy to support Greek cities against Rome and won every battle but lost the war. He was both a role model and a warning to Hannibal.

Quintus Fabius Maximus Verucosus (d. 203 B.C.) Dictator in 217 and a prominent general and politician during most of the rest of the Second Punic War, he led the Roman policy of delay and attrition that stymied Hannibal in Italy.

Scipio Africanus or Publius Cornelius Scipio Africanus (236–183 B.C.) Rome's greatest general of the Second Punic War, he conquered Spain and North Africa and defeated Hannibal at Zama.

Cato, Marcus Porcius or Cato the Younger (95–46 B.C.) Caesar's most bitter and most principled enemy, his suicide made him a symbol of republican liberty.

Cicero, Marcus Tullius (106–43 B.C.) Rome's greatest orator, Cicero hesitated during the civil war before supporting Pompey; eventually, he received a pardon from Caesar. He is most important to us for the light his letters and speeches throw on Roman public life.

Cleopatra or Cleopatra VII (69–30 B.C.) Queen of Egypt and mistress of Julius Caesar and, later, Mark Antony, she was a brilliant stateswoman who skillfully maneuvered for political power and to try to preserve her kingdom's independence.

Gaius Julius Caesar (100–44 B.C.) The greatest general of the later Roman republic and perhaps of all Roman history, he was also a shrewd politician and an excellent writer.

Lucius Domitius Ahenobarbus (d. 48 B.C.) Roman politician and enemy of Caesar, whom he fought at Corfinium, Massilia, and Pharsalus.

Mark Antony or Marcus Antonius (83–30 B.C.) One of Caesar's leading commanders, he proved a better general than politician.

Metellus Scipio or Quintus Caecilius Metellus Pius Scipio (d. 46 B.C.) Governor of Syria, he commanded the center of Pompey's lines at Pharsalus and fled to North Africa, where he led the opposition to Caesar and was defeated at Thapsus. He killed himself afterward.

Pharnaces II (63–47 B.C.) King of Bosporus (in modern Turkey) and son of Mithradates, a famous enemy of Rome, Pharnaces suffered a crushing defeat against Caesar at Zela and was killed soon after by a domestic enemy.

Pompey or Gnaeus Pompeius Magnus (106–48 B.C.) Second only to Caesar as a Roman commander and statesman in the late republic, he went from being Caesar's ally to his leading opponent—and the result was civil war.

Titus Labienus (ca. 100–45 B.C.) Caesar's second-in-command in Gaul, he defected to Pompey and fought to the bitter end against his former chief.

MASTERS *of* COMMAND

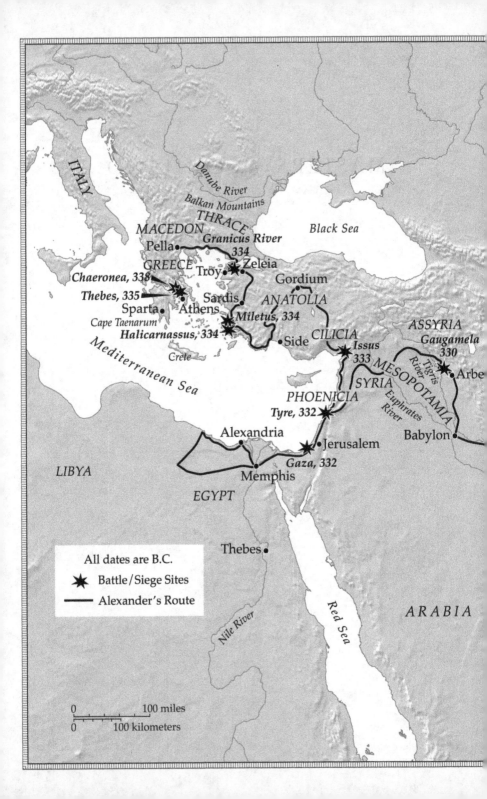

ITALY

Danube River

Balkan Mountains

THRACE

MACEDON

Pella

GREECE

Chaeronea, 338

Thebes, 335

Sparta

Athens

Cape Taenarum

Halicarnassus, 334

Crete

Troy

Granicus River
334

Zeleia

Black Sea

Gordium

Sardis

ANATOLIA

Miletus, 334

Side

CILICIA

Issus
333

ASSYRIA

Gaugamela
330

Tigris River

Arbe

MESOPOTAMIA

Euphrates River

Mediterranean Sea

SYRIA

PHOENICIA

Tyre, 332

Babylon

Alexandria

Gaza, 332

Jerusalem

LIBYA

Memphis

EGYPT

Thebes

Nile River

Red Sea

ARABIA

All dates are B.C.

★ Battle/Siege Sites

——— Alexander's Route

0   100 miles

0   100 kilometers

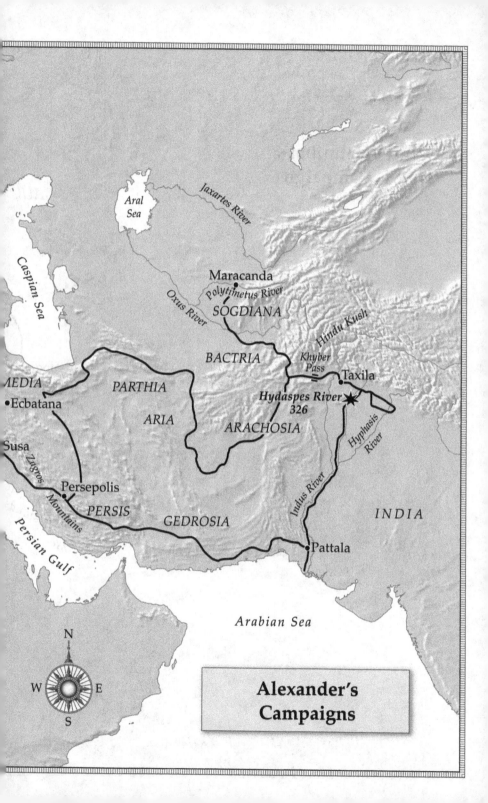

Aral Sea

Caspian Sea

Jaxartes River

Oxus River

Maracanda

Polytimetus River

SOGDIANA

Hindu Kush

BACTRIA

Khyber Pass

Taxila

MEDIA

PARTHIA

Ecbatana

ARIA

ARACHOSIA

Hydaspes River
326

Hyphasis River

Susa

Zagros Mountains

Persepolis

PERSIS

GEDROSIA

Indus River

INDIA

Persian Gulf

Pattala

Arabian Sea

N
W   E
S

**Alexander's
Campaigns**

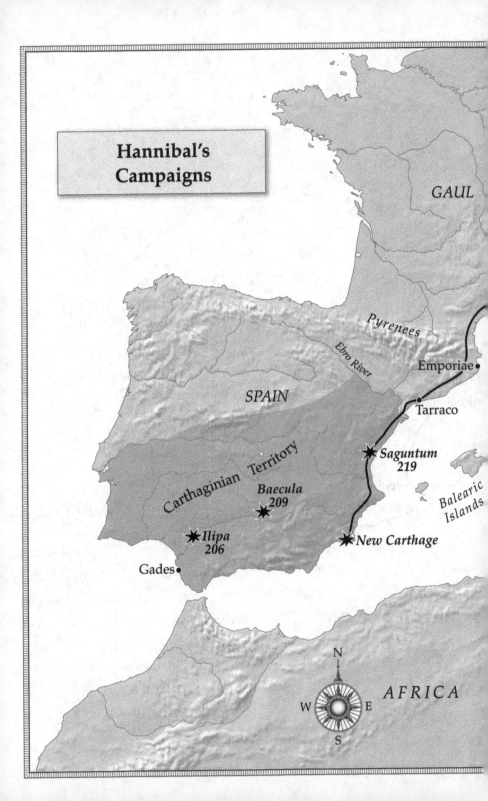

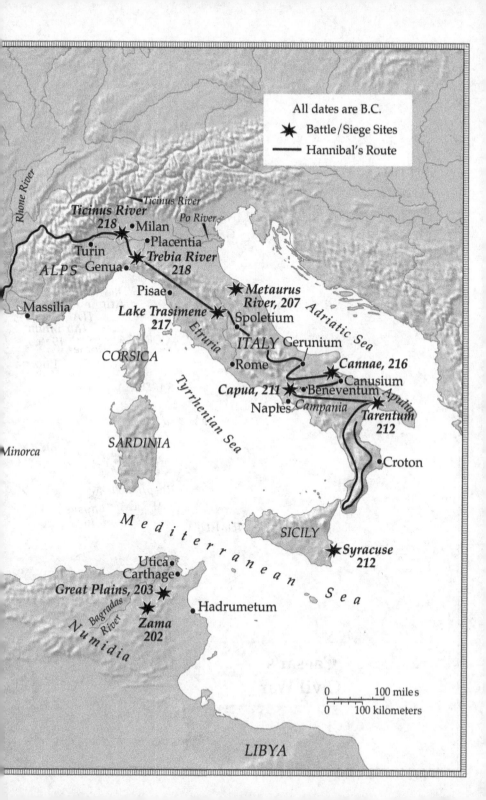

All dates are B.C.
★ Battle/Siege Sites
— Hannibal's Route

Rhone River

Ticinus River
218

Ticinus River

Po River

•Milan
•Placentia

Trebia River
218

Turin

ALPS Genua

Pisae•

Metaurus River, 207

Spoletium

Lake Trasimene
217

Etruria

ITALY Gerunium

•Rome

Cannae, 216

Canusium

Capua, 211 •Beneventum

Naples• *Campania*

Apulia

Tarentum
212

Adriatic Sea

CORSICA

Tyrrhenian Sea

SARDINIA

Minorca

•Croton

Massilia

Mediterranean Sea

SICILY

Syracuse
212

Utica•
Carthage•

Great Plains, 203 ★

Bagradas River

Hadrumetum•

Zama
202

Numidia

0   100 miles
0   100 kilometers

LIBYA

Caesar's
Civil War

Danube River

Black Sea

ARMENIA

yrrachium
48

Philippi
42

PONTUS

Zela
47

PARTHIAN
EMPIRE

a

MACEDONIA

ANATOLIA

Brundisium
49

THESSALY

Corcyra

Actium
31

Pharsalus
48

ASIA

Tarsus

ACHAEA

CILICIA

•Antioch

SYRIA

S e a

JUDAEA

Alexandria
48-47

EGYPT

Nile River

Red Sea

All dates are B.C.

★ Battle/Siege Sites

0   100   200 miles

0   100 200 300 kilometers

I

TEN QUALITIES OF SUCCESSFUL COMMANDERS

YOU COULDN'T MISS THE KING. THE BATTLE WAS ALREADY A MUDDLE OF MEN and horses in motion and yet he was unmistakable. He was short but muscular and he sat on a huge black steed. Shining in his splendid armor, with tall white plumes fixed on either side of his helmet, Alexander the Great, king of Macedon, led the second wave of the Companion Cavalry. A blast of bugles and a roar of battle cries had sent them off, galloping across the shallow Granicus River and up onto the opposite bank, under the waiting eyes of Persia's finest horsemen. Flush with victory over the first wave of the Macedonian attack, the Persians charged the enemy with loud shouts.

Two Persian brothers zeroed in on Alexander himself. Rhoesaces and Sphithridates were both aristocrats; Sphithridates was governor of Ionia, a wealthy province on what is today Turkey's Aegean coast. The brothers charged and Sphithridates split Alexander's helmet with his scimitar and grazed Alexander's hair. Alexander struck back and drove his wooden lance into Spithridates's chest. As Spithridates died, his brother swung his sword at Alexander's naked head and aimed a deathblow. In the split second before he made contact his arm was sliced off by the deft sword of Cleitus the Black, a Macedonian officer. Alexander was saved. It was a May day in northwestern Anatolia (Turkey) in 334 B.C.

• • •

One hundred eighteen years later, the din of battle sounded across the rolling hills of southern Italy, where the armies of Rome and Carthage were locked in a death struggle outside the little town of Cannae. As the Roman legions marched steadily forward, the Carthaginians gritted their teeth and retreated, taking casualties as they went. Would they collapse under the Roman onslaught or would they draw the enemy into a trap?

Both sides' commanders led from the front. The Roman consul Paullus plunged into the thick of things, urging his infantry to crush the foe. His Carthaginian opponent faced him not far away, in the center of the Carthaginian infantry line, positioned where he had been since the start of the fighting hours earlier. Hannibal of Carthage commanded his troops in person.

Hannibal rode on horseback, wearing a mail breastplate and a plumed helmet, and carrying a round shield. His face was famous for its bright and fiery look. He had only one good eye, having lost the vision in his right eye to disease during a long, hard march a year earlier.

The battle had reached its deciding moment. Just a little longer and the Carthaginians could spring their trap, but they would be hard-pressed to hold on against Rome's power. Knowing this, Hannibal rode among the soldiers, heartening and cheering on his men and even trading blows with the Roman enemy. If the risk he was taking didn't kill him, Hannibal would achieve triumph. It was the afternoon of August 2, 216 B.C.

One hundred sixty-eight years later, in the spring of 48 B.C., civil war gripped Rome. The conflict raged first in Italy, Spain, and southern France. Then the central front moved eastward. The focus shifted to the coast of Epirus (today Albania), the naval gateway to the Adriatic Sea and Italy. Two great generals, Pompey and Caesar, were jockeying for position on the land outside the strategic port city of Dyrrachium (modern Durrës, Albania). Each man led a large army, camped outside of town.

They played a waiting game, punctuated by bursts of fighting. Each army tried to outflank the other and starve it out through a series of walls, moats, forts, and towers across the hilly terrain. Suddenly, in early May, boredom gave way to a bloody engagement. Deserters from Caesar's army revealed a weak point in their lines. Pompey used the information to attack and take Caesar by surprise. But Caesar rallied and launched a counterattack that same day. It started out well, but then his men found themselves in a maze of abandoned walls and ditches. When they were assaulted in turn, they panicked.

Caesar was there, among his men, an example of courage. Tall and sinewy, he stood firm. Soldiers ran by in retreat, still holding their battle standards—long poles lined with metal disks and topped with a carved image of a human hand. Caesar grabbed the standards with his own hands and commanded the men to stop. His words were usually persuasive and his black eyes shone with vigor. Yet not a single man stopped; some looked at the ground in shame, and some even threw away their standards. Finally, one of the standard bearers, with his pole upside down, dared to thrust the sharp end of it at Caesar himself. The commander's bodyguards cut off his arm at the last moment and saved Caesar's life. If not for them, the civil war might have ended on the spot.

Three generals, three battles, and one pattern: a life thrown into the thick of combat. But combat was only the price of admission. These weren't just commanders—they were soldier-statesmen conquering an empire. Alexander the Great, Hannibal, and Julius Caesar are the big three of ancient military history. Alexander set the pattern. Hannibal came a little more than a century later, calling Alexander the greatest general of all time. Caesar appeared about 150 years later and wept, as a young man, when he saw a statue of Alexander, lamenting that he, Caesar, hadn't conquered anything yet.

Each was a master of war. They had to look far beyond the battlefield. They had to decide not only how to fight but whom to fight and why. They had to define victory and know when to end the war. They had to envision the postwar world and to design a new world order that would bring stability and lasting power. In short, they were not only field commanders but also statesmen.

Yet each would probably want to be remembered as a battle hero. Never mind the long hours of silent contemplation, the continual hashing out of plans in conferences, the negotiations for war-winning alliances, the tedious details of stocking granaries or removing wagons stuck in the mud. The thick of bloody battle—primitive, elemental—is where they felt most at home.

In battle, they were heroic. As field commanders, leaders of the army in combat and on campaign, they were peerless. As strategists, they have a mixed record. Their war plans reached for the skies, but only Alexander and Caesar got there. As statesmen all three fell short. Neither Alexander nor Caesar, much less Hannibal, ever solved the problem of how to bring about or how to maintain the new world order that each one sought.

Alexander (356–323 B.C.) conquered the largest empire the world had yet known—Persia. But he died just short of turning thirty-three, after suffering a humiliating mutiny by his men and without having provided for his succession or a plan to administer his vast new domain. His empire immediately collapsed into civil war and chaos. Fifty years later, it consisted of half a dozen new kingdoms, all governed by Alexander's fellow Greeks, but none ruled by his family. Far from establishing a dynasty, Alexander was the last of his line to reign.

Hannibal (247–183 B.C.) took command of a colonial empire in Spain founded by his father and expanded by his brother-in-law. Then Rome challenged his control. Rome and Carthage were blood enemies, having already fought a major war over Sicily, which Rome had won. Now, with the support of his home government in Carthage, Hannibal launched a war to defang Rome once and for all. He accomplished the spectacular feat of crossing the Alps in the snow with his army and his elephants, and marched into Italy. There he handed Rome its greatest battlefield defeats, including one of the most thorough victories in the annals of warfare, Cannae (216 B.C.) Yet he lost the war. Like Alexander, he was the last member of his family to hold political power in his state.

Caesar (100–44 B.C.) followed up the epoch-making conquest of Gaul by fighting and winning a civil war against the vast wealth and manpower of the Roman republic. Caesar began a legislative program to change the republic into a monarchy, but politics bored him. He was more interested in starting a new campaign against the Parthians (an Iranian kingdom). Yet before he could leave for the front he was stabbed to death by a crowd of Roman senators, at the foot of his enemy's statue on the Ides of March. Caesar did establish a dynasty, though—or rather, his great-nephew Octavian (63 B.C.–A.D. 14) did. In his will, Caesar named Octavian as his adopted son and heir, but Octavian had to fight for fifteen long and bloody years before the rest of the Roman world accepted him. Octavian is better known by the name he later chose—Augustus, Rome's first emperor.

Each of the three generals was a military prodigy—and a gambler. They confronted empires: enemies with far larger armies than their own; enemies who enjoyed strategic command of the sea; and enemies with the home-court advantage. Yet these generals risked everything for victory.

All three led their forces in a dramatic sweep into enemy territory: Caesar crossed the Rubicon, Hannibal crossed the Alps, and Alexander crossed the Dardanelles. Alexander began a long war in the Persian empire (334–323 B.C.), Hannibal began a struggle with Rome known today as the Second Punic War (218–201 B.C.), and Caesar started the civil war (49–45 B.C.). Each man next experienced a mix of success and failure, and then went on to win a smashing victory in battle. Yet in the end Hannibal lost his war and Alexander and Caesar won empty victories.

I wrote this book to explain why. The story of these three supreme commanders is as fresh today as it was two thousand years ago. It offers lessons for leaders in many walks of life, from the war room to the boardroom—lessons and warnings.

THE TEN KEYS TO SUCCESS

When Theodore Ayrault Dodge dubbed Alexander, Hannibal, and Caesar as "great captains" in 1889—in a book of that name—most of his readers admired imperial ambition. Today, after the bloody twentieth century, we are less sure of it. The grandeur of these three great generals inspires but their lethality is terrifying. They are three gods of war, yet they are also three devils. We admire these men for the same reason that we fear them, because they seem to be superhuman in some ways. They stand for greatness—and for ambiguity. They were great but not good. Or, rather, the good in them was mixed with evil.

All the more reason to ask what accounts for the great commanders' success—their virtues or their vices? Each had his own style. Alexander appears in the biblical Book of Daniel as a one-horned he-goat, forceful and impetuous, but I prefer to think of him as a horse—spirited, speedy, tough, and more than able to haul a heavy load when needed. Hannibal was a great feline predator, like a leopard—cunning, strong, agile, nimble, stealthy, and opportunistic. Caesar was a wolf—fast and relentless, a skillful and murderous hunter.

But the main reason for their success was the things they held in common. They knew how to play the game of war and they brought certain qualities to it. Let's begin by describing those qualities and then we'll turn to the game.

Some of these qualities are admirable, others not. Some are admirable only in moderation. But conquerors are rarely moderate, least of all Alexander, Hannibal, and Caesar.

Ten qualities underlay the wartime success of these three great commanders. The first nine are ambition, judgment, leadership, audacity, agility, infrastructure, strategy, terror, and branding. The tenth is different, as it is something that happens to a commander rather than something he has—the quality of Divine Providence.

1. Ambition

The Greeks said it best. Their word for "ambition" is *philotimia*, which literally means "love of honor." Their word for "drive" is *horme*, which has overtones of emotion—think of our word "hormone." And a third Greek word, *megalopsychia*, translates poorly into English but we need it to understand these great leaders. It means "greatness of soul," referring to a passionate drive to achieve great things and to be rewarded with supreme honor.

Enter Alexander or Hannibal or Caesar.

They were members of what Abraham Lincoln once called "the tribe of the eagle." They brimmed over with talent. Their self-assurance knew no limits. Men of towering ambition, they thirsted and burned for distinction. Nothing less than the conquest of new worlds would satisfy them.

Their aims were lofty but also egotistical and unjust. Alexander spread democracy and Greek civilization but he attacked Persia to conquer an empire, not to right a wrong. Hannibal wanted to free his country from Rome's chokehold but he rejected negotiation in order to rival Alexander's conquests. Caesar stood up for the interests of ordinary people but he burned to be the first man in Rome and he didn't hesitate to overturn the republic.

The great commanders were not accountants who encourage CEOs to downsize their plans. They could no more stop conquering than lions can stop hunting.

2. Judgment

Good judgment, guided by education, intuition, and experience, defines all three commanders' success in war. When it comes to politics, though, Caesar is in a class of his own, followed by Alexander and Hannibal in a distant third.

They were immensely intelligent but they each had something more—a quality known as strategic intuition. When faced with a new situation, each could draw from past experience and come up with the right answer. They knew how to operate without perfect information and they were unflappable under pressure. They were able to think creatively, rapidly, and effectively. And they could read others like a book. They knew war but they also knew people.

They did not need on-the-job training. Before they crossed the Hellespont, the Alps, or the Rubicon, our three leaders had all acquired proficiency in the art of war.

Alexander and Hannibal learned at the feet of their famous warrior fathers—Philip II, the all-conquering king of Macedon, and Hamilcar Barca, the Carthaginian general who fought Rome to a standstill. Caesar came from an aristocratic family and he practiced the traditional arts of the Roman nobility—oratory and war. By the time he crossed the Rubicon in 49 B.C., at age fifty, he had gone to the greatest of all schools of war: he had conquered Gaul (that is, the equivalent of most of modern-day France as well as Belgium).

Although super-competent as soldiers, each of the three commanders had his blind spot. Alexander ignored navies, Hannibal ignored sieges, and Caesar barely knew logistics. These were significant disabilities.

Before he became a conqueror, Caesar was a politician and he mastered the power game in Rome. Before invading Persia, Alexander got the hang of Macedon's court intrigue and backstabbing, but that was a far cry from governing a huge empire. When he attacked Rome, Hannibal had not set foot in Carthage since the age of nine—nearly twenty years before—and when it came to domestic politics, he barely knew his ABCs. He would eventually pay for his ignorance.

3. Leadership

They had iron in their souls. The great commanders were decisive, forceful, and assured. They had staffs whom they consulted—and frequently over-ruled. They thrived on giving orders. Men obeyed, and not just because of their rank: they obeyed because their commander had earned their respect. The men had learned to trust their leader with their lives.

They breathed dignity. Only Alexander was a king but Hannibal and Caesar were lordly. Yet they all had the common touch, especially that politician Caesar.

"I didn't follow the cause. I followed the man—and he was my friend."

With these simple words, a lieutenant of Caesar summed up a secret of the great commanders' success. They appealed to their followers not just as conquerors or chiefs but also as men. They had those special personal qualities that inspired others on a deep, emotional level. More than oratorical skill, although that mattered, there was the simple but eloquent gesture. The sight of Hannibal in his army cloak, sleeping on the ground with his men, or Alexander in the desert, refusing a helmet full of water while his soldiers went thirsty, or Caesar sleeping on the porch of a requisitioned hut so his frail friend Oppius could rest inside—these scenes did more to inspire the soldiers' confidence than a hundred speeches.

Not that the commanders relied on friendship to manage their armies—far from it. Skilled actors, they could fire up an army or douse its passion. Caesar once stopped a mutiny with a single word: "citizens." By addressing his men with a civilian title he brought them back to their senses—and reminded them how much they craved their chief's approval.

They were masters of reward and punishment. They used honors and cash prizes to foster bravery. They paid the troops well—or faced mutinies. They were big-hearted and wanted everyone to know it—they kept relatively little loot for themselves but doled it out to their friends.

When it came to their best troops, such as Alexander's Macedonians or

Hannibal's Africans, they did everything they could to keep casualties to a minimum. Meanwhile, they left no soldier in doubt that, if worst came to worst, widows and orphans would receive lavish benefits.

They stoked the fear factor by punishing anyone who crossed them, men and officers alike. Beatings, executions, and even crucifixions—these too were tools of leadership.

4. Audacity

Honor was at the heart of their character. Courage was the red blood of their veins. But the warrior virtue that best embodies Alexander, Hannibal, and Caesar alike is audacity.

Each of them was, in his own way, scaling Mount Everest. The king of little Macedon was not meant to conquer Persia's vast empire. The governor of Gaul was not supposed to topple the Roman senate and its armies. And it was unimaginable that the Carthaginian commander of southern Spain should cross both river and mountain and invade Italy. But they dared to do what couldn't be done.

"Because he loved honor, he loved danger"—what Plutarch said of Caesar in battle applies to Alexander and Hannibal as well. They fought in the thick of things. It was dangerous: during his invasion of the Persian empire, Alexander had seven recorded wounds, at least three of them serious, as well as one serious illness from which he recovered. It was also effective, because a general who shared his men's risks won his men's hearts.

They were bold in the military campaigns they designed. Although most generals are risk-averse most of the time, these three were risk takers. They always tried to seize the initiative. Each one gambled that he could destroy the enemy's center of gravity before the enemy could destroy his. Like all successful leaders, the three also knew when *not* to be audacious.

Alexander, Hannibal, and Caesar each occasionally took a wild risk, but usually they calculated the odds. They raced out in front but rarely without first securing their base. Still, they each believed in their invincible destiny and good fortune, which led them to gamble and sometimes fail. Few men bounced back as quickly from failure as they did.

5. Agility

They were soldiers for all seasons. Or at least for most seasons: change on the battlefield was their friend, but even their agility had its limits. And once off the battlefield and into politics, they faced more difficult challenges.

When the conditions of combat changed, they retooled. Having excelled at conventional warfare in western Asia, Alexander switched to counterinsurgency when faced with a guerrilla war in Central Asia. Hannibal shifted effortlessly between set battles and ambushes. Caesar was at home on the battlefield, but he threw himself into urban warfare in Alexandria and managed to pull off a victory.

Speed was their watchword, mobility their hallmark. Alexander's thundering heavy cavalry, Hannibal's agile light horsemen, and Caesar's lightning infantry thrusts—these were the agents of success. In their hands, even elephants could be made to move with grace, as when Hannibal's elephants were cajoled onto rafts across the Rhône.

They traveled light, with little in the way of a supply train. Their men lived off the land—Alexander's less precariously than either Hannibal's or Caesar's, since the Macedonians paid more attention to logistics and did the advance work necessary to secure supplies.

They were masters of multitasking. Caesar dictated letters on horseback, with a secretary mounted on either side, each taking down a different piece. They were Herculean workaholics who managed time with the deftness of a prizefighter. Only the need for sleep and sex, said Alexander, reminded him that he was human.

But agility had its limits. Alexander was nearly stymied by the Persian fleet. Hannibal paid dearly for his inability to conduct sieges in Italy. Caesar nearly starved his army during the poorly conceived siege of Dyrrachium.

Nor do agile warriors necessarily make good politicians. War is clarity; politics is frustration. Alexander conquered the Persian empire with gusto but he quickly lost interest in managing its affairs. Hannibal discovered that winning allies in Italy was easier than bending them to his will. Caesar found the battlefield less challenging than the Forum; his downfall came not from senatorial armies but from daggers in the Senate Chamber.

6. Infrastructure

To win a war takes certain material things: arms and armor, ships, food, money, money, and more money. With enough money, you can buy the rest. You can even acquire manpower—even disciplined and veteran manpower—that is, mercenaries.

The one thing that money can't buy is synergy. It can't buy a combined-arms force (light and heavy infantry and cavalry as well as engineers) that is trained to fight together as a coherent whole—and welded to its leader. You have to build that on your own.

And build it our three generals did. They each inherited a dazzling instrument and then honed it into something even sharper and more deadly.

Philip II built the Macedonian army and Alexander added the crowning touch by leading the cavalry to victory in Philip's greatest battle—Chaeronea. Then, after Philip's death, Alexander rode at the army's head in its years of glory in Asia. Hannibal inherited the men who had carved out a new Carthaginian empire in Spain for his father, Hamilcar. Caesar took the Roman legions and made them his own. Fired in the crucible of the Gallic wars, they were the finest army in the Roman world.

7. Strategy

In its original, ancient Greek sense, strategy refers to generalship overall, from battle tactics to the art of operations (weaving battles together in pursuit of a larger goal) to war strategy (how to win a war). Add to these what we now call grand strategy—the broader political goal that a war serves. Great commanders must master them all.

Alexander, Hannibal, and Caesar all had an instinctive grasp of operations. However, Caesar's mastery of tactics did not match Alexander's or Hannibal's.

Hannibal, in particular, was the master of surprise. His march over the Alps left the enemy breathless. He ran circles around the Romans with an array of unheard-of tricks, managed to pry open the gates of a strong city, unleashed a cavalry charge from a hiding place in the enemy's rear, and shuttled his army to freedom one night right under the Romans' noses.

Neither Alexander nor Caesar was in Hannibal's league but they had a few cons of their own. When the Persians blocked a mountain pass into the heart of Iran, Alexander successfully rode through the hills and surprised them from the rear. When Caesar faced Pompey in a do-or-die battle, Caesar hid his best troops until the enemy cavalry charged—then he pulled out his men and broke the cavalry's momentum.

But when it came to war strategy, Alexander and Caesar turned the tables on Hannibal. They thought ahead and they were dogged. Knowing that he could not beat Persia at sea, Alexander stooped to conquer Persia's Mediterranean seaports—while putting off the big battle that he craved. Thinking ahead to a showdown with Pompey, Caesar shipped the loot he won in Gaul back home to the ordinary people of Italy—in effect, he bought their votes. Hannibal was less painstaking. He loved speed and sorcery but he had no interest in grinding down Rome's allies one by one.

For all his success, Hannibal failed at long-term thinking. His battlefield triumphs stunned but did not slay Rome. When the enemy bounced back, Hannibal had no Plan B. We don't know who was more to blame, Hannibal or his home government, but we do know who had the last laugh—Rome.

All three commanders had a grand strategy. Alexander wanted to conquer the Persian empire, Hannibal to break Rome's power for good, and Caesar to achieve political supremacy. But those goals left many, many details to work out.

8. Terror

They were willing to kill innocents and everyone knew it. That too was a secret of their success.

Scene from a civil war: when a young public official tried to stop Caesar from breaking into the treasury in Rome, Caesar raised his voice and threatened to kill him if he didn't get out of the way. "And young man," he said, "you have to know that it was harder for me to say this than it would be to do it." The terrified official left.

But threatening a government official's life was nothing compared to massacring entire cities, as the great commanders did. Caesar sacked the small Greek city of Gomphi as punishment for its betraying him. Alexander destroyed the great Greek metropolis of Thebes just to show what he did to rebels. Even worse would come later in Central and South Asia, where the angry Macedonians massacred town after town.

Caesar did the same in Gaul, where the ancient biographer Plutarch says he killed a million people and enslaved a million more. Exaggerations—but close enough to the truth that most Italians were quick to surrender when he crossed the Rubicon. Caesar then cleverly played against type and pardoned his enemies, which won the applause of a relieved public.

The first thing Hannibal did when he reached Italy in 218 was to massacre the people of Turin—a small place in those days—in order to break resistance in the surrounding area. When he finally left Italy fifteen years later, in 203, Hannibal slaughtered those Italians who refused to go with him—and he didn't hesitate to follow them into the grounds of a temple to do so. Or so the Romans claimed.

9. Branding

Men with imperial ambitions don't go to war over little things like border disputes. They need grand causes and clear symbols.

All three were chameleons. None was a man of the people but all played the populist.

Alexander began as an avenger and a liberator and he ended up as a demigod. He promised payback for Persia's invasion of Greece 150 years earlier, proclaimed the liberation of the Greek cities that he conquered, and made them democracies, whether they liked it or not. Once he reached Iran, he put on selected items of Persian dress and insisted that his men now salaam in his presence, Persian style, in a nod to his new, Eastern subjects. Meanwhile, he told his Greek allies to worship him as the son of the god Zeus.

Hannibal too stood for vengeance and liberation and he walked his own pathway to the gods. To Carthage, he promised vengeance for its earlier defeat by Rome; to Italians, he promised freedom from Roman domination. He claimed the support of the Carthaginian god Melqart—or Hercules. And he encouraged his Celtic followers to consider him a hero out of their myths.

Caesar went to great pains to show that he was no mere provincial governor in revolt against the lawful government of Rome. He said that he was fighting for the rights of the Roman people and for his own good name—

the latter a principle dear to Roman hearts. Caesar also drew a bright line between himself and earlier generals who had marched on Rome. They had sealed their wars with reigns of terror, but his policy was mercy.

As far as the gods, Caesar's family traced its ancestry back to Venus. Caesar received divine honors from the Senate while still alive and was deified after his death. But Caesar acquired something else that was worth still more—celebrity. His *Commentaries on the Gallic War* made him a symbol of military prowess. By the time he crossed the Rubicon two years later, Caesar's reputation served as a force multiplier.

10. Divine Providence

Napoleon asked for generals who were not only good but also lucky. He would have had many occasions to be pleased with Alexander, Hannibal, and Caesar. But only Divine Providence, and not mere luck, can explain the guidance and protection needed to reach the heights they did. Although the previous nine factors were necessary, Divine Providence was essential.

Divine Providence guided the steps of young men born to be conquerors, like Alexander and Hannibal, and also the steps of a middle-aged politician who went to war and turned out to be the greatest general of all—Caesar. Only Divine Providence can lead a man's foes off the cliff. Without having to lift a finger, for example, Alexander saw his worst enemy die suddenly.

The Romans played into Hannibal's hands by launching their biggest army against him. He was waiting at Cannae. There, Hannibal achieved one of the world's greatest battlefield victories, but he failed to follow up Cannae with a march on Rome—and that cost him the war.

As the saying goes, man plans, God laughs.

THE FIVE STAGES OF WAR

A great leader knows the rhythm of war. That is critical because in war, as in most things, timing is everything. Success is not only a matter of the ten qualities just discussed, but of knowing when to deploy them. That goes especially for the kind of war that Alexander, Hannibal, and Caesar all had in mind.

Their three wars all followed a similar pattern. Each began with a combination of attack and defense, in keeping with a basic rule of combat: every time you throw a punch, you create an opening for your opponent to attack, so you need to protect yourself. Accordingly, our generals invaded the enemy's country while anticipating an enemy counterattack. Each ran into trouble early on, because in war things never go as planned, but then quickly regrouped. Next came a great victory in a pitched battle that shattered the enemy's offensive capability. Then the three each tried to finish the job by depriving the enemy of his money and manpower—two of them succeeded. The last step was to reap the fruits of victory in a peace agreement for the postwar world, but none of the captains achieved this.

Their three wars followed a similar pattern but then, most wars do. In spite of many changes in technology, since ancient times the principles of war have changed as little as human nature has.

Each of these wars consisted of five phases. I call them the five stages of warfare: (1) attack, (2) resistance, (3) clash, (4) closing the net, and (5) knowing when to stop.

In the **attack** stage, the decision to go to war leads to the outbreak of fighting guided by a plan. The war plan is crucial—as the saying goes, failing to plan is planning to fail. But every plan runs into obstacles—call them **resistance.** In that stage, the attacker has to overcome those obstacles or fail. Our generals succeeded and forced their opponents to engage in a **clash**—the battle or battles that left the invading army supreme. But winning a battle is not enough. A successful general has to bring the enemy to his knees by using whatever it takes—pursuit, siege, blockade, counterinsurgency, or other tactics. He has to bring to bear political and financial as well as military resources. He needs to be ready for second-guessing at home and insurgency abroad. **Closing the net** is the most complex and challenging stage of all. Finally, a soldier-statesman has the advantage of **knowing when to stop.** He ends the fighting at a time and in a manner that does more than cease hostilities—it lays the groundwork for the postwar world.

Most people probably think of war as a three-stage process: attack, fight, win or lose. But that model is wrong because it simplifies and distorts the nature of war. We cannot understand war without allowing for its unpredictability and its fundamentally political nature.

The great commanders knew this. They didn't just plan to win. They anticipated failure and they knew how to rebound from it. They put battlefield success into context. They knew that you could win a battle and still lose the war. They also understood that military victory does not equal political success.

War is unpredictable. Many ancient soldiers worshiped Fortune or Luck, and not without reason. Their commanders made careful plans, but no planner knows every hill or what lies behind it; no forecaster can control the weather or predict what Providence has in store. And then, there is the enemy. War is not shadowboxing; war is a match against a moving target. The enemy has a way of doing fancy dancing and tripping up the best-laid plans.

For example, the Persians unleashed a counterattack by sea against Alexander's base in Greece, and the Romans launched a strike against Hannibal's stronghold in Spain. Both Alexander and Hannibal flubbed their responses, but Alexander was lucky. Hannibal took a hard hit. Pompey might have attacked Caesar's base in Italy from Spain, but Caesar beat him to the punch by invading Spain first.

Politics constrains war in two ways. No general can carry out military acts unless he commands the support of his men on the battlefield and his backers at home. No military victory can bear fruit unless it forces the enemy to do your will. It is no use winning a battle if the enemy is able to fight on to victory. Peace negotiations can prove treacherous, and many a general has won the war but lost the peace. For example, the general Lysander (d. 395 B.C.) led Sparta to victory against Athens in the Peloponnesian War (431–404 B.C.), but his postwar policies were so heavy-handed that his allies turned on him and Sparta threw him out of office. That gave Athens an opening to rise again as a military threat. In modern times, the French army defeated the rebels militarily in the Algerian War (1954–1962), but at so high a cost that the French government, with popular support, decided to give up. Algeria, after more than a century as a French colony, became an independent state.

When we look closely at the nature of war—its unpredictability and political nature—we understand why this five-stage model is so useful. The five-stage model fits not just the wars of Alexander, Hannibal, and Caesar but war generally, including more recent wars such as Iraq and Afghanistan. It describes conventional warfare best, but it also fits guerrilla wars and wars of attrition, where the clash is not a set battle but a battle nonetheless, however long or amorphous.

Although Alexander, Hannibal, and Caesar are known as masters of conventional warfare, they offer lessons for unconventional warfare as well, from Alexander's retooling his army into a force flexible enough to defeat Afghanistan's nomads and mountain fighters, to Hannibal's tactical cunning in the Italian hills, to Caesar's street-fighting in Alexandria, to the hearts-and-minds initiatives that all three generals used on enemy populations.

GREATNESS ISN'T WHAT IT USED TO BE

We historians are supposed to be objective but the three subjects of this book make that hard. They excite the passions from love to hate and often a little of each. Maybe the world still loves heroes. Biographers certainly do. They run the risk of falling in love with their subjects, and these subjects—especially Alexander and Caesar—have had many biographers. But ancient heroes serve many and various modern agendas.

Take Alexander. He was a conqueror but history records him as an icon. To liberals, he was a visionary; to conservatives, he was a champion of Western civilization; and to more than one religious tradition, he was nearly a saint. Jewish tradition records that Alexander visited the Temple in Jerusalem and showed it respect. Ever since, "Alexander" has been a common Jewish name—and remains so today, even among Orthodox Jews. Christians believe that Alexander was preparing the way of the Lord by bringing Greek civilization to the East and by laying the groundwork for the unification of humanity. Because he was the "son of a god," because he claimed to make men free, and because he died young, Alexander appears to some to prefigure Christ. Islam too remembers Alexander, and possibly in its holiest text: many scholars believe that Dhul-Qarnain, a figure mentioned in the Quran, and considered by many to be a prophet, actually refers to Alexander.

But you don't have to be religious to revere Alexander. Nationalists from Greece to India all claim him. Gay-rights activists see him as a protogay because he loved men as well as women. A female scholar, however, told me she looks down on Alexander as a male fantasy figure who represents the struggle between adventure and responsibility. Some brand Alexander as a butcher and a brute. Most historians, though, sing Alexander's praises.

Caesar is no one's idea of a saint, but he casts a shadow over every scholar even so. Caesar is the gatekeeper of his own reputation, because his brilliant books *The Gallic War* and *The Civil War* dominate the ancient historical record. For a modern advocate, Caesar has the best—Shakespeare, who endowed the man with tragic dignity. Still, Caesar's deeds speak for themselves and they don't always win admirers. He invaded Gaul without just cause and made rivers of blood run there. Then he started a civil war in Rome, less for any principle than for his own selfish good. He ended up as a dictator who destroyed the freedom of the Roman republic. Caesarism still stands today for military or imperial dictatorship and for political absolutism.

With Hannibal we have the opposite problem. Because he failed to defeat Rome, Hannibal might appear a loser rather than the champion that he was. Hannibal wins the hearts of underdogs, which sometimes leads to strange bedfellows. As a boy Sigmund Freud idolized Hannibal as a "Semite" who took on Rome the way Freud resisted anti-Semitism in Catholic Vienna. African Americans have traditionally considered Hannibal a black hero. He was probably not dark-skinned, although many thousands of troops in his army were.

Still, Hannibal's underdog appeal rests on solid ground. After taking on an arrogant empire and shaking it to its core, he lost everything. But he maintained his dignity. Hannibal in defeat reinvented himself as an administrator, restarted the struggle against Rome in the East, and refused to let the enemy humiliate him by marching in triumph. He died beaten but unbowed.

Great generals must be ready to die young, and many conquerors throughout history have. They also must face the ever-present possibility of failure. Conquest is not an easy job. Success requires a combination of military greatness and supreme political skill. Very few people excel at both.

Our generals today do not try to excel at both, and that is a good thing. They bow to civilian authority. They do not decide whether to go to war, only how to fight a war, and even on that point they must yield to the politicians. They do not decide political strategy, only military strategy. It is a good thing not to put political and military power in the hands of one man.

They do lose sleep over killing people. They don't fight wars of aggression, only of defense. To be sure, sometimes defense requires attacking another state that is plotting against us or oppressing its own people or occupying land that is rightfully ours, but all that is a far cry from declaring someone else's soil to be "spear-won" land, as Alexander did.

The great commanders of the ancient world lacked the humility called for in great statesmen. They were great men but not benefactors of the human race; they came to destroy more than to fulfill. In many ways, their examples are to be honored in the breach. And yet, they do have something to teach us.

No man has ever outdone Alexander's feat of conquering such a large empire in such a short time at such a young age. No strategist has ever pulled off a more daring invasion than Hannibal's march from Spain over the Pyrenees, the Rhône, and the Alps into Italy. No battlefield commander has ever won a more complete tactical victory than Hannibal's at Cannae. No general has ever thrown the dice as boldly as Caesar did when he crossed the Adriatic Sea on the eve of winter without warships or supplies—and won the war.

No one ever understood better than these three that war is politics. No conqueror has ever dared to co-opt the conquered as brilliantly as Alexander did when he declared himself to be the king of Asia—and acted the part. No invader has ever rallied the invaded as smoothly as Hannibal did when he entered Italy to the cry of "Italy for the Italians." No soldier-statesman has ever combined the carrot—pardons—with the stick—military force—as deftly as Caesar.

And then, at the moment of triumph, no one ever forgot the rule that war is politics as completely—or as disastrously—as they. Flush with victory and drunk with success, each man did the one thing that no successful general can ever dare do: he succumbed to his own vanity. Modern generals are not immune to excessive pride. But, in democracies, at any rate, laws prevent any one individual from doing too much damage. History tells a cautionary tale.

2

ATTACK

A TWENTY-TWO-YEAR-OLD SAT IN THE HELMSMAN'S SEAT AND STEERED THE admiral's flagship southward across the steel blue water of the Hellespont, the narrow channel separating Europe and Asia. As the boat neared its destination, he threw a spear from the ship and plunged it into the ground. Then, wearing a full suit of armor, he was the first man to jump off and step onto the Asian shore. The effect was to mark the land as "spear-won," territory that the gods had given him to take by force. He had thirty-seven thousand men with him to make good on his claim that spring day in 334 B.C.

About a hundred years later and a thousand miles away, a twenty-nine-year-old led an army. He slogged through some of the most forbidding terrain in the world, the snow-covered Alps, with forty thousand soldiers on foot and eight thousand on horseback. And to top it off—thirty-seven elephants! Only about half of the men would survive that brutal crossing, but on the November day in 218 B.C. when they walked out of the hills, they marched into Roman territory and upended Italy. Seventeen years of war and destruction would follow.

A little more than 150 years later and three hundred miles to the south, a fifty-one-year-old with just five thousand men under his command crossed a river in the northern Italian plain. But that river—really little more than a stream—marked the boundary between his province, where he could legally lead an army, and Italy proper, where he could not. His short journey on a late autumn day signaled the start of nearly thirty years of civil war from one end of Rome's Mediterranean empire to the other. It was January 12,

49 B.C., by the flawed Roman calendar then in use—about November 24, 50 B.C., by the solar calendar that we use today.

Alexander the Great, in the first anecdote, Hannibal, in the second, and Julius Caesar, in the third, each illustrates a point: history often focuses on a frontier crossing as the start of a great war. Alexander's Persian expedition began with the crossing of the Hellespont. The Second Punic War began when Hannibal left Spain, marched through southern Gaul, and crossed over the Alps into Italy. The Roman Civil War began when Caesar crossed the Rubicon.

But frontier crossings are an anticlimax. They mark the outbreak of a war, not its cause. Caesar might have said, "The die is cast," when he traversed the Rubicon, but the game had already begun. Five days earlier the Roman senate had declared Caesar an outlaw, thereby forcing him either to fight or give up his political and military career (and possibly his life). But the collision course between Caesar and the Senate had been obvious for months, if not a year earlier. At least a month before crossing the Rubicon, Caesar had ordered two legions in France to cross the Alps and join him in Italy. When Alexander navigated the Hellespont he was continuing a war begun three years earlier by his father. When Hannibal marched over the Alps he was pursuing a war with Rome that had broken out a year earlier in Spain. And if the ancient sources can be believed, Hannibal had been expecting to fight that war since he was a boy.

Well before they saw the Rubicon and the Alps and the Hellespont, Caesar and Hannibal and Alexander had each decided to go to war. That decision was the most important choice that each of them would ever make. Why did each man choose war?

WHY WAR?
Alexander: Like Father, Like Son

Alexander's war on the Persian empire was not a case of self-defense. Neither he nor his country had anything to fear from Persia. As the historian Polybius (ca. 200–118 B.C.) pointed out in ancient times, Alexander fought a war of conquest; in fact, the war was his legacy bequeathed to him by his father, King Philip II. Past Greek successes against the Persians had convinced Philip that the Persian empire was ripe for the taking; there was no doubt about "the splendor of the great prize to which the war promised."

Brainy and sophisticated, Philip was in touch with the Greek intellectuals of his day. One book might have interested him especially, *The Education of Cyrus* by the Athenian writer and soldier Xenophon. Xenophon offered a fictionalized but gripping account of how Cyrus, king of a small corner of southwestern Iran, founded the mighty Persian empire by force of arms. Xenophon's Cyrus was a man of honor and courage who attracted the best men of his day by the force of his character. Whether or not Philip had read the book, he had probably heard of it. And if he had, he surely asked himself, "If Cyrus could do it, why can't I?"

When it came to ambition, Alexander was his father's equal. He, too, aimed at conquering the Persian empire. It was a tall order but Alexander was a man of destiny. He was born to fight this war. Like his father, he had the personality of a conqueror, with a passionate conviction of his ability and even of his divinity. Philip hinted in public that the twelve Olympian gods should add him to their ranks. Alexander simply proclaimed himself a god.

Alexander believed that he was descended from the mythical Greek hero Achilles. From childhood on, Alexander identified with him. Branding himself as a second Achilles was a two-edged sword. Achilles was not only Greece's greatest warrior but also its most selfish. Compared to his own honor, he cared nothing for his country. He chose glory over long life. Achilles loved war and had little interest in hearth and home. For Alexander the parallels would prove all too fitting.

He certainly had a knack for war. His courage and skill stood out in his adolescence. Even before Philip's death, Alexander showed himself to be a great cavalry commander and a great leader of men. But even if he had been given to timidity or self-doubt, he would have had to squelch the emotions. The consequences of not going to war would have been dire. Alexander had to prove that he was his father's son. At the age of twenty-two, he also had to show that he could carry out a grown man's responsibilities.

Alexander's father, Philip, had survived twenty-three years on the notoriously unstable throne of Macedon by devoting nearly his entire reign to war. His successful expansion abroad underwrote his popularity at home, but in the end, he was assassinated. Philip's last military act had been to start the long-planned invasion of Persian Anatolia by sending advance forces.

One other thing: Philip had spent practically everything in the Macedonian treasury to pay for his military force. By the time Alexander invaded Persia, Macedon, the richest kingdom in Europe, was broke. Alexander had to fight his way to solvency or face ruin.

Had Alexander not continued the war, he would have been branded a coward and would probably have ended up like his father—dead at the hands of one of his own hawkish countrymen.

Hannibal: The Family Business

Hannibal too sprang from a famous father. Hamilcar Barca emerged as a great general during the First Punic War (264–241 B.C.), a struggle with Rome for control of Sicily. Although Carthage lost the war, Hamilcar won every battle. Afterward, he returned home and achieved even greater success by defeating a savage mercenaries' revolt (239 B.C.). Under Hamilcar, the Barcas became Carthage's first family of war.

As good a politician as he was a general, Hamilcar championed the common people in a city dominated by a wealthy elite. He rode a wave of popular support to get a commission to fight in Spain. There, Hamilcar won a new empire, in southern Spain, as a replacement for the empire that Carthage had lost in Sicily. Spain had gold and silver mines and a plentiful supply of soldiers, and Carthage now controlled them. The city regained its power.

Hamilcar brought his nine-year-old son Hannibal with him to Spain. The boy grew up in an armed camp, guided by two brilliant soldiers—his father and his uncle—and gifted with the genetic endowment of his family. Hannibal had two brothers: Hasdrubal and Mago. Hamilcar called his sons "the lion's brood"—and Hannibal was the alpha male of the pride. Raised to be the consummate commander, he did not disappoint when he reached manhood.

"He was by his very nature truly a marvelous man," says Polybius of Hannibal, "with a personality suited by its original constitution to carry out anything that lies within human affairs." He was a man of extremes. His mind was quick and astute but his body was indifferent to pain. He had a sense of humor and a violent temper. He was a man of honor but his critics said he ignored his promises when it suited him and that he had a weakness for money.

Hannibal's bold and courageous heart yearned to carry out ambitious deeds. Physically imposing, he looked every inch the commander. He was born to be a leader of men, and won the love and loyalty of his troops.

Heroic, expansionist, and blessed by Carthage's gods—that's how the Barca family advertised their "brand." They paid special attention to Melqart, a god of heroism and history. The royal god of Tyre—mother city of Carthage—Melqart made Carthaginians proud of their past. In Spain, Melqart's temple stood on an island in the Atlantic Ocean, off Gades (modern Cadiz), and symbolized the courage to face the vast unknown. Greeks associated Melqart with their hero, Heracles, and the Barcas advertised the connection on their coins. Displayed in profile, Melqart-Heracles is a tough-looking customer, bull-necked and bearded, with a victory wreath on his head and a club over his shoulder. The reverse side of the coin adds to the image of ferocity by depicting a war elephant.

Hannibal's ambition shone as brightly as the Barca silver coins. As a young man, Hannibal studied with a Greek tutor. I suspect that of all the heroes of Greece, Alexander the Great was Hannibal's favorite. As an adult, he certainly imitated the Macedonian—he walked in Alexander's footsteps by invading a great empire with a small but elite army, and by proclaiming himself a liberator on a divine mission.

But Hannibal was a son of Carthage. Like his country, he was dynamic, expansionist—and hard for us to reconstruct. Rome destroyed Carthage in 146 B.C., in an act of utter annihilation that many scholars today consider to be genocide. Thanks to archaeology, some of Carthage's material culture has been unearthed, but very little Carthaginian writing survives.

The real Carthage was wealthy, dynamic, and cruel. Its economy rested on commerce and on agricultural wealth. Its armies and navies fought from Spain to Libya, while its seafarers voyaged as far as Ireland and West Africa. Its elite admired Greek culture and couldn't get enough of it. Its politicians punished defeated generals by crucifixion. Its parents sacrificed their own children as gifts to the angry gods in times of crisis—archaeology demonstrates that the testimony of Greek writers on this point was no myth.

Hannibal was Carthage's most famous son, but no Carthaginian records about him survive. Our sources for Caesar are excellent and those for Alexander are not bad, but for knowledge of Hannibal, we depend almost exclusively on Greek and Roman writers, especially Polybius and Livy. We simply know less about Hannibal than the other two commanders. Historians' conclusions about Hannibal contain an element of guesswork.

To return to Hamilcar: he was a loyal citizen of Carthage but he enjoyed almost absolute power in Spain. Although he had political enemies in the Council of Elders that dominated Carthaginian politics, he had far more supporters. The Barca faction believed in national greatness through war and empire. And it was determined to stand up to Rome.

Rome disappointed Carthage by taking Sicily in the First Punic War, but it added humiliation shortly afterward by seizing another Carthaginian island—Sardinia. It was a clear treaty violation but Carthage was too weak to do anything about it at the time. But that changed. Between Spain's resources and the Barcas' talent for war, Carthage could say "never again!" Indeed, the Greek and Roman sources claim, the Barcas actively planned a war of revenge.

The story goes that when Hannibal was a boy in 237 B.C., Hamilcar made him swear a solemn oath of eternal enmity toward Rome. Whether this story is true, Hannibal's actions on the eve of war show how little he trusted Rome.

When Hamilcar died in 228 B.C., his son-in-law, Hasdrubal the Handsome, replaced him. Hasdrubal the Handsome gave Carthaginian Spain a capital at a town he named Carthage (modern-day Cartagena), a great harbor in southeastern Spain. (The Romans later called it New Carthage and, to avoid confusion, so shall we.) If Hasdrubal too planned war with Rome, he was assassinated in 221 before he could act on it. The army in Spain chose a successor by acclamation, and the Carthaginian people confirmed it. Their man was Hannibal, now twenty-six and commander of the Spanish empire that his father had founded. Hannibal quickly displayed his aptitude for war by storming through much of central Spain and expanding Carthage's empire.

Rome had watched the rise of Carthaginian power in Spain with admiration and fear. Hannibal and his father (and uncle) had put into effect a revolution. When they began, Carthage lay prostrate at the feet of Rome. Now Rome began to fear that it might end up prostrate at the feet of Carthage.

So Rome used the Spanish city of Saguntum (modern Sagunto) as a wedge into Carthaginian Spain. Saguntum had been stirring up Spanish tribes against Hannibal. When the Carthaginians insisted on counterat-tacking Saguntum, Rome threatened retaliation. Hannibal would not budge. He was, writes Polybius, "young, full of martial ardor, encouraged by the success of his enterprises, and spurred on by his long-standing enmity to Rome."

Rome claimed that Carthage had violated its treaty obligations by at-tacking Saguntum, a Roman ally, as guaranteed by a treaty between Rome and Hasdrubal, when he had commanded in Spain. But Carthage challenged Rome on legal grounds while modern scholars question whether Saguntum was Rome's ally or merely its "friend"—a status that allowed Rome to champion Saguntum without committing to its defense.

By refusing to stand down, Hannibal faced certain war with Rome. The alternative, however, would have meant letting Rome begin expanding in Spain. No one with any knowledge of Roman history could doubt where that would eventually lead: an ever-tightening grip on Carthage's Spanish empire. The question was, how could Carthage stop it?

One possibility was appeasement. Accept Rome's superiority, make concessions, and settle down to being a second-rate power in Rome's orbit. Another possibility was to fight but to stand on the defensive. Let Rome exhaust itself trying to beat Carthaginian armies on their home ground in Spain and probably also in North Africa. With a brilliant general like Hannibal on their side, eventually the Carthaginians would wear out the Romans.

The third possibility, and the one that Hannibal chose, was audacity. He would attack and shock the enemy by invading Italy—an extension of his father Hamilcar's raids. Hannibal reasoned that his victories in Italy would make Rome's allies defect to him, and that would force Rome to sue for peace. Never again would Carthage have to worry about Roman aggression. Attack Rome—that was the Barca way.

Like Alexander, then, Hannibal took up with gusto the family business and the military offensive that it demanded.

Caesar: No Chance for Peace

Caesar's is a more complicated story. Unlike Alexander or Hannibal, Caesar was not the son of a great general. Although he came from an old, patrician

Roman family, Caesar was a self-made warrior. Nor had he risen to the top at an early age, like the other two generals. But Caesar did not suffer from an inferiority complex. His family claimed descent from Rome's legendary ancestor Aeneas, and through Aeneas, the goddess Venus. At age sixteen, Caesar was a priest of Jupiter and, late in life, he allowed the Senate to grant him divine honors.

He was a man of immense ambition. As success mounted upon success, Caesar wanted to become the most powerful Roman of all—or, as he put it bluntly, to be first man in Rome.

A superb soldier, the ambitious Caesar climbed the military ladder steadily. By the time he crossed the Rubicon in 49 B.C., at age fifty, he had gone to the greatest school of all: he had conquered Gaul. It was one of the most brutal, thorough, and profitable victories in Rome's long history.

Besides being a brilliant general, Caesar was a gifted demagogue and a shrewd politician. He planned to leverage his success in Gaul into further power and honor in Rome and then another great command, this time against the Parthians (an Iranian empire). But the many political enemies whom he had made in his meteoric rise had no intention of letting that happen. As he piled success upon success in Gaul, as he acquired gigantic wealth, power, and military force, a rising political chorus in Rome called for his head.

Caesar ran the greatest risks of all by not going to war. If he had kept the peace, he would have had to give up his office as governor of Gaul, the province that he had conquered for Rome. He would have had to return to Italy as a private citizen, where prominent senators said they would immediately prosecute him for various illegalities in his prior career. Caesar could expect that, as in a recent trial at Rome, his political enemy Pompey would have the courthouse surrounded by soldiers, in order to "persuade" the jurors how to vote. The result would almost certainly be condemnation, with exile or execution to follow. It would be the end of Caesar's public career and possibly his life. By going to war, Caesar had a better chance of achieving his long-term ambition of supreme power.

Caesar's rise took place against the background of the crisis of the Roman republic. The great city that had conquered an empire was in poor shape. By the time Caesar crossed the Rubicon, Rome had witnessed ninety years of intermittent turmoil on the home front, including riots and assassinations (133–121 B.C.), an allied revolt (90–88 B.C.), a slave war (73–71 B.C.), and a debtors' rebellion (63 B.C.). Worst of all was a civil war (86–82 B.C.) that made it clear that a determined general with a veteran army could trample on the political power of the Roman senate. A longtime rivalry between the Roman generals Marius and Sulla ended with Sulla conquering his own country, massacring his enemies, and becoming dictator for life. His early death (79 B.C.) allowed the Senate to reestablish its authority. When Caesar crossed the Rubicon, Rome had been a republic again for thirty years, but generals like Pompey and Caesar cast a shadow on its freedom.

Like Caesar, Pompey too insisted on being the first man in Rome. Born in 106 B.C., he made his name as a general while still in his twenties by fighting for Sulla in the civil war. Sulla called him Pompeius Magnus, "Pompey the Great." Another, less flattering nickname also dated to this era: "the teenage butcher," probably referring to his slaughter of captured opponents.

The rest of Pompey's military career played out over a vast canvas for nearly fifteen years between 76 and 63 B.C. First he ground down the Roman rebel Sertorius during a five-year-long struggle in Spain. Then Pompey took credit for beating the rebel gladiator Spartacus in Italy (another general, Marcus Licinius Crassus, did most of the work). Finally there came a series of spectacular victories in the eastern Mediterranean: over the pirates, whom he put out of business; over the rebel Mithradates, whom he drove to suicide; and over a swath of territory extending from the Black Sea to the Jordan River, all of which he put under Rome's control.

Pompey spent the years between 63 and 49 B.C. back in Rome. He was more than happy to run roughshod over the Senate's powers during that period and to dominate politics through a series of backroom deals with Caesar and Crassus. But Crassus fell in battle (53 B.C.) and Caesar won immortality in Gaul.

Pompey could not bear the thought of Caesar coming back from Gaul and dominating Roman politics, so he discovered the virtues of Rome's good old republican system of government. He decided to ride to the Senate's rescue and take up arms on its behalf. The senators did not trust him but they needed his military skill.

"The Republic is not the question at issue," as Cicero would soon write. "The struggle is over who is to be king." In 49 B.C., Pompey and the Senate made uneasy allies. A ruthless enemy like Caesar could exploit their mutual suspicion.

Unlike Alexander or Hannibal, Caesar did not fight the war he wanted; he would have preferred to lead an army against Parthia rather than against fellow Romans. But he didn't shrink from civil war when it became necessary.

Caesar's domestic enemies treated him unfairly, but by crossing the Rubicon, Caesar did worse: he engaged in treason. He was a rebel general attacking the legitimate government of his country. A more modest man would have spared his country.

In his *Civil War*, Caesar offered two justifications for his action. He told his soldiers, in a public meeting, that he was fighting to defend the power of Rome's tribunes—the representatives of the people. Caesar also emphasized the matter of rank (*dignitas* in Latin). The issue, Caesar told his soldiers in a public meeting, was the "reputation and rank" of their commander. To Pompey, Caesar wrote that he had always considered "the rank of the republic" more important than life, and the rank in question was "a benefit granted to me [Caesar] by the Roman people"—that is, his command in Gaul. Men noticed what Caesar was saying. As Cicero wrote to a confidant, "He [Caesar] says he is doing everything for the sake of rank." To the Romans, rank was a core value, the way freedom or security or community is a core value to modern electorates. By defending himself, Caesar claimed to be defending the Roman way of life.

Or so he said. It is hard not to think that "the liberty of the people," "the sacrosanct status of the tribunes," "the rank of the nobles," to him were all spelled "Caesar."

MILITARY STRATEGIES

So much for the reasons why Alexander, Hannibal, and Caesar each went to war. How did they plan to win? This is no small question because there were excellent reasons why each of them should have lost.

They shared a similarly bleak strategic situation at the outset. Each man was about to invade a country whose military force outnumbered him in manpower and money. Each man faced an enemy who had command of the sea. Hannibal and Caesar both lacked navies; Alexander's navy could not compete with his enemy's.

Yet each man expected victory. Each one's story was a classic case of something that has happened again and again in history. A ruthless general with a hardened, elite, and small army tries to knock out a flabby giant. Sometimes it works: Hernando Cortés, for instance, began with only six hundred men when he marched on the Aztecs in 1519; by 1521 he had conquered Mexico. Sometimes it fails, as when Robert E. Lee invaded Pennsylvania in 1863 and lost at Gettysburg or when Hitler invaded Russia in 1941 and later lost at Stalingrad.

Our three commanders shared certain advantages. In spite of relative deficiencies in money or manpower, they had a distinct advantage in infrastructure. They all led experienced armies with a record of dominance in pitched battle—that is, a formal engagement planned beforehand and fought on chosen ground. Each was a constant campaigner, a master of mobility who pushed his army forward. All were great leaders, gifted with the ability to inspire the troops and shrewd enough to keep a steady stream of material rewards flowing to them. They had outstanding moral and physical qualities, such as courage, patience, vigor, and stamina, but their intellectual qualities were even more important. Each man combined a superior intellect with a decisive and resolute will. They lacked nothing in audacity. All were bold; none was risk-averse. Foresight, aptitude, and sheer brainpower are essential to a great commander; good judgment, especially in a crisis, is the most important quality of all. Each had a passionate conviction of his destiny and ability, not to say his divinity.

Each of the three commanders had a rare combination of instinct and arrogance. Each had the good judgment to size up his enemy correctly. Great men think they know their enemy and they have contempt for him. And one of the things that makes them great is that they are usually right. Alexander, for example, knew the Persians could not resist battle, just as Hannibal knew that neither could the Romans. Caesar knew that Pompey could not seize the day.

All three men were gifted with strategic vision. Each had a plan for victory: a blueprint for translating battlefield success into reality. Yet each man was an improviser and an opportunist, quick to take advantage of any possibility that happened to open.

For Hannibal, the argument boiled down, we might suspect, to science; to Caesar, character; and to Alexander, culture. Alexander had learned from his tutor, the philosopher Aristotle, that Persians were barbarians, without a

Greek's love of freedom or the willingness to stand steadfastly and die for it. "The enemy would have won that day, if they had a general," is Caesar's blistering appraisal of Pompey's leadership on a day of hard fighting in 48 B.C. Hannibal knew that, with his ability to combine infantry and cavalry, to maneuver, and to employ deceit, he was the master of military science—he was an artist of the battlefield; by comparison, the Romans were mere hammer drivers.

Alexander: Looking for a Fight

Alexander led one of history's most victorious armies and one of its most versatile. He had inherited it from his father, Philip, king of Macedon and founder of its military greatness. Philip was brilliant. By applying the latest advances in Greek military technology to Macedon's backward army, he forged a disciplined, professional, year-round force.

Macedon, with its plains and horses, was cavalry country, and Philip raised cavalry to new importance. The Macedonian heavy cavalry, now known as the Companion Cavalry, benefited from new recruitment and training, new weapons, new tactics, and new doctrine. The sons of the aristocracy went to court as teenagers and were trained as cavalrymen. They were outfitted with extra-long lances that gave them added reach compared with their enemies. They learned to fight in a wedge-shaped formation that was both more maneuverable than an in-line formation and more effective at penetrating the enemy line. Their doctrine was cunning aggression: they scanned the enemy line for a gap and then shot through it with murderous intensity. In short, the new Macedonian cavalry excelled at shock attack.

Alexander invaded Persian territory with eighteen hundred Companion Cavalry. They were organized in eight squadrons of which the Royal Squadron was the most elite; Alexander himself rode in the Royal Squadron's lead. Although small in number, the Companion Cavalry was one of the most effective units of horsemen in military history.

The cavalry spearheaded Macedonian victories but it couldn't have done so without the help of the other units in the Macedonian army, which Philip also revolutionized. Macedonian heavy infantrymen fought in a closely packed unit, the phalanx, like earlier Greek infantrymen. But they carried extra-long pikes to keep the enemy at a distance and they trained year-round. An elite infantry corps, known as the *hypaspists*, linked up the cavalry and infantry. Their job was to minimize the gap that inevitably opened when the cavalry sped ahead of the slower-marching infantry. Specialized units of slingers, archers, and javelin men raised the army's ability to meet all challenges. So did Philip's mastery of the technology of siegecraft, which he brought to a level of efficiency unseen since centuries before in the Near East.

A Macedonian battle represented an orchestrated balance of cavalry and infantry, with specialized units also playing a part. The standard tactic was to place the infantry in the center of the line and the cavalry on the flanks, with the best cavalry on the right wing. Typically, the Macedonian heavy infantrymen would first hold the enemy and try to create a weak spot in its line. The cavalry would then spring into action and rip open the enemy formation. Light-armed infantry, specially trained to dart among horses, helped the cavalry along. Then the heavy infantry would follow and finish the job.

Although the core of his army was Macedonian, Alexander's soldiers also included a number of reliable allies. Cavalry from Thessaly (in central Greece), Agrianian javelin-men from the mountains of what is today southern Serbia, and Cretan slingers and archers stood out. So did the mercenaries, who were employed in large numbers.

Alexander had a superb group of general officers to rely on, led by Philip's marshals. Although the young king surely itched to replace them with his own men, he was too shrewd to do so. He knew that Philip's men represented Macedon's proud and close-knit nobility. They had the troops' support and besides, he had no one to match their skill or experience. Alexander had a fingertip feel for political as well as military reality. So he kept Philip's generals. Meanwhile, Alexander bonded with his soldiers by displaying strategic insight, courage in battle, and limitless self-confidence.

Between the leaders and the men they led, Alexander's was one of history's greatest armies. If the Persians decided to fight conventional battles, then the Macedonians had a real chance of winning, despite massive inferiority in money and manpower. But if the Persians chose a different strategy, one based on a combination of unconventional warfare on land and a naval offensive at sea, then they might have rendered Alexander's army a splendid but irrelevant machine. Even great armies can lose wars if the enemy is cunning, determined, and resourceful.

The Persians ruled the largest empire in history to that date, stretching from Central Asia to Egypt, and including perhaps one-fifth of the world's population. With their huge sources of military manpower, the Persians substantially outnumbered the Macedonians. Great horsemen, the Persians had excellent cavalry and they made up for their weakness in infantry by hiring first-class Greek mercenary infantrymen. But their inexperience, lack of trusted generals, and—in the case of the cavalry—inferior equipment put the Persians at a great disadvantage against the Macedonians in battle.

The Greeks called Persia's emperor the "Great King." The adjective "good" probably better fit the current occupant of the throne, Darius III. He was a fine battlefield commander and an excellent military organizer. He was a shrewd political operator and a cunning diplomat. But he lacked experience and legitimacy: like Alexander, he was a new king (his reign began in 336 B.C.), but unlike him, Darius was neither the heir to the throne nor a king's son. Born Codomanus, he was a fine military man but he did not have his eye on the throne. Darius became king only after the long-reigning Persian monarch Artaxerxes III (r. 358–338) and his son Arses (r. 338–336) had each been murdered by his chief minister. Darius was their distant cousin. Many Persians looked on Darius as a usurper and gave him less than their full support. Alexander had a seasoned corps of generals committed to a common purpose, but Darius suffered from divided and inexperienced advisors.

When it came to size and resources, the Persian empire experienced a real difference between reality and appearance. Many of the provinces at either end of the empire were barely under Persian control. Egypt, for example, was perpetually in revolt, most recently in the 340s; the satraps (provincial governors) of Anatolia mounted a revolt in the 360s that smoldered until the 340s; the provinces of Central and South Asia were more or less independent.

Still, in spite of Persia's disadvantages, a brilliant leader with a sure touch and a dollop of luck could have defeated Alexander. Unfortunately, Darius, although courageous, intelligent, and an excellent organizer, lacked Alexander's skill and experience as a field commander.

Still, Darius knew enough to turn to Persia's tried-and-true policy against Greek invasion: a naval counteroffensive. This strategy had stopped Sparta in 395 B.C. after it invaded Anatolia. It looked promising now in 334, when Macedon's navy was small and unreliable, consisting almost

entirely of Athenian allies, although most Athenians resented Macedonian
hegemony. Persia's navy was big and trustworthy. If it made a serious push
across the Aegean Sea, Persia could raise a rebellion in Alexander's rear, in
the Greek city-states. The Persian navy might defeat Alexander while his
invasion was just beginning.

Hannibal: Force and Fraud

Few generals have ever approached the battlefield as well armed in force
and fraud as Hannibal. Few have ever pulled off greater feats of mobility. As
with the wigs and disguises that he wore to foil assassins, Hannibal was full
of tricks. But he was also a deadly battlefield puncher.

Hannibal's army consisted of a varied mix of men and abilities. Indeed,
one of his greatest achievements was turning them into a cohesive whole.

The Roman army in Hannibal's day consisted of citizen-soldiers. Ordinary Roman males, most of them farmers, served their country as soldiers.
Fighting beside them were soldiers from allied cities in Italy, most of whom
were also citizen-soldiers.

Carthage's army was totally different. Only some of the officers were
Carthaginian; the troops represented other nationalities. Some were mercenaries but most had been recruited from the various peoples in North Africa
and Spain under Carthaginian rule. Some were inexperienced but others
had soldiered long enough to be considered professionals. Hannibal's best
troops were North Africans—Libyans and Numidians (today, Algerians).
Next came the Spaniards, to whom he soon added northern Italian Celts. As
infantrymen, the best of them—the Libyans—rivaled Rome's famed legionaries, but they could not match their numbers. What gave Hannibal an edge
was his horsemen and his ability to maneuver them. He used cavalry more
successfully than any general since Alexander, a century earlier.

Hannibal's father, Hamilcar Barca, had learned how to win battles from
Greek military experts. His method was to hold the enemy in the center
while enveloping him on the wings and even the rear. It was not an easy maneuver to carry out but when accomplished it could be devastating. Hannibal, who learned these tactics from his father, carried them out brilliantly.
Hannibal commanded both heavy and light cavalry. Together, these infantry
could run rings around Roman cavalry. Hannibal's cavalrymen were trained

to fight in tandem with his infantrymen. Combined, they represented a deadly one-two punch. Because they were professionals, Hannibal's men had the training to carry out maneuvers that Rome's citizen-soldiers could only dream of. Meanwhile, his elephants would shield Hannibal's infantry and terrify the enemy. The result would be state-of-the-art military science.

Hannibal's army had certain advantages of command and experience. He had a fine corps of supporting generals. In Italy officers like Maharbal, son of Himilco; Hanno, son of Bomilcar; and one Hasdrubal (not Hannibal's brother) would rip Roman armies to pieces. But Hannibal's generals did not do well on their own without his guiding hand, starting with his two brothers, Mago and Hasdrubal. The one exception, Mottones, Hannibal's hand-picked cavalry commander in Sicily, shone in battle but fell afoul of Carthaginian political in-fighting. He turned traitor and became a Roman citizen—and general!

As for the Carthaginian army, Polybius describes Hannibal's men thus: they "had been trained in actual warfare constantly from their earliest youth, they had a general who had been brought up together with them and was accustomed from childhood to operations in the field, they had won many battles in Spain. . . ."

Not that Hannibal could afford to ignore the deadly cohesion and stead-fastness of the Roman legions! Unlike most of Rome's opponents, however, he had a chance of beating Rome. A tactical giant, Hannibal reckoned that his superior generalship could defeat the Romans in battle and cause them enormous casualties. But he would have to move with devastating speed and overwhelming force. Otherwise, he might end up like Pyrrhus.

King Pyrrhus of Epirus invaded southern Italy in 280 B.C. A charismatic general like Hannibal, Pyrrhus too had a small but experienced army complete with cavalry and elephants. Unlike Hannibal, he even had many Italian allies. Pyrrhus won two major pitched battles against Rome but suffered such severe losses as to render them "Pyrrhic victories"—the term we still use today. More important, Rome refused to concede. Rome's central Italian allies held steadfast and provided new troops, but Pyrrhus's manpower was running out.

Furthermore, Rome won the support of a key ally from outside Italy. Ironically, it was Carthage that feared that Pyrrhus would invade its territory in Sicily. That indeed happened, but Pyrrhus did no better in Sicily than in Italy. Meanwhile, Rome pummeled his Italian allies, so Pyrrhus returned to help them, only to be defeated in battle. In 275, Pyrrhus went home, having accomplished nothing.

Hannibal risked a similar fate. In fact, he risked worse, because in Pyrrhus's day, Rome had no fleet. Now it had a great navy, which meant that it could counterattack in Spain. Carthage did not have much of a navy of its own, having lost its fleet in the First Punic War.

In 218 B.C., Rome had 220 warships, while Carthage had only one hundred. But the numbers tell only part of the story. Since winning the First Punic War, Rome's sailors had developed expertise and guts. Carthage's sailors had stagnated. In 218 Carthage needed not only more ships but also a new and bolder naval culture. Its admirals included no Hannibals.

Geography was another problem. Rome controlled the vital ports in Sicily and Sardinia. Ancient navies needed to make frequent stops on shore, so whoever controlled the harbors of these central Mediterranean islands controlled the sea-lanes.

For all these reasons, Hannibal could not ship his forces to Italy. He had no other invasion route but a grueling, thousand-mile overland march from southern Spain to northern Italy. And that might cost him vital manpower.

The key to Rome's strength was its confederacy. Between 350 and 270 B.C. Rome had conquered all of the communities of Italy south of the Po and Rubicon rivers. It was a large area to control and Rome used various strategies to do so, from annexing territory, building roads, and planting colonies to intervening as needed in order to install friendly politicians in power.

But two Roman policies stand out in importance. First, Rome turned itself into a population giant by granting Roman citizenship to many of the conquered peoples. By 225 B.C. Rome's population, in the city of Rome and Roman territory all over Italy, was close to one million free people, of whom 300,000 were adult males and so therefore, liable for military service. Second, Rome required its allies to contribute soldiers to the Roman army. In 225, allied troops amounted to 460,000 men. So Rome had a total of 760,000 potential soldiers.

This was a staggering number, especially considering Hannibal's forces, about 60,000 men when he first left Spain but a mere 26,000 men when he reached northern Italy after his devastating march. How, then, did he plan to defeat Rome?

The answer was to crack the Roman confederacy. Hannibal planned to shock Italy by handing Rome such big defeats in battle that the allies would start defecting to him, first in a trickle and then a flood. Their actions would add to Hannibal's manpower and subtract from Rome's. Rome might hold out at first, but eventually Hannibal would win away so many of Rome's allied troops that Rome would come to the bargaining table.

To make his task slightly easier, Hannibal didn't plan to destroy Rome, merely to defang it. He was fighting, he said, only for "honor and empire." He wanted to protect Carthage's empire in Spain and to get back Sardinia, and probably Sicily as well.

For Hannibal, then, victory depended on two things: battle victories and allied defections. Could he achieve his goal?

Polybius didn't think so. The historian criticized Hannibal for going to war on emotional grounds rather than rational analysis: Hannibal was "wholly under the influence of unreasoning and violent anger." Rome was just too strong and Hannibal should never have invaded Italy, according to Polybius.

Polybius is a formidable historian, but he doesn't give audacity its due. It would be fairer to say this: Hannibal had a well-thought-out if highly risky plan. It began with a long and dangerous march followed by a rapid series of hammer blows to Rome's homeland, so hard and fast that Rome's Italian confederacy would crack. It also called for diplomatic finesse in dealing with Rome's Italian allies and political shrewdness in managing the home government in Carthage.

Not since Alexander had any general displayed so much offensive ability. If anyone could do it, Hannibal could, but was Rome too strong?

Caesar: Speed Kills

As he made his plans on the far side of the Rubicon, Caesar might have calculated his military strengths and weaknesses. His greatest strength by far was his army. Caesar's army was not merely good, it was his. Eight years in Gaul had tied the men to him by blood and iron and faith. The army believed in Caesar.

He, in turn, played them like a lute. He overlooked their lapses and foibles but came down hard on deserters. He never called them "soldiers" but always "fellow soldiers." After a massacre in Gaul, he swore not to cut his hair or beard until he had avenged the dead—and, as everyone knew, he was vain about his looks, so it was a sacrifice indeed.

Caesar's army worshiped his brains, his courage, his charity, and his charisma. Thirty thousand fighting men saw him as their captain, their patron, their leader, and even their father. In Gaul he gave them victory and profit. The men never lacked for material rewards: Caesar saw to that. Now, he promised them the first rank in the Roman state.

True, civil war offered fewer sources of loot than foreign conflict, and that would generate tension. Yet Caesar's political skills would keep his men happy, and besides, civil war offered the thrill of the illicit, the knowledge that every man in his army had made himself an outlaw once he crossed the Rubicon. The prospect of victory or death wove extraordinary ties between leader and led. It was, in short, a love story.

Caesar's forces at the Rubicon were small in number but reinforcements were on the way. Meanwhile, he had the men of the Thirteenth Legion. Veterans of Gaul, they were experienced and self-controlled. They knew how to infiltrate a town and then suddenly make their presence known. One legion—five thousand men—was big enough to lay siege to a small city, and Caesar's army was expert in sieges. Once his numbers increased, they could do the same to big cities.

Nor was there any doubt about their ability to move fast. Alexander and Hannibal were speedy but Caesar was quicksilver—an athlete of the battlefield. Rarely has a general understood better that speed kills. Neither did Caesar lack stamina. His army combined the speed of a cheetah with the endurance of an ant.

Once he had more soldiers, Caesar would relish meeting the enemy in battle. He might have guessed, however, that Pompey would not want to risk his men against Caesar's veterans. More likely, Caesar would have to outrun and outmaneuver Pompey, and catch him in a town that he could besiege or maybe even take by storm.

Caesar knew Pompey personally and seems to have had genuine affection for him, but Caesar had no doubt about his own superiority as a general. Whether he thought that Pompey had lost his skill or that he had never had it, Caesar was convinced that he was better.

It didn't matter. Whatever Pompey might have been able to do, he suffered one big disadvantage: he lacked supreme command. Instead, he shared command with several leading senators. His army lacked the unity at the top that victory usually requires. Caesar, the undisputed chief, did not have to wrestle with other generals. He was not a committee chairman but a leader.

Balanced against this advantage was a big military disadvantage: Caesar had no navy. If he could not beat his enemies in Italy, they could escape by ship and live to fight another day. And perhaps Pompey was not quite so inferior as Caesar might have thought. It was all the more reason for Caesar to move with speed and decisiveness.

Caesar was enough of a realist to know that he would probably not catch Pompey in a decisive battle in Italy. To win the war, Caesar would have to overcome his weakness at sea, transport his army abroad, and force Pompey into a do-or-die battle. Could he do it? That would be Caesar's greatest test.

Targets Hard and Soft

When Alexander and Caesar each launched their wars, the enemy—the Persian empire or the Roman republic—had already been weakened by decades of regional rebellions and civil war. Mercenaries and adventurers in force had already crisscrossed the Aegean Sea for years when Alexander invaded. Caesar was not the first rebel general to march on Rome. Neither Darius's Persia nor Pompey's Rome offered a united front to the invader; each suffered from factionalism.

By contrast, the Roman republic attacked by Hannibal stood relatively united. Rome's Italian confederacy was vulnerable in northern Italy, where the Celts had only recently lost their freedom to Rome and southern Italy too had its share of *independistas*. But the core of Rome's Italian confederacy in central Italy was rock solid. To win the war, Hannibal had to break that rock. If that was not impossible, neither was it easy.

So Hannibal faced a tougher job than either Caesar or Alexander did. Domestic politics did not make his task easier. Hannibal was not a king or a dictator but a general of the Carthaginian state. Although Spain gave him a power base, he would need support from Carthage unless he defeated Rome very rapidly. And that support was not guaranteed.

Most Carthaginians were eager to fight their hated Roman enemy, but that doesn't mean they supported Hannibal's war plans. Some disagreed with his strategy, while others distrusted him or disliked the Barcas. And Hannibal had last seen Carthage when he was nine years old. His knowledge of domestic politics could hardly match his familiarity with the field of arms.

The other two commanders also faced problems on the home front. Alexander was a king loathed by most of the Greek city-states that were, in theory, his allies. Many of Alexander's Greek allies were itching to rebel and join Persia. Caesar was no king but a rebel provincial general against lawful authority; he lacked legitimacy. Even if Caesar conquered Italy, he had no fleet to pry open the sea-lanes needed to get grain supplies through; if Pompey took to the sea, he could starve Italy.

All in all, Hannibal had the most difficult task. To crack Rome's Central Italian confederacy would take the application of great resources in infrastructure to precisely the right point. Hannibal had to procure those resources from the Carthaginian government and he had to direct them against the proper target. That would require a grasp both of strategy and of politics. The war would prove if Hannibal had it.

POLITICAL STRATEGIES

All three men fought wars with a strongly political dimension. Like most generals today, none had the luxury of following military logic alone. Each had to take politics into account as well.

Alexander: Politician and General

Alexander's march into the Persian empire was not merely an invasion route but a form of information warfare, aimed at two audiences: the Persian army and Greek public opinion. His message to Persia was that he was coming in force. For two years, the Macedonian army in Anatolia had consisted of a 10,000-man advance force. Now, in 334, nearly 50,000 Macedonians—an additional 32,000 infantry and 5,000 cavalry—had invaded, along with a fleet of 160 warships and numerous transports. To the Greeks, Alexander presented his expedition as revenge—he marketed it as a Panhellenic crusade to avenge the Persians' invasion of 480 b.c. That was long ago but most Greeks still thought of the Persians as "the barbarian," as their ancestors had.

But Alexander had to shore up weak support—indeed, the threat of rebellion—from his Greek rear, including the unreliable Athenian navy. He had to show that he was pro-Greek and that any Greeks who supported Persia would be dealt with severely. He did that by a combination of branding and brutal reprisals.

In order to emphasize the theme of Greek revenge, Alexander led the Macedonian army eastward toward the Hellespont on about the same route that the Persian king Xerxes had followed when he marched westward in his doomed invasion of Greece in 480 b.c. Alexander crossed the Hellespont from Sestos to Abydos, the very place where Xerxes had bridged the channel (they went by ship) in the opposite direction. While crossing the Hellespont, Alexander made sacrifices to the gods and poured a libation to the water, in contrast with Xerxes, who had his men whip the Hellespont and toss chains in it to "punish" the water for a destructive storm, acts that the Greeks considered impious.

When he landed near Abydos, Alexander strode onto the shore of Asia in full armor. He had already thrown a spear from the ship: a sign, as he later put it, that he considered the Persian empire a spear-won land from the gods. For good measure, Alexander went to the nearby city of Troy or, rather, Ilion, the Greek city built on the site of Troy. Xerxes had made a similar pilgrimage there in 480, and Alexander could do no less.

Having waged a propaganda campaign to demonstrate his devotion to the cause of Greece, Alexander now returned to the main purpose of his trip to Anatolia: he rejoined his army.

Alexander invaded the Persian empire in 334 b.c. with a clear war plan but an open-ended goal. At a minimum he wanted to conquer western Anatolia (modern Turkey) and add it to his kingdom. At a maximum—well, there is reason to think that Philip had aimed at conquering the entire Persian empire in all of its vastness. This included both Persia's other holdings in Western Asia—Syria, Palestine, Egypt, and Mesopotamia—and lands lying farther eastward—the Iranian plateau and all or part of modern Kazakhstan, Afghanistan, Tajikistan, Uzbekistan, Pakistan, and northwestern India. It was a huge ambition, and to some it would probably have seemed like a mythological tale. No one could rule an empire this big without becoming an absolute monarch; Alexander's advisors knew this, and many of them eventually recoiled in horror from the prospect. But it probably seemed unlikely at first, since the Persian empire was no pushover. Although it had demonstrated military weakness in recent years, Persia still had huge advantages in money, manpower, ships, and local knowledge.

Each step in Alexander's campaign was in itself a tall order. Take Anatolia. To conquer it, Alexander had to keep the Persian navy from opening a second front in Greece as well as defeat the Persian army in Anatolia. He also had to win allies and find food for his men. Last but not least, he had to raise money, because war is expensive, and the Macedonian treasury was empty.

In 334 B.C. Alexander was twenty-two and had sat on the throne for only two years. Yet he was already an experienced field commander. At age sixteen, Philip made him regent of Macedonia, and Alexander led a rapid expedition to Thrace that put down a rebellion and turned a city into a Macedonian military outpost called Alexandropolis. At age eighteen, under Philip's supervision, Alexander led the Macedonian cavalry on the war-winning charge that conquered Greece at the Battle of Chaeronea (338 B.C.). At twenty, he became king. In the next two years as commander-in-chief of the Macedonian army, he marched his armies a thousand miles, suppressed rebellions in Greece and the Balkans, and destroyed Thebes, Greece's single most powerful land power. He also extended his empire's northern frontier to the Danube River, won a series of victories on his own without the help of Philip's best generals, and executed both precisely planned operations and brilliant improvisations. Alexander demonstrated other skills as well, such as his mastery of combined-arms operations, in which he used cavalry and light-armed and heavy-armed infantry. He showed himself able to scramble when needed, by sizing up both enemy and terrain on the spot and issuing precisely the right orders. He was very inventive. On one occasion, he had his men cut steps up the cliff face of a mountain, and on another occasion, he ordered them to throw together a scratch fleet to cross the Danube. His most creative manuever of all was history's first recorded use of field artillery.

Alexander had earned the love of his soldiers. He also earned the fear of Macedon's Greek and Balkan allies but he didn't trust them. Nowadays, the province of Macedonia (not to be confused with the independent country to the north) is an integral part of Greece, but in Alexander's era, many Greeks looked on Macedonians as savages, and would have been glad to revolt, given a chance. The Persian navy represented that chance. To discourage the Greeks, Alexander left 13,500 soldiers (27 percent—i.e., more than one quarter—of his total forces) in Macedonia when he invaded Persia. Their job was to be ready to invade any Greek city-state that joined the Persians.

Every major city-state on the Greek mainland except Sparta had joined Alexander's coalition. Sparta stubbornly held out. Its great days were behind it, however, and it was now mainly a small and out-of-the way place with a glorious name. Even if its refusal smarted, Sparta was not worth the trouble to conquer.

Alexander also planned a political response to the threatened Persian naval offensive. As he drove the Persians out of the Greek cities of Anatolia, he advertised himself as a liberator for all Greeks. But he also showed himself to be a killer: in his first battle he executed most Greek mercenaries caught fighting for Persia, which was a brutal act, considering that captured mercenaries were usually easily encouraged to change sides. He wanted to make a political more than a military point in order to discourage other Greeks from fighting for Persia.

Hannibal: The Diplomat

When he marched against Rome in 218 b.c., Hannibal was already an accomplished commander. He had spent two years conquering hostile Spanish tribes and then turning to Rome's Spanish ally, Saguntum. He laid siege to the city and took it after eight months. When Rome declared war, Hannibal was ready with a daring plan: an overland march across the Pyrenees and the hostile territory of southern France and the Alps—with elephants, no less.

Hannibal had crushed his Spanish enemies and earned the love of his men. He offered military prowess and leadership skill, to which he added public relations. He used religion deftly to appeal to the various Celtic peoples in his army. Unlike Alexander, Hannibal never claimed to be a god, but he avowed divine patronage. He branded himself as a new Hercules. Before leaving New Carthage, he made a special trip to Gades to pray at the shrine of Melqart, the Punic Hercules. In the Alps, there was talk of a god—plausibly, Hercules—leading Hannibal through the mountains. On the march through northern Spain, Hannibal reported a dream of a young man sent by the king of the gods to guide him to Italy and to ravage its land like a giant serpent.

In spite of that serpent, Hannibal was a diplomat who planned to win the support of potential allies in enemy territory. Rome had conquered the peoples of central and southern Italy one by one. Many of them chafed under its rule. But a bigger problem was Rome's fragile control of the Celts, whose tribes comprised the majority of the population of the Po valley and most of today's northern Italy (including Piedmont, Lombardy, the Veneto, and Emilia-Romagna). They had launched a great rebellion between 225 and 222 B.C. and were still simmering in discontent after defeat by Rome. Before setting out on his expedition, Hannibal sent ambassadors to the Celts and won promises of support from some tribes.

Meanwhile, in central and southern Italy, the population did not express anti-Roman sentiments as openly, but these regions too were rich in subterranean feelings of resentment. Hannibal planned to raise them up. He would tell Italians that he had come not as a conqueror but a liberator. After each of his victories he enslaved Romans but freed any Italians that his men had captured.

Hannibal's comparison of himself to Hercules—Heracles to Greeks— played well in southern Italy. Pyrrhus too had likened himself to Heracles, and so had the greatest Greek conqueror of all, Alexander.

Hannibal had two other political audiences to think of, one in Spain and the other in North Africa. Some Spanish tribes still smarted under Carthaginian rule; should Hannibal falter in Italy, the news might spark their rebellion. When he marched to Italy, therefore, he left soldiers, ships, and elephants behind in Spain under the command of his brother Hasdrubal to keep the Spaniards in line.

Even more important for Hannibal was the politics of Carthage's government. Hannibal protected Carthage by sending sixteen thousand soldiers from Spain to North Africa when he left for Italy. Carthage had supported Hannibal when Rome demanded his head, after the siege of Saguntum. The city had fought rather than hand over Hannibal, but they also wanted to keep Spain—and knew they had to protect Hannibal to do so. When it came to the Italian campaign, they might have felt differently.

As at Rome, so in Carthage a council of elders or senate played a leading role in the government. Its members had mixed feelings about Hannibal's war. On the one hand, they hated Rome, but on the other hand, many of them distrusted Hannibal. The Barca family had won Carthage a lucrative province in Spain but had also won itself a power base. If Hannibal now added Italy to his sphere of influence, he would tower over Carthage. Political titans always make councils of elders nervous. "Safety in numbers" is usually their motto.

So the Carthaginian senate supported Hannibal but not in every particular. Many senators had their own agenda—winning back the lost colonies in Sicily and Sardinia. They saw the war in Italy as a means to that end. Should Hannibal stumble there, they were ready to open new fronts in the islands and to turn to new commanders—preferably ones with lesser political ambitions.

To win the war in Italy, therefore, Hannibal had to be far more than a great general. He had also to be a first-class diplomat, an able propagandist, and a cunning domestic politician.

Caesar: Shock and Awe Commander

What the Barca family had built in Spain, Caesar achieved in Gaul: conquest of a rich province that was all but his own property. Unlike Hannibal, however, who had left Carthage for good at the age of nine to follow his father to Spain, Caesar had built a career in Rome before going to Gaul: he was already a veteran politician when, in his forties, he became a conqueror. Caesar's actions both before and after crossing the Rubicon demonstrate his mastery of the art of being a political general—of being, in short, Caesar.

Caesar used his victory in Gaul well. To advertise his success he wrote a literary classic, *The Gallic War,* in which he branded himself as a military giant. From its famous opening—"All Gaul is divided into three parts"—Caesar proclaimed to the Roman people his military and political skill; after all, "divide and conquer" was the oldest maxim of Roman warfare. The book drove home the power of Caesar's military. It was quick, efficient, ruthless, and utterly ready to commit acts of terror: Caesar was said to have been responsible for a million deaths in the conquest of Gaul and a million more enslaved, many of them civilians.

While in Gaul, Caesar kept a finger on the pulse of politics in Rome.

Gaul was a vast province, big enough to allow Caesar to spend his winters in Ravenna in northern Italy, just 200 miles from Rome. In 49 B.C., northern Italy was not considered Roman territory; it was a foreign province, under the rule of a Roman governor—Caesar. Northern Italy was called Cisalpine Gaul, "Gaul on this side [the south side] of the Alps," and it was part of Caesar's Gallic command. While wintering in Ravenna, Caesar commanded one legion. His other legions were north of the Alps, but three of them were poised to reach him quickly.

Having made his name as a populist before going to Gaul, Caesar continued the tradition by sending loot home to fund public works projects. He offered the Roman people a program of welfare benefits, which made him more popular than the grandees in the Roman senate, who jealously guarded their own property. But unlike many politicians, Caesar did not crow at his opponents' mistakes.

Caesar faced two main groups of opponents at the time he crossed the Rubicon: conservatives in the Senate and Pompey and his supporters. The senators stood on principle: they could not abide the thought of one man dominating Roman politics as a dictator, as the dictator Sulla had (82–79 B.C.). They saw Caesar as what might now be called a "red dictator," someone whose populist policies might yield absolute power. Pompey didn't care about principle; he cared about Pompey. Before Caesar had conquered Gaul, Pompey had been the dominant military-political figure in Rome. Now, his star was waning and Caesar's was a supernova. Pompey would not share power with Caesar; the senators could not bear submitting to a fellow aristocrat turned populist demagogue. Not that they relished cooperation with Pompey, himself a dominant figure, but the senators correctly saw him as less of a threat to them than was Caesar. So they ordered Caesar's arrest, and he responded by crossing the Rubicon with his army, aimed at Rome.

Many had doubted that Caesar would dare take this step, and for a good reason: he had only one legion in Italy, that is, five thousand men. Pompey had two legions (eight thousand to ten thousand men) and the authority to raise 130,000 new troops, to be led by himself and various prominent senators. Pompey also had seven legions in Spain and, although far off, they could be moved to Italy. Caesar had ten legions north of the Alps; as it turned out, three were ready to join him about a month later. Besides, he no doubt knew what a general would later say: "It is not the big armies that win battles; it is the good ones."

If it seems surprising that neither side had a large army ready, remember, as Pompey and Caesar both did, that in a civil war, less is more. Both knew that the public wanted peace, so neither general wanted the blame for having provoked war. Each was willing to risk a lack of preparation in order to dodge responsibility for the war. The result was that once war broke out, the two sides each had to play catch-up. That favored Caesar.

Caesar had sole and supreme command of his forces, while Pompey had to share command with a committee of senators, each pulling in his own direction. Pompey and his allies in the Senate distrusted each other as much as Hitler and Stalin did after they agreed to carve up Poland together.

If Caesar coldly appraised Pompey before Caesar crossed the Rubicon, he would have had to admit that he faced a great general. Among Pompey's achievements were victories in North Africa, Spain, the eastern Mediterranean from Anatolia to Judea, and on the high seas against the pirates. He was shrewd, disciplined, and a superb organizer. Yet, while Caesar had stormed through Gaul, Pompey had gotten used to a life of civilian ease: it had been nearly fifteen years since he had commanded in the field. On top of that, Pompey's military specialty was defense. Caesar, on the other hand, specialized in what is today called shock and awe.

A good general needs to figure out how his enemy thinks. Before crossing the Rubicon, Caesar probably guessed Pompey's strategy: rather than risk fighting Caesar's hardened veterans of Gaul, Pompey would raise new troops quickly in Italy and then evacuate them to Greece. There he could train them into a great army, return with them to Italy, and defeat Caesar.

Caesar knew that Pompey held two aces. Unlike Caesar, Pompey had a navy, which meant that, after fleeing Italy, he could return in force by way of the sea. The East, furthermore, was his base, just as Gaul was Caesar's base. Pompey had conquered much of the eastern Mediterranean for Rome in the 60s B.C., leaving him a gigantic network of men who owed him favors.

But Pompey needed time. He needed time to persuade the senators that it really made sense to evacuate Italy. Many of them would refuse to concede to Caesar the psychological advantage of controlling Italy's "sacred soil"—a point made by none other than Napoleon, who studied ancient history while living out his exile. Pompey also needed time to recruit new troops in Italy. Unfortunately for Pompey, Caesar was the thief of time. The war was a race, and in military terms, Caesar was a champion runner.

THREE EARLY VICTORIES—MORE TO COME

By the time they invaded enemy territory, Alexander, Hannibal, and Caesar had each shown that he was dangerous. Each wielded the equivalent of a dagger: a loyal, veteran, and victorious army. Only two defenses were possible: to fight with equal force or to retreat. Retreat repels most soldiers but sometimes it is necessary for future victory, despite the accompanying shame. A retreat makes it possible to harass the enemy in skirmishes as they give chase, to deny him food by purposely destroying one's own resources (a "scorched-earth" policy), and to regroup to fight again another day.

But still, retreat denies the men a fight, and few soldiers will tolerate that. Most armies choose to stand and fight, as the Persians did against Alexander and the Romans did against Hannibal.

Alexander: A Quick Early Victory

Things could hardly have gone better for Alexander as his army invaded Anatolia in spring 334. Getting from Europe to Asia required ferrying across the narrow waterway of the Hellespont (or Dardanelles as we know it). A strategic bottleneck, the Hellespont attracted antiquity's naval battles the way a canvas ring attracts boxers, but Persia's mighty fleet was nowhere to be seen. The Macedonians controlled both shores at the crossing point, and ancient navies did not like to fight without a friendly shore to retreat to. Alexander's forces crossed unmolested and landed near Troy. They totaled about 50,000 men.

Their logistical base, however, was made of sand. Alexander had only a month's worth of supplies. Worse still, he had no money. Macedon had spent its last drachma in putting together the invasion force. To feed his men, Alexander would have to persuade or force the cities of Anatolia to open their gates—and their granaries.

Darius did not take the Macedonian threat lightly. He saw to it that the five satraps of Anatolia's great provinces met and pooled their military resources under the guidance of the leading mercenary general of the day. But that general did not have absolute command. In retrospect, Darius made a mistake by allowing a divided command when he should have enforced a single, united policy. Committees do not make good generals.

As Alexander's army arrived on Asian soil, a council of Persian commanders met about seventy-five miles to the east, in the small city of Zeleia. Those present included satraps and members of the royal family as well as the greatest mercenary commander of the age, Memnon of Rhodes, a man "famous for his good judgment as a general."

Memnon was Greek. It might seem surprising to find a Greek among Persia's commanders, but it was a common sight. Persians made great cavalrymen but only mediocre infantrymen, while Greeks made excellent infantrymen. When it came to war, the Persian government was pragmatic and relatively open-minded, so it hired Greek soldiers and Greek generals.

Memnon came from the premier mercenary family of the age. He and his brother Mentor had spent twenty years in Persian service, where they rose to top positions. Yet they had married into Persia's first family of rebellion, the family of Artabazus, satrap of Phrygia (an important area in northwestern Turkey). Mentor married Artabazus's daughter Barsine; when Mentor died in 340, Barsine married Memnon. (Artabazus, by the way, married Mentor and Memnon's sister.) In the 350s, Artabazus rebelled against the then Persian king Artaxerxes III. The tide of war ebbed and flowed until 352, when Artabazus and Memnon fled to Macedon and the court of Philip II. Mentor went to Egypt and eventually ended up back in the good graces of Artaxerxes III by helping to put down a rebellion there. In exchange, Artabazus and Memnon were pardoned and allowed to return to Persian territory in 343. They brought firsthand knowledge of Macedonian plans and power. When Darius III became king in 336, Memnon and Artabazus both served him loyally.

Memnon leveraged his knowledge of Macedon into a series of victories against Alexander's advance forces in Anatolia from 336 to 335. In one battle, he even defeated the Macedonian commanding general, the great veteran Parmenio, and drove him back toward the Hellespont. But Memnon was shrewd, and he did not overestimate his success. He knew that it was one thing to defeat a small advance force and quite another to take on the main army led by its king.

Memnon knew just how seasoned and ruthless young Alexander was. Memnon concluded that a conventional battle against Macedon was too

dangerous, because of the Persians' inferiority in infantry. Instead, he "advocated a policy of . . . ravaging the land and through the shortage of supplies
keeping the Macedonians from advancing further." At the same time, he was
pressing for a naval offensive.

Led by the local satrap, the men gathered at Zeleia rejected Memnon's
advice. They considered it their duty to defend their land, not to destroy it.
They might also have disliked taking advice from a foreigner like Memnon.
Some might even have questioned his loyalty, considering that the Macedonians had spared his estates near Troy from ravaging. (This was a bit of
psychological warfare aimed at making the Persians distrust Memnon.)

The Persians at Zeleia decided to fight a pitched battle. They knew that
Alexander outnumbered them in infantry but they probably also knew that
most of Alexander's 30,000 infantrymen were untested and untrustworthy
allied troops. Persia had 6,000 veteran and reliable Greek mercenaries.
Persia had the numerical edge in cavalry, 20,000 to 5,000. The Persians
planned to make the Macedonians fight a cavalry battle. And they knew that
they could fight on ground of their own choosing, because Alexander had to
come to them.

As long as the Persians had an army near Zeleia, Alexander could not
march south, because the enemy might then cut his communications with
the Hellespont. So Alexander marched toward Zeleia, about three days away
from Troy. As the enemy might have guessed, he left most of his 30,000
infantrymen behind; he took only 12,000 heavy infantrymen, all trusted
Macedonians, as well as 1,000 light-armed troops from Thrace. He also
brought his entire cavalry, 5,000 men.

The Persian army made its stand on the main east-west road, west of
Zeleia. As Alexander's army marched eastward, his scouts reported the location of the Persians at the far end of the Plain of Adrasteia, on the east bank
of the Granicus River. The defenders had chosen good ground. Although
the river was not deep (only about three feet in May), it was fast-flowing,
slippery, and protected by steep and muddy banks. The Macedonians would
have no easy time getting their men across and in good order. The Persians
planned to take advantage of disarray in the enemy ranks to execute a strategy of decapitation. They would target Alexander and kill him.

It was already afternoon when the Macedonians located the Persians.
Alexander's advisors recommended delaying until the next day, in the hope

that the enemy would withdraw from the damp river edge overnight, which would allow the Macedonians to cross in the morning. Alexander insisted on immediate battle. Usually a good psychologist, he knew that action would inspire his men and frighten the enemy.

The Persian cavalry lined the east bank of the Granicus, covering both the lip of the bank and a flat area going back about three hundred yards. They held their infantry, all Greek mercenaries, in reserve on the high ground behind them, knowing it would be pointless to deploy them against an enemy who outnumbered them. The infantry could be called in later, if needed.

On the other side of the river, Alexander's Macedonians did not follow suit, but arranged their infantry between their cavalry on either wing. Alexander and the Macedonian cavalry held the Macedonian right wing; Parmenio and the allied, Thessalian cavalry occupied the left wing. As usual, the cavalry would strike first. They could not make a frontal assault, but their scouts had found a few gentle, gravel slopes along the steep banks of the river. The cavalry aimed for them as crossing places.

And so, the two waves of riders, with which this book started, attacked the Persians. Alexander began with a cunning move. He sent in a squadron of about one thousand cavalrymen, to draw the enemy off the bank and into the river. It succeeded, at a cost of heavy Macedonian casualties. Having forced the enemy to break up its line, Alexander now attacked. He led his men in oblique order heading upstream, that is, going farther to his right, in order to do two things. Alexander wanted both to outflank the Persians and to ensure that his men would present a solid front to the enemy rather than emerge from the river in column, where they could be picked off one by one. No novice, he had proven himself four years earlier by leading a cavalry charge against the Greeks at the Battle of Chaeronea.

The Persians were no tactical novices either. A wedge-shaped unit of horsemen, led by some of Persia's leading men, bore down on the enemy. They aimed for Alexander, hoping to cut out the heart of the invasion by killing its leader. They almost succeeded. In fact, they would have changed history, had not Cleitus saved his king from Rhoesaces's nearly fatal attack, as we saw in chapter 1.

Once the Macedonians rescued Alexander, their assault proved devastating to the Persians. For all the elegance of Alexander's opening moves,

Granicus came down to a brawl. The sources talk of shoving and of "horses fighting entangled with horses and men entangled with men." Alexander's men had better equipment and technical expertise, and many of them, especially his bodyguard, were simply big and strong. The Macedonians had cornel wood lances, heavy thrusting weapons that greatly outperformed the Persians' light javelins, which were throwing weapons. A twelve-foot lance, with the weight of a galloping horse and rider behind it, could crush a skull, and the Macedonians aimed at the faces of the Persians and their horses. While Macedonian horsemen pushed the Persians back, Thracian light troops, who intermingled with the cavalry, added to the Persians' woes. They were specialists at darting in and out of horsemen and hurling their javelins.

Meanwhile, in the center of the line, the Macedonian infantry advanced. With terrifying efficiency, and with their huge pikes held out before them, the men of the phalanx crossed the river, climbed the opposite bank, and forced the enemy back. The Persian center broke and the cavalry turned and fled. On the Macedonian left, the Thessalian cavalry fought with distinction. Persia's Greek mercenaries stood in the rear, amazed and horrified at what was happening; apparently no one ordered them into action.

Alexander and his men won a great victory. It was a tribute to the army's professionalism and its power and it reflected well on Alexander's boldness as a field commander and courage as a warrior. But it also left an opening to the Persians, who had, after all, nearly killed their enemy's king. Yet the Persians had access to huge manpower resources. If they mustered a big enough army, with plenty of Greek mercenaries and enough cavalry to surround the Macedonians on the wings, they stood a chance in battle.

Except for the squadron of one thousand cavalrymen, Macedonian casualties were light, although probably not as light as the pro-Macedonian sources claim: supposedly, just eighty-five cavalry and thirty infantry died. Macedonian casualty figures would increase in the battles ahead, but all in all, they stayed fairly low. That was one key to Alexander's success: he spared his men.

He also lavished kindness on them. After the battle, Alexander made sure his wounded were treated well and went to the trouble of visiting them himself. He had the Macedonian dead buried with their weapons; he exempted their surviving families from taxes. Finally, he commissioned a bronze statue group in honor of the twenty-five Macedonian Companion Cavalry who fell in the first attack. Alexander gave the job to Lysippus, the most famous sculptor of the day, and had the statues erected in Macedonia.

Persian casualties were high. About a thousand Persian cavalrymen were killed. Eight Persian generals fell in the battle, including two satraps, the commander of the mercenaries, and two royal in-laws and a former king's grandson. Another satrap escaped and committed suicide soon afterward. Memnon escaped as well, but he planned to keep up the fight.

The six thousand Greek mercenaries fared much worse. Because the fighting was all but over, the Greeks expected to be able to surrender. Instead, the Macedonians surrounded them and attacked. The Greeks defended themselves, and the Macedonians took casualties, but in the end it was a massacre. Only two thousand Greeks survived. They were sent to Macedon to do hard labor. Even by ancient standards, this was brutal, but the point was not military but political. Alexander wanted to brand any Greek who opposed him as a traitor. The message was aimed not only at Greeks in Persian service but also at potential rebels on the Greek home front.

To underline the message, Alexander sent three hundred captured Persian suits of armor to the Parthenon in Athens, with the inscription: "Alexander son of Philip and the Greeks except the Spartans, from the barbarians living in Asia." In Greek terms, the inscription meant that Alexander was fighting for all Greece in a clash of civilizations against a savage enemy living on another continent. For all Greeks, that is, except the Spartans! This was an insult: in the old days, Sparta had stood against Persia at Thermopylae. Now, Macedon claimed to be the new Sparta. That would make Alexander a great hero, like Sparta's legendary King Leonidas—except, of course, that unlike Leonidas, who died at Thermopylae, Alexander planned to live.

Hannibal: A Two-fisted Victory and Thirty-seven Elephants

The most impressive thing about Hannibal and his army as they exited from the Alps about November 218 B.C. was that they were there at all. They had just completed one of the great epic marches in the history of warfare. It was approximately a five-month, thousand-mile struggle against both natural and human enemies. Besides traversing the Pyrenees and the Rhône, they had to cross the Alps in the snows of late autumn. They fought hostile tribesmen and evaded a Roman expeditionary force. They suffered desertion, disease, battle casualties, and starvation. And then there were the elephants, those stunning beasts that Hannibal's men ferried over the Rhône and drove through icy Alpine passes.

When the Carthaginian high command was debating the proposed march from Spain to Italy, one of Hannibal's generals warned him of the dangers. The general, who was also named Hannibal but with the fierce nickname of "the Gladiator," painted a picture of terrible logistical obstacles. The men would have to eat human flesh in order to survive, said Hannibal the Gladiator. That was an exaggeration, but not much.

Success had not come cheap. When Hannibal left Spain's New Carthage in or around June, he had 90,000 infantrymen, 12,000 cavalrymen, and 37 elephants. He gave 15,000 troops to his brother Hasdrubal to hold central and southern Spain, while he gave 11,000 troops to pacify northeastern Spain; another 10,000 troops were sent home. Hannibal crossed the Pyrenees into France with 50,000 infantry, 9,000 cavalry, and the elephants. When he reached the Rhône about October, he had 38,000 infantry, 8,000 cavalry, and thirty-seven elephants; most of the recent losses were due to desertion. Then, he crossed the Alps in about fifteen days. By the end of November, about five months after starting his journey, he reached Italy with only 20,000 infantry and 6,000 cavalry—the Alpine trek had cost him nearly half his remaining soldiers. Some died in combat with the hostile mountain peoples, while others succumbed to the snow and cold. Many others simply deserted. No doubt Hannibal had expected some losses on the march, but probably not on this scale.

Polybius emphasizes how much the elephants helped Hannibal's army in the Alps. Neither he nor any other source mentions the loss of any elephants there, although they do state heavy losses among horses and pack animals. Perhaps all of Hannibal's original thirty-seven elephants survived the Alps.

Desertion was the prime cause of Hannibal's losses in manpower. The good news, however, was that most of his best troops were still with him. They came from North Africa, and that was too far to run home to. Most of the deserters were probably Spaniards. Yet, they were good soldiers too.

Hannibal's ability to hold the best part of his army together under awful conditions is a tribute to his leadership. Still, there is no way to get around it. Hannibal left Spain with 59,000 men and reached Italy with 26,000 men. In the campaign season that followed, his main problem was a lack of manpower. So, Hannibal's initial losses haunted him for years to come.

Hannibal's remaining army was in bad shape by the time it reached Italy. "For his men had not only suffered terribly from the toil of ascent and descent of the passes and the roughness of the road," writes one ancient writer, "but they were also in wretched condition owing to the scarcity of provisions and neglect of their persons, many having fallen into a state of utter despondency from prolonged toil and want of food."

Given the size and shape of the army that staggered into Italy in November 218, the war might have been over. Hannibal could not defeat Rome in the long run without substantial reinforcements. But in the short run, Hannibal turned things around, which is a tribute to his leadership and to his men's toughness. Not only that—he went on to win battlefield victory after victory, which seems almost miraculous.

Like Alexander, Hannibal drove his men hard but he knew their limits. They needed rest, which Hannibal gave them. The men also needed food, but the only way to get food was to fight the enemy and take his resources—hard work, but victory would restore both the Carthaginians' bodies and their morale.

Within a month or so of arriving in Italy, Hannibal achieved that victory, indeed several victories. He gave a virtuoso display of his skill as a commander. As a diplomat, he alternated between policies of terror and appeasement and won gains with both. As a manager, Hannibal proved that he knew men as well as he knew war. As a commander, he applied a combination of cunning, ingenuity, and fortitude that defeated Roman armies twice, first in a cavalry skirmish and then in a pitched battle. And he accomplished it all by the winter solstice, about December 22 or 23, 218 B.C.

But the Romans racked up a string of accomplishments as well. They demonstrated that they could think strategically. Although they could not match Hannibal's tactical skill, they showed guts and endurance. The Roman infantry—the famed legions—could throw a powerful punch, and Hannibal now knew it from personal experience. Like the Carthaginians, the Romans exhibited mobility and speed in their operations. Indeed, a neutral observer at the end of the year 218 would have gasped at the distances that the two sides had each covered, at the rapidity with which they had moved, and at the flexibility with which they shuffled pieces on the military chessboard.

When it came to strategic surprise, however, Hannibal had the edge. The Romans expected him to stand on the defensive, so they were stunned by his aggressive march to Italy.

After leaving the Alps, Hannibal headed for the Po River Valley, where his agents had already made contact the previous spring with the largest Celtic tribes—Rome's longtime enemies. The mighty Po flows from the Alps to the Adriatic. Whoever controlled its valley controlled northern Italy. The Romans had fought the Celts for control of this area and only recently emerged on top. First Hannibal had to pass through the area around modern Turin, whose Celtic inhabitants were not friendly to him. He attacked their main town and slaughtered the residents. The other tribes around Turin learned their lesson and joined him.

The Romans, meanwhile, hurried to the scene. After declaring war on Carthage the previous summer, they had decided on a two-pronged offensive, with attacks in both Spain and North Africa. When news of Hannibal's approach in southern France came, they cancelled the African offensive but decided to keep up the pressure on Spain, Hannibal's base. Rome wisely recognized that the struggle might be long, and so it was crucial to prevent Hannibal's Spanish reinforcements from joining him.

Before Hannibal's arrival in Italy, Rome had sent troops to the Po River Valley to deal with Celtic unrest. Just a few months before, it had also founded two new military colonies in the valley, one at Cremona and the other at Placentia (Piacenza), each in a strategic location. As Hannibal approached, even more Roman troops marched to northern Italy under the command of Tiberius Sempronius Longus, one of the two consuls (chief officials, annually elected) for 218 B.C. The other consul, Publius Cornelius Scipio, was in charge of the Spanish expedition, but he turned command in Spain over to his lieutenant (and brother) and made haste to northern Italy as well.

The campaign of November to December 218 focused on the strategic triangle represented by three points, the cities of Placentia, Clastidium, and Ticinum. Placentia, the new Roman colony on the central Po, stood just east of the valley of the Trebbia River and the pass that led to the northern

Italian port city of Pisa. Farther west of Placentia, a spur of the Appenines reached up from the south and nearly touched the Po, making this a strategic chokepoint. Just west of that lay Clastidium (modern Casteggio), a Celtic fort that the Romans had taken over and turned into one of their strongholds. Both Placentia and Clastidium lay on the south side of the Po. On the north side, just east of Clastidium, the Ticinus River flowed into it. A few miles upstream on the Ticinus lay Ticinum (modern Pavia), a Celtic settlement. Whoever held these three cities had the key to the Po River Valley.

Scipio, the first Roman on the scene, was also the first Roman to taste battle with Hannibal. Using Placentia as a base, he went on the offensive. Scipio's engineers threw makeshift bridges over the Po and the Ticinus and he ordered his troops to cross the rivers in search of Hannibal. On the plain somewhere to the west of the Ticinus and north of the Po, Scipio found him. The date was about late November 218.

The flat plain was classic cavalry country, or it would have been had it not been pockmarked by woods, swamps, and streams. Those features rendered it perfect for the kind of ambushes and suprises that Hannibal loved to carry out. He was a tactical master, not least in exploiting geographical features to the maximum. Hannibal most likely employed such tactics in this terrain.

The Ticinus River was more a cavalry skirmish than a proper battle. Cavalry was never Rome's strongpoint; the Roman army was primarily an army of foot soldiers. Hannibal's cavalry both outnumbered and outclassed the Romans. His heavy cavalry consisted of Spaniards, and Hannibal attacked the Romans with them in the center. Meanwhile, he made good use of his light cavalry, the dazzling horsemen from Numidia (modern Algeria). Specialists at harassing and breaking up enemy formations, the Numidian horsemen at the Ticinus River rode around the Roman flank and charged their rear. Not only did the Romans turn and flee, but they almost lost their commander, Scipio. His wounded body was dragged to safety and, according to one tradition, he was saved by his nineteen-year-old son, also named Cornelius Scipio (later Scipio Africanus), the very man who would eventually defeat Hannibal, sixteen years later.

Scipio had badly underestimated Hannibal. Perhaps that is understandable, given both Hannibal's youth and the information that Scipio probably received about the poor state of Hannibal's army after it had straggled out of the Alps. Or maybe Scipio had a chip on his shoulder. When the Carthaginians had crossed the Rhône in southern France in October, Scipio had tried—and failed—to reach them in time to stop them. Humiliated, he then returned to Italy.

After their defeat across the Ticinus, the Romans retreated rapidly, leaving forces beyond to break up the bridges after them. They regrouped to the southeast near the Roman colony at Placentia on the Po. Hannibal followed, picking up Celtic allies and Roman prisoners along the way. He gained entry to Clastidium, when its commander opened the gates: he and the men in his garrison were Roman allies from southern Italy. The Carthaginian turned the occasion into a propaganda event, treating the prisoners ostentatiously well and even honoring their leader. By trying to woo Rome's allies, Hannibal made war on the political as well as the military front. Meanwhile, a group of Rome's Celtic allies left Scipio's camp to join Hannibal and made a different kind of statement. They killed some of the Romans and cut off their heads to bring with them.

The two sides encamped in the valley of the Trebia (Trebbia) River, west of Placentia and south of its confluence with the Po. In early December, Tiberius Sempronius Longus and his troops joined Scipio and his men. Hannibal's army had grown to 28,000 infantry but the Romans, with 36,000 to 38,000 infantry, outnumbered him. Yet Hannibal had 10,000 cavalry while Rome had only 4,000. Finally, there were still about thirty-seven elephants.

The two sides sparred and skirmished. One raid almost turned into an all-out battle, as Hannibal's hard-pressed soldiers retreated in disorder. But Hannibal demonstrated his iron grip on his troops. He sent out officers and buglers with specific instructions. The men in retreat had to stand and hold their ground, but that was that; he would not let them go on the offensive. Hannibal refused to be drawn into a battle except on his terms, that is, in a place, at a time, and under circumstances that he had carefully chosen beforehand. He was, as we might say today, a control freak.

But Hannibal did have a general engagement in mind at the Trebia, and on carefully selected ground. He chose the wide fields west of the river, where the flat and treeless plain was crisscrossed with gullies.

Hannibal knew that the Romans practically smelled ambushes when they entered the woods and would be on their guard. The open country, though, would invite Roman carelessness, Hannibal reasoned. One night, he managed to hide two thousand men in an overgrown gully behind the likely Roman battle line.

Hannibal knew his enemy. As Polybius wrote, Hannibal understood that nothing is "more essential to a general than the knowledge of his opponent's principles and character." A general has to envision the weak spots not only in his enemy's body but in his mind. Hannibal did just that and Polybius was all admiration.

The next morning, Hannibal lured the Romans out to battle, under Sempronius's command. The Numidian cavalry taunted the Romans and they took the bait. Having seen the Carthaginians retreat, Sempronius might have mistakenly thought that he had them on the run.

Before going out to fight, Hannibal prepared his troops carefully. He fed them a good breakfast, warmed them around the campfires, and told them to rub themselves down with olive oil as protection against the cold. The Romans, however, had no time for breakfast and did not protect themselves with oil. The Carthaginians had only a short distance to go to reach the battlefield. The Romans had to travel farther, and they had to cross the river. The water was cold and breast high, leaving them drenched and tired by the time they reached the enemy. It was the winter solstice, around December 22 or 23, 218 B.C.

As at the Ticinus, Hannibal planned to win by enveloping his enemy's flanks. He arranged his infantry in the center and divided the cavalry between the two wings. Hannibal divided the elephants too and placed them in front of the infantry on either wing. Roman armies deployed their legions in three lines, with the cavalry on the flanks, and Tiberius Sempronius Longus did so as well. In the battle that followed, Rome's always powerful legionaries held their own against the Carthaginian center. But the Carthaginians overwhelmed the enemy's wings. After driving the Roman cavalry from the field, Hannibal's men used a combination of cavalry, skirmishers, and elephants to break the Roman flanks. Meanwhile, the two thousand Carthaginians hidden in the gulley rose up and attacked the Romans in the rear.

The Roman legionaries in the center—ten thousand men—managed to escape by punching through the enemy line. Most of the cavalry escaped as well. But two-thirds of the Roman army—about twenty-eight thousand men—was killed or captured. Hannibal's losses consisted mainly of Celtic infantrymen in his center. Wintry weather after the battle killed most of Hannibal's surviving elephants.

Tiberius Sempronius Longus did not dare send the truth about the battle to Rome; instead, he sent a message that a storm had deprived him of victory. Hannibal was a tempest, all right, but one whose cunning and agility left Rome in shock.

As the truth about the Trebia percolated to Rome, Hannibal struck another propaganda blow. While barely keeping his Roman prisoners alive, he treated the Italians respectfully. He called an assembly in which he said that, "he had come above all to give the Italians back their freedom and to help them recover the cities and the territories which the Romans had taken away." Then he sent them home without asking for any ransom.

Hannibal delivered a dual message: slaughter and liberation. The question was whether it would drive a wedge between Rome and its allies.

Caesar: The Audacity of Terror and the Sting of Clemency

Caesar made his first move with a wolf's speed and agility. Before crossing the Rubicon he sent centurions in civilian clothes into Rimini, a key city at the junction of two Roman roads. On January 12, 49 B.C. (November 24, 50 B.C. by the solar calendar), Caesar crossed the Rubicon. By the time he marched on the city with his legion, Caesar's men had opened the gates. Rimini surrendered. It was a sign of things to come.

As one ancient writer says of Caesar, "He thought surprise, daring, and taking quick advantage of the moment could achieve more than preparing for a regular invasion; he wanted to panic his enemies." Another says that because Caesar "used to depend on the surprise caused by his speed and the terror caused by his audacity, rather than on the immensity of his preparations, he decided, with his 5,000 men, to be the first to attack in this great war and to seize the strategic positions in Italy before the enemy." Such methods worked.

Within a month, Caesar and his men took the major towns in northern and central Italy. They did not need to shed any blood. In some places the enemy fled, in other places, they surrendered, either on their own initiative or because of local pressure. Italians reacted with horror to find in their backyard the army that had conquered Gaul.

Meanwhile, Pompey left Rome, first to Capua and then to Luceria, a city on the Apulian plain. It takes a shrewd and seasoned commander to engage in a fighting retreat; Pompey was such a general. Critics accused him of cowardice, but Pompey and his lieutenants were raising troops in central and southern Italy and then moving them south. They kept just one step ahead of Caesar's advance. Things went rather smoothly until Corfinium.

Corfinium sums up the politics of the civil war in Italy. It was the only place that offered any real resistance to Caesar. But Corfinium wasn't just a military operation; it was a "new type of conquest," as Caesar himself said. Corfinium symbolizes the brilliance of his policy—and its risks.

Geography made Corfinium. It sat high in the Apennines, in a fertile valley hemmed in by mountains. The town lay about 100 miles due east of Rome on the ancient via Valeria, the highway to the Adriatic Sea. Other strongholds nearby controlled roads to the south and west.

About forty years earlier, in 90 B.C., the Italian rebels against Rome had chosen Corfinium as their capital in the Social War (91–88 B.C.). They renamed it Italica and gave it a new forum and Senate house, but they soon surrendered the town to Rome. Apparently, there was no struggle— otherwise Rome would have destroyed the city's fortification walls, which still stood in 49 B.C. Elsewhere in Italy, the Social War was hard fought. Rome put down the rebellion but agreed to the allies' demand for Roman citizenship.

The city's strategic position remained obvious. As he marched south, Caesar could not afford to bypass Corfinium and leave a strong enemy force in his rear. If the enemy chose to make a stand there, he would have to fight. And so it happened.

In February 49 (by the Roman calendar: December 50 by the solar calendar), as Caesar approached from the north, Lucius Domitius Ahenobarbus decided to dig in at Corfinium. Domitius was a man of grand gestures and extreme opinions, famous for bringing one hundred African lions to the arena and for marrying the sister of Cato, the archconservative of the Roman senate. How appropriate that the emperor Nero was Domitius's great-great-great-grandson!

When it came to Caesar, Domitius was a fire-eater. He came from a rich family whose prominence extended to the dawn of the Roman republic. Domitius had often publicly attacked Caesar and, for that matter, Pompey too, before Pompey split with Caesar. Domitius had once threatened to recall Caesar from Gaul; the Senate had recently appointed him to replace Caesar as governor there. An ex-consul, Domitius was now a leading general of the Senate's armies.

In the second week of February, he decided to stand his ground at Corfinium. Pompey had already evacuated his forces to Luceria, about one hundred miles southeast of Corfinium. Domitius might have joined Pompey there, but he reasoned that it was better to make a stand in a stronghold on the road to Rome than in open country far from the capital. He had no small force of men in and around Corfinium, having raised twelve cohorts of troops from the tough mountain peoples in the vicinity. Pompey's lieutenants brought another nineteen cohorts from central Italy, for a total of thirty-one cohorts: on paper, about fifteen thousand men. But fearing that Caesar would cut Domitius off, Pompey sent an urgent message to withdraw.

By now, Caesar had two legions, or eight thousand to ten thousand men. He arrived at Corfinium on February 15 and set up camp outside the city walls. Seven of Domitius's cohorts in a neighboring town immediately defected to Caesar. Two days later, another legion, twenty-two newly recruited cohorts from Gaul and three hundred foreign cavalry joined Caesar, for a total of about 27,000 to 30,000 men. Caesar outnumbered Domitius by about two to one.

When Caesar reached Corfinium, Domitius had sent messengers to Pompey, asking him to come quickly with his forces to block the passes, cut off Caesar's supplies, and trap him between their two armies. While he was waiting for help to arrive, Domitius organized his troops in defensive positions, arranged artillery on the city walls, and called an assembly in which he pledged a piece of his own land as a reward to each soldier.

It was no use, however. Winters in Corfinium are mild enough for military operations, and Caesar moved with vigor. He added a second camp on the far side of town; he fortified both camps with great earthworks. Then he prepared to lay siege to Corfinium by building walls and forts to surround it. For good reason Caesar was known as a great engineer! Pompey, meanwhile, wrote back to Domitius. His reply arrived on February 19 and stated a clear no. Far from bringing his forces to Corfinium, Pompey again advised Domitius to get his army out and join him in Luceria; doing anything else was too risky. Pompey would have ordered Domitius to join him if he could, but he wasn't able to. Unlike Caesar, Pompey lacked supreme command.

What Pompey did insist on, though, was that he had neither advised nor wanted Domitius to make a stand at Corfinium. Far from fighting in Italy, Pompey decided to evacuate the peninsula. He would move east, and with the help of his vast contacts in the Greek world build a new army. If Domitius knew that, he didn't agree. If Pompey left Italy and stormed back to victory with help from his friends in the East, he would owe the Senate nothing. But if they beat Caesar at Corfinium now, the Senate would share the credit. Pompey was unmoved, stating that he could not possibly stand up to Caesar's veterans.

So Domitius was left on his own. He tried to rally his men but they knew a hopeless situation when they saw one. They were trapped in the mountains and under siege by the best army in the Roman world. Claiming that their general was trying to escape, his own officers arrested Domitius. Whatever the real story, Domitius made a good gift for Caesar, to whom they promptly offered to surrender. It was February 21. Pompey had already left Luceria and moved farther south, to the heel of the Italian boot.

In only seven days, the great fortress of Corfinium had fallen. That, however, is not the most striking part of the story; that distinction belongs to what happened next, when it was time for Caesar to take vengeance: nothing. Caesar prevented his soldiers from entering the city and looting it. Meanwhile, he received the elite among the town's defenders: fifty men, including senators, public officials, and their sons. Caesar pardoned all of them. Domitius asked for death; Caesar not only gave him life but returned the six million sesterces (Roman coins) that Domitius had brought to town (and which the town authorities had turned over to Caesar). "This he did," wrote Caesar, "in order not to seem more self-controlled in regard to men's lives than their money."

It was a remarkable display of generosity, and Caesar knew it. In a letter that he wrote to Cicero the following month, Caesar pointed out his determination not to follow the bloody road of Sulla the dictator, who had killed thousands in Italy. "Let this be the new type of conquest," Caesar wrote, "to fortify ourselves with pity and generosity."

Caesar's policy was generous but also political: he wanted to win the goodwill of all Italians. He also wanted to win the support of Domitius's soldiers, whom he immediately ordered to join him by taking a loyalty oath. Caesar had not only added fifteen thousand soldiers to his army, but he had deprived Pompey of them. Because it was a civil war it was not unusual for men to switch sides.

By his policy of clemency, Caesar branded himself as a conqueror who displayed generosity—but with a bite. In Roman eyes, clemency was a gift to a defeated, foreign opponent. There was, then, an insult in Caesar's gesture, and everyone knew it. Cicero, for example, called it "insidious clemency." Caesar's opponents would never forgive him his mercy. No wonder that many of the men who stabbed him to death on the Ides of March, five years later, had been pardoned by Caesar.

THE ESSENCE OF DECISION

Starting a war is not like taking out a certificate of deposit. There is no guaranteed rate of return. Think of war, rather, as a high-tech start-up. If a commander has done his job properly, the enterprise will rest on a firm foundation, but it is a risk, even so. There are no sure things in war. From Caesar at the Rubicon to the present day, war remains a high-stakes gamble.

Yet the paradox is that our three generals each would have found peace too risky. Peace would have cost Caesar his career and possibly his life. The Macedonians would never have tolerated Alexander if he had refused to invade Persia. Hannibal's fear of Rome might have contained an element of paranoia, but it was shared by most of Carthage's power brokers. Daredevil though they sometimes were, Alexander, Hannibal, and Caesar each played it safe by going to war. Peace was a sure thing—and it spelled ruin. War was risky but when risk is the only way out, it is the smart move.

Not that their wars were easy; far from it. But Alexander, Hannibal, and Caesar each made it look easy, and therein lies part of their greatness. Alexander had an empty treasury, a restive rear, and a record mostly of failure by his advance troops in Anatolia up to that point. Caesar had only one legion to pit against the Roman state. Hannibal had even bigger problems, above all, the daunting journey from Spain to northern Italy. By the time he crossed the Alps, about five months after starting out, he had lost nearly half his forces. Yet more important, he *had* made the trip—and then went on to win a battle.

Like any good general, Hannibal had prepared as carefully as possible. "Men are apt to think in great crises that when all has been done they still have something left to do and when all has been said that they have not yet said enough," wrote Thucydides around 400 B.C., and the words continue to ring true. Yet they don't tell the whole story.

Success in war depends not only on knowing yourself but your enemy. Within a month of stepping onto enemy soil, Alexander, Hannibal, and Caesar had the right to feel that they had judged their enemy correctly. Alexander had counted on the Persians challenging him to a pitched battle rather than adopting a scorched-earth policy. Hannibal had made a similar assessment about the Romans. Events proved each of them correct. The battles of the Granicus River, the Ticinus River, and the Trebia respectively were triumphs for the two invading war machines.

Caesar might have hoped that Pompey would do him the favor of engaging Caesar's veteran army in a pitched battle, but that wasn't likely, as Caesar surely had known. Pompey's more probable policy would not have been a mystery to a man of Caesar's wiles: recruiting soldiers and rapidly withdrawing them eastward. The best that Caesar could have hoped for was to chase Pompey out of Italy before he could raise many troops. Domitius's clumsy stand at Corfinium was a lucky break for Caesar. But six weeks after crossing the Rubicon, Caesar had still not caught Pompey nor stopped him from leaving Italy with his army.

Of the three generals, Alexander had the best war so far. He had brought his army across the Hellespont without opposition, won a pitched battle at the cost of few casualties, and stood poised to take control of Anatolia's western provinces and their resources. Caesar captured an enemy army led by a clumsy foe and he scored propaganda points through generous behavior, but he had yet to catch his main opponent, Pompey, and his army. Hannibal had the most difficult war because of his punishing losses on the march to Italy. In the long run, he needed reinforcements. Still, Hannibal had held his men together, reached Italy and hooked up with his allies, and he had smashed the Roman army, all considerable successes.

Alexander, Hannibal, and Caesar had each begun his war well. But none of them had the luxury of mistaking beginner's luck for final victory. Their wars, like any new enterprise, would be judged by their ultimate achievements, not their initial performances—even though those performances had been spectacular.

Wars, in fact, have a way of getting more complicated the longer they go on. Once hostilities begin they take on a logic of their own. Having survived the initial shock, each side tends to increase its investment, which decreases its willingness to give in. The result: what might have seemed like a decisive move before the war turns out to be just an opening gambit once the fighting is under way.

In the opening stages of war, Persia, Rome, and the coalition of Pompey and the Senate had all been hit hard. But none of them was ready to quit.

For Alexander, Hannibal, and Caesar, therefore, the wars had just begun.

3

RESISTANCE

O N AN AUTUMN MORNING IN 334 B.C., ALEXANDER, KING OF MACEDON, looked down from a hillside and surveyed his prize. Below, in a natural theater, lay the great city of Halicarnassus, with the blue sea sparkling beyond it. The city was Persia's main naval base on Anatolia's Aegean coast, and it had fallen to Alexander's army after a long siege.

But the Persians didn't go before putting up a stiff fight, and they left in good order one morning after burning down half the town the night before. Worse still for Alexander, the Persians didn't precisely leave. They withdrew from most of the city but kept the two fortified citadels (one a hill, one an island) that flanked the harbor. Halicarnassus was a Persian naval base before Alexander's siege and it remained a Persian naval base afterward.

And so, as Alexander's men marched into Halicarnassus, they could watch Persian warships sail serenely in and out of town as if the battle had never happened. In one of those ships sat the enemy commander, the chief strategist of the war that was not going as Alexander had planned— Memnon of Rhodes.

About a hundred years later and 3,500 miles away, on a spring day in 217 B.C., another commander's war plan began to come unhinged. On that day two fleets, one Carthaginian and the other Roman, met in battle just off the northeast coast of Spain. They were near the delta of the Ebro River. The commanders represented the two greatest military families of the war: Hasdrubal, Hannibal's brother, led the Carthaginians, and Gnaeus Cornelius Scipio, uncle of the later Scipio Africanus, led the Romans.

The Carthaginians outnumbered the enemy forty ships to thirty-five, and they had a land army to support them; the Romans had only the marines aboard ship. But the Romans were much hungrier for a win. Knowing that their own men held the shore, the Carthaginians gave up practically as soon as the enemy drew blood. Hasdrubal probably watched in shame as they ran their ships aground on the beach and fled. The Romans dared to row in close and towed off twenty-five of the enemy's ships—nearly two-thirds of Hasdrubal's flotilla.

It wasn't a decisive operation, and Carthage still had command of Spain. But it was an ominous sign of a growing threat in Hannibal's rear. Hannibal had trusted his brother Hasdrubal to hold Carthage's Spanish base while he defeated Rome in Italy. If Hasdrubal failed, if he lost control of Spain to Rome, then Hannibal's entire war plan might come tumbling down.

A little more than 150 years later and eight hundred miles to the east, in the gathering darkness of a winter evening in southern Italy, disappointment struck again. Julius Caesar's men stood on a quay and faced the sight of an enemy navy that had escaped from under their noses. Two weeks earlier, Pompey and 27,000 soldiers had arrived in the fortified port city of Brundisium, where a fleet awaited them. He planned to sail his troops across the Adriatic Sea to northern Greece, where he would build a new and bigger army, aided by his many allies in the East. Since he controlled the sea, Pompey knew that he could return the following year and fight from a position of strength.

Caesar planned to stop him. He had one part of his army lay siege to Brundisium and the other part try to close off the harbor, outside its walls, by building a mole across it. But Pompey fought back.

In the end, when Caesar's troops broke into Brundisium, there was nothing left of Pompey's forces except two ships stuck in Caesar's breakwater. All the rest had escaped. Pompey had succeeded in breaking out of his great opponent's trap.

"No battle plan survives contact with the enemy." When he wrote his famous maxim, German General Helmuth von Moltke (1800–1891) was thinking of the Franco-Prussian War of 1870–71 but he might have had our three commanders in mind. Soon after going to war, each of them had to rewrite his plans.

Alexander discovered just how much harm the Persian fleet could do him under the command of a great admiral. Hannibal faced an enemy who side-stepped his attack in Italy but threatened his rear in Spain. Caesar met an enemy who rebuffed him and regrouped for a counterattack. All three men faced frustration.

Military thinkers, ancient and modern, would certainly sympathize. Most generals and kings, wrote Polybius, think only about success; they "do not envision the consequences of misfortune or consider at all how they should behave and what they should do in the event of disaster, although . . . [it] takes great foresight."

The American admiral James Stockdale put it succinctly: "The challenge of education is not to prepare a person for success, but to prepare him for failure."

How prepared for failure were Alexander, Hannibal, and Caesar? Did they adjust with agility?

ALEXANDER

After smashing the Persians at the Granicus, Alexander was free to get down to business. That business was decidedly *not* marching eastward against Darius. Not yet. Alexander's immediate need was to get food for his men and money to pay them. That in turn meant winning over the cities of western Anatolia, most of which were Greek. With his army to remind them who was in charge Alexander offered carrots and sticks. To popular acclaim, he replaced oligarchies with democracies. This was less idealism than pragmatism on Alexander's part. Aristotle had taught him that democracies were more stable than oligarchies. In western Anatolia, where Persia had long supported oligarchy, democrats were Macedon's natural allies. He also imposed taxes, nicely relabeled as "contributions." The locals cheered for democracy and accepted taxation with the resignation of people who were used to conquerors. Alexander claimed he had come to "liberate" these cities, but they knew better than to take him at face value.

Before turning eastward, Alexander had to control the west. So far, he had won a battle but not the war. The Persian navy commanded the Aegean; a new Persian army could march westward in massive numbers. Alexander's forces were still relatively small and poor. He would soon need reinforcements to replace men lost in battle or to sickness or left behind to garrison conquered territory.

There would still be dozens of twists and turns in the conflict. Each resulted from a Persian counterattack; each tested Alexander. The three most important are Memnon's naval offensive, the battle of Issus, and the siege of Tyre.

Wooden Walls: Persia's First Counterattack

Four hundred Persian galleys—"wooden walls," as a Greek once called warships—dominated the eastern Mediterranean. With its naval superiority, Persia could cut the enemy's communications, land in Greece, and raise a revolt against Macedon. That would force Alexander to return home or risk losing Macedon, his native land and the source of future reinforcements. Alexander could solve the problem by beating the Persian fleet, but how could he polish off a much better navy?

By doing it on land! Alexander claimed that by using his army and siege train to capture Persia's seaports, he could deny the enemy the use of its fleet. The Persians weren't buying, though.

Memnon of Rhodes was both the brains and the muscle behind Persia's naval policy. His strategic audacity and tactical toughness equaled Alexander's, but unlike Alexander, Memnon was not king; Darius was. As a foreigner and one linked with a rival Persian family, Memnon never won Darius's complete trust. In fact, Memnon was forced to send his wife and children to Darius as hostages in order to hold his command. But when Memnon fought, he made Alexander sweat.

The first round took place in summer 334 at Miletus, a key port on the Aegean coast of Anatolia. The Persian navy didn't perform as well as some hoped, and we might wonder whether Memnon was there, as one source—but only one source—states. In any case, the mere presence of the Persian fleet spooked Alexander, as it turned out. It happened as follows:

Miletus sat on a narrow peninsula in the Gulf of Latmos, protected by the strategic island of Lade nearby. A pro-Persian party governed the city with the support of a garrison of Greek mercenaries. As Alexander's army approached by land, the pro-Persians got the good news that Persia's fleet of four hundred ships was on its way. But Alexander's navy of 160 ships reached Miletus first. Whoever controlled the island of Lade controlled access to Miletus, so the Macedonians landed at Lade and garrisoned it with five hundred men. The Persians were compelled to anchor across the Gulf of Latmos, about three miles away. (Ancient navies always needed a friendly shore to find food and water and to anchor at night.)

Meanwhile, the Macedonians debated strategy. Alexander's chief subordinate was Parmenio, a much older man, a political power in his own right, and Philip's greatest general. Alexander respected Parmenio but distrusted him. Parmenio now advised a naval battle but Alexander refused to risk it against an enemy that was superior both in numbers and experience. He worried that his "allies" back in Greece were so restive that they would rise in revolt at the mere news of a Macedonian defeat at sea.

Instead of fighting a naval battle, Alexander used his fleet as a shield. His ships held the Persian fleet at a distance while, on land, his army laid siege to Miletus. His engines quickly broke through the walls and took the city. Some of the enemy garrison tried to swim to safety but Alexander's navy captured them. Still, Alexander feared that the Persian fleet would come back and defeat his navy, so he sent a unit of cavalrymen on a long march around the Gulf to the Persians' anchorage, where they destroyed the enemies' shore parties. Now the Persians had to sail off to the island of Samos for supplies, an additional five miles away. The battle for Miletus was effectively over.

Alexander's fleet had played a role in the victory, but he was not impressed. It was his army that captured the city and his cavalry that drove the Persian fleet away. Besides, Alexander never entirely trusted the sailors, who came from his less-than-loyal Greek allies. He considered the navy a bad bargain, given the expense of paying the sailors and keeping the ships in trim. So Alexander made a bold decision: he sent most of the fleet home.

Alexander dismissed 140 ships, keeping only 20 Athenian vessels to carry siege equipment; incidentally, the several thousand Athenian sailors were virtual hostages. It was a major blunder. As the Miletus campaign showed, Alexander's fleet was of limited use but it was not useless. Worse, no navy meant no defense against a Persian thrust across the Aegean. If the Persians chose to strike, Alexander had left them a wide-open target.

Alexander took risks but usually with carefully planned forethought. Dismissing his navy was different. Suddenly Alexander gave up one of the foundations of his strategy and replaced it with an untested theory: that it was possible to defeat sea power on land. This decision was a mistake. As a Macedonian, Alexander came from a nation of landlubbers. Maybe he just plain distrusted ships.

The Persian fleet now sailed south to Halicarnassus, another major naval base on the Aegean coast. Alexander fought hard—on land—to take the city, while Memnon fought even harder to organize its defense. At Halicarnassus, unlike at Miletus, the Persians had control of the sea, which gave Memnon's forces mobility and access to supplies.

In the end, Halicarnassus gave Alexander a tactical victory but a strategic defeat. Alexander forced Memnon to withdraw from the town—but not from the fortified port, which remained in Persian hands. During the siege Memnon inflicted high casualties on the Macedonians. He also defeated Alexander's attack on the neighboring port city of Myndus by sending naval reinforcements to the Persian garrison there. Memnon evacuated most of his soldiers from Halicarnassus to the nearby island of Cos. But the Persians retained a naval presence on Anatolia's Aegean coast: in their garrison at Halicarnassus, at Myndus, and in two port cities farther south, Cnidus and Caunus, neither of which was easy to attack by land. In short, Alexander did not drive the Persian fleet from all bases on the Anatolian coast.

It was the end of the year 334 B.C. and it marked Memnon's moment. The veteran warrior finally convinced Darius to let him launch a major naval offensive, made up of three hundred ships and fifteen thousand mercenary soldiers. Since Alexander had virtually no navy, this force could sweep across the Aegean Sea and bring the war to Greece. It was what Churchill would later call a "soft underbelly" strategy: attacking the enemy not where he was strong and protected, but where he was weak.

Memnon began his naval offensive in spring 333. Right away he took several important Aegean islands allied to Alexander, including Chios and all of Lesbos except the big city of Mytilene, which fell after a siege. According to one source, the Persians also retook Miletus.

Alexander was concerned. His gamble of dissolving his navy now seemed foolhardy. It was time to revise his plans. He sent a huge sum to Greece in order to raise a new fleet but it would not be ready for months.

Then he continued southward and eastward, to Anatolia's Mediterranean coast, where he could deny Persia access to an important source of sailors and ship timber as well as capture additional ports. Deprived of these ports, Persian ships found it much riskier to travel between the Aegean and Persia's major naval bases in Phoenicia (modern Lebanon). Alexander did another thing as well: he raised money from the rich cities in southern Anatolia. If they refused to be "liberated," he marched on them.

All the while, Alexander kept his eye on Memnon and the Aegean. After leaving Halicarnassus, he divided his forces. He kept half of his army with him and sent the rest, under Parmenio, to the city of Gordium in north-central Anatolia. Gordium was the perfect pivot point. From there, Parmenio could march back to Macedonia, if Memnon attacked, or send reinforcements to Alexander, if needed.

Alexander cultivated an image of action. But except for his dismissal of his fleet, his overall policy during his first year in Anatolia was slow and deliberate. The myth was different. Nothing symbolizes it better than an event at Gordium in spring 333. There, Alexander "fulfilled" a prophecy that he would conquer the Persian empire by untying an immensely intricate knot: he "untied" the knot by cutting it with his sword. The man who cut the Gordian knot had no patience for the slow and deliberate way of doing things. He was a dashing young hero forging always forward. But that was just the myth.

In fact, Alexander was cautious enough to know when to call off an attack, even if it allowed his enemies to boast that they had beaten the mighty Alexander. Myndus, the port near Halicarnassus, was just one example of his holding back; he did the same with the cities of Termessus and Syllium, both located just inland from Anatolia's Mediterranean coast. A good commander knows when to retreat, and Alexander did. He had bigger problems, after all.

For a moment in spring 333, it looked as if Alexander's early victories might fall victim to Persia's counterattack. But Divine Providence smiled: in June, Memnon died of an illness. His nephew, Pharnabazus, and his deputy, Autophradates, continued the campaign, but they were lesser men. They couldn't match Memnon's skill at war, his knowledge of Macedon, or his clout with Darius.

Memnon's death was a turning point. Had he lived, he might have lit a fire in Greece. He would probably have conquered other strategic Greek islands and landed on the mainland with fifteen thousand Greek mercenaries.

Important city-states were ready to join the Persians in the fight, especially Sparta, which had never accepted Macedonian rule. In 331, these states actually did rebel against Macedon, but it was too late. By then, Alexander had acquired so much loot that he could finance a new mercenary army to add to the small force that he had left behind to defend Macedon. They crushed the rebels. But a rebellion in 333 would have forced Alexander to march back home to defend Macedon. That would not have been easy if Memnon had blockaded the Hellespont.

In May 333 it seemed that Alexander's policy had failed: he could not stop Persia's naval offensive without a navy of his own. But in June, Memnon's death saved him.

Darius ended the naval offensive. He decided to withdraw most of the mercenaries from the fleet and transfer them to the mainland. Had Memnon survived, he might have persuaded the Persian king to reconsider. As it was, Darius decided to take resources from the war at sea, where the enemy was weak, and transfer them to a battle on land, where the enemy was strong.

The Battle of Issus: Persia's Second Counterattack

It is the most famous face-off in the history of art. A mosaic from Pompeii shows the scene. Alexander the Great, spear in hand, charges on horseback against Darius of Persia. Three Persian cavalrymen and a row of pikes are all that come between the two warrior-kings. Driving ever forward, with his horsemen riding beside him, Alexander is poised to kill Darius. The Persian king is in danger and he knows it: he stands wide-eyed on his chariot, facing Alexander. But Darius's charioteer is ready: having turned the horses away from Alexander, he pulls the reins and cracks a whip to spur a rapid escape.

Frozen in time, the moment captures the climax of a dramatic clash of kings: the battle of Issus, on or around November 1, 333 B.C. On an autumn afternoon, the Macedonian and Persian armies fought over the fate of empire. The Macedonians were a winning and experienced force but the Persians had strengths too and they outnumbered the Macedonians two to one.

Issus is known as a clash of kings that highlighted Alexander's heroism. That's no accident. Like the Kennedys or Princess Diana, Alexander had a knack for public relations and he highlighted his valor. But, in truth, Issus demanded other qualities; not Alexander's heroism so much as his coolness, steadiness, and caution won the battle.

The die was cast for combat by spring 333 when Darius gathered an army. He knew, of course, of the risk of fighting the Macedonians in pitched battle. But Darius's own army was no pushover. The Persian king was aware that Alexander was heading south and east. In fact, by summer 333, Alexander reached Cilicia, the fertile and wealthy plain on Turkey's southern coast and the gateway to Syria. In the months before, he had rejoined Parmenio and the rest of the army at Gordium, where he received four thousand to six thousand reinforcements, mostly from Macedonia.

Not wanting to risk Alexander's entry into the heart of the empire in Mesopotamia (modern Iraq), Darius chose to fight him in Syria. The Persian had to respond quickly, which meant that he had no time to gather all of the empire's far-flung forces. In particular, Darius would have to do without the great horsemen of Central Asia. But he would gather a strong army, even so.

By September, Darius and his soldiers were ready to march. October 333 saw them camped on the plains of Syria, with the tall Amanus Mountains lying to the west and Cilicia—and the Macedonians—beyond. Alexander had surely heard of Darius's plans, but he was shocked to discover how close the enemy was: in Syria, less than a week's march away.

Both armies wanted to fight, but in entirely different places. The Persians wanted the contest on the wide plains of Syria, where they could spread out and make use of their superior numbers. Alexander hoped to fight in a narrow space between the mountains and the sea, where the Persians could not deploy their army comfortably. There was suitable terrain around Issus, a coastal city at the head of the Gulf of Issus (today, Turkey's Gulf of Iskenderun). There, a coastal strip, only several miles wide, stretches from the Amanus Mountains to the Mediterranean. As it turned out, Alexander got to fight *where* he wanted but not *as* he wanted.

It happened like this: Alexander, encamped in the west, refused to take the bait and cross the mountains to head for Syria and the Persians. So, either out of impatience or because his army was running out of food, Darius decided to cross the mountains himself and fight Alexander in Cilicia, where the broad coastal plains would make an acceptable substitute for his preferred battlefield in Syria. Darius entered Cilicia via the Amanus Gates

(Turkey's Bahçe Pass). But Alexander had already left. He was marching south past Issus and along the narrow Mediterranean coast toward Syria.

Darius now followed, which was good for Alexander, except that Alexander expected Darius to march toward him from the south, after crossing the Amanus range via the Syrian Gates (Turkey's Belen Pass).

But Darius surprised Alexander by coming from the north, via the Amanus Gates. When Darius reached the Mediterranean at Issus, he found himself in Alexander's rear, cutting off the Macedonians from their supplies. What a shock for Alexander! A lesser general would have been nonplussed by Darius's unexpected arrival behind him, but Alexander stayed calm. He was a cavalryman, after all, and cavalrymen are used to operating far from their home base. The crisis brought out the best in the Macedonian king.

It was evening. After his men ate, Alexander marched the entire army toward the Persians, covering a distance of about ten miles. After camping in a narrow pass, at dawn the next morning they began marching about another ten miles toward the Persians and then fanning out into battle order.

Without breaking a sweat, Alexander turned his army around rapidly and deployed it for battle. He displayed agility and audacity. Above all, he displayed strategic intuition. He was able to assess the situation quickly and come up with the right solution.

Darius should have tried to draw Alexander back northward, into the plain. But surprise is a force multiplier that dramatically increases an army's effectiveness, and maybe the Persians thought they had caught Alexander off guard. Or perhaps, as one source says, it was too dangerous to retreat with Alexander ready for battle. And so, the Persians stood and fought.

The two forces met on the steep-banked Pinarus River, which ran from the winding foothills of the Amanus Mountains to the Mediterranean, where it reached a level beach. (It is almost certainly to be identified with to-day's Payas Çay.) Here, according to the ancient sources, the plain was about one-and-a-half miles wide. The game of moves and misdirection had ended, to Alexander's distinct advantage. Darius had wanted to fight on the plain and Alexander to fight in the narrows; Alexander had won.

It is clear that Alexander was greatly outnumbered. An educated guess is that he had nearly 30,000 infantry and about 5,000 cavalry. Darius's forces were 65,000 infantry, including 15,000 Greek mercenaries and 15,000 cavalry. The mercenaries were first rate, but the other Persian infantrymen were not.

Alexander positioned his troops on the south bank of the Pinarus. He arranged them in what would become his classic battle order. The Macedonian phalanx stood in the center of the line, to tie down the Greek mercenaries opposite them. On the left wing, allied cavalry and light-armed troops took a defensive stance, under the command of the veteran general Parmenio. The right wing was the Macedonians' striking arm, spearheaded by the Companion Cavalry and led by Alexander himself. Their task was to look for an opening in the enemy line and pour through it.

Alexander followed a simple strategy at Issus: decapitation. By tradition, the Persian king stood at or near the center of his battle line, behind a protective infantry force. At Issus, Darius stood closer to his left flank. Alexander aimed straight for Darius, hoping to overpower his guards—the weaker Persian infantry, not the Greek mercenaries—and force the Persian king to run for his life. He figured that when Darius's army heard that their leader had fled in fear, they would give up—even if they happened to be winning on their part of the battlefield. Alexander's greatest hope was to kill Darius; that would shake the Persian political system and might even cause its collapse.

Darius took up a position on the steep, northern bank of the Pinarus. It was good defensive ground, but he needed to go on the offensive. That was a job for the cavalry; the infantry would absorb the enemy's attack. The Persians posted their cavalry on the wings and their infantry in the center. Ideally, they hoped to fight on a wide battlefield, but unfortunately for Darius, Issus was narrow. Had he fought on the plain, Darius would have enveloped the Macedonian army with his superior numbers of cavalry. But at Issus, the Mediterranean and the mountains protected the Macedonian flanks. Darius needed a new plan.

He got one, proving himself a quick and creative thinker. Darius recognized two weaknesses in the Macedonian army: the phalanx (in the Macedonian center) and the allied cavalry (on the Macedonian left wing). He was confident that his Greek mercenary phalanx could hold the Macedonian phalanx, but he wasn't sure that his cavalry on the Persian right wing could break through the enemy cavalry opposite it. So he added power to his punch by transferring most of the cavalry on the Persian left wing to the Persian right wing, which he hoped would help the Persians to break through the enemy line near the sea. Unfortunately, that left the Persians' left wing, which stood near the foothills of the mountains, vulnerable. Darius tried to defend that wing by sending light-armed troops, armed with missiles, such as javelins and arrows, into the foothills, where they could circle around and take the enemy in the rear.

Both moves looked promising, but Alexander parried them. He too proved up to the challenge of readjusting under pressure. He placed archers and javelin-men in the foothills on his right to deflect Darius's thrust. Then, just before the battle began, Alexander moved the best of his allied cavalry, the Thessalians, to his left wing—and he did so in secret, by moving them behind his lines. Once again, Alexander displayed his strategic intuition.

It probably took all morning to get the armies into position; the battle began in the afternoon. The two armies were already in sight of each other but not yet in javelin range. The sources report that Alexander rode ahead of his front standards and called out his commanders by name to encourage them. No doubt the Persians did something similar. Then came two final moves to inspire the men. In both armies the trumpeters signaled the attack and the men shouted their battle cries. The roar echoed off the thickly wooded mountains.

The battle confounded expectations. In the center, Darius's Greek mercenaries not only held off the Macedonian phalanx, but they found gaps in it and made the Macedonians pay in blood. On the Macedonian left, Parmenio led a tough defense that kept the Persian cavalry from advancing. Darius's blow was stopped. Meanwhile, the Macedonians unleashed their own strike from their right wing.

Alexander led his Companion Cavalry across the Pinarus, up the opposite bank, and into the Persian infantry. The sources disagree about whether they charged across or simply cantered. Once they reached the Persians, the Companion Cavalry cut through them until Alexander was fighting in sight of Darius. Now there took place the famous confrontation of the two kings with which this section began. After realizing that his position was hopeless, Darius turned and fled. He was not a coward but a realist. He understood that he had lost a battle but could still win the war—as long as he survived.

Alexander, meanwhile, passed another test of his judgment. Despite the temptation to ride after Darius, he was mature enough to put first things first: he now turned toward his center to help his phalanx. That turned the tide, and the Macedonians pushed the Greek mercenaries back. Alexander received a minor thigh wound in the fighting. Meanwhile, Parmenio and the Thessalians on the Macedonian left launched a counterdrive against the Persian cavalry. Whether because of that thrust or the news of Darius's flight, the Persians turned and galloped off toward safety. But their own infantry blocked the way, and many men were trampled to death.

Macedonian casualties were higher at Issus than at the Granicus. The sources, who probably underestimate, report five hundred Macedonian deaths and four thousand wounded. Persian losses were much, much higher: an army that tries to run away over rugged terrain is bound to suffer. No reliable Persian casualty figures exist.

Issus turned out as it did for three reasons: prebattle maneuvers, the skill of the Macedonian army, and the good judgment of Alexander. No fool, Alexander knew how much he relied on his generals. Without the heroic defense on the left wing by Parmenio, for example, the Persians might have taken Alexander in the rear and the result would have been a very different story. The Persians were far from incompetent. They fought well but the Macedonians outclassed them.

Darius had organizational and tactical skills, and he was quick on his feet. But he lacked Alexander's self-confidence and single-mindedness, and Alexander's gifts as a battlefield commander. Besides, compared with Macedon's military machine, the Persian army was brittle and inexperienced.

Issus was a great victory for Alexander but it didn't decide the war. Darius survived, as did part of his army. He still controlled most of a vast empire, with huge military and financial resources at his disposal, including the Mediterranean's preeminent fleet.

In fact, Alexander might have been frustrated with the battle's outcome. He had come close to killing the one man who, more than any army, stood between him and control of an empire. Now, Alexander would have to fight him again or negotiate with him.

But the contest would not continue at the same level as before. Alexander had improved his position enormously. As an added bonus to battlefield victory, he captured money and very important people. Persian kings brought their family to the battlefield, probably as a sign of confidence. Forced to run for his life, Darius left behind his mother, principal wife, daughters and son, all of whom fell into Alexander's hands. They were now hostages. Alexander also sent Parmenio rushing to Damascus, where he captured more than three thousand talents (about 175,000 pounds) of gold and silver as well as additional hostages. One of the hostages, Memnon's widow, Barsine, eventually became Alexander's mistress.

Walls and Words: Persia's Third Counterattack

Issus dealt Darius a bitter blow but not a fatal defeat. He decided to reopen the war at sea in the Aegean and try once again to raise a revolt in Greece. All would not be quiet on the western front—not if Darius could help it.

Alexander knew it, and so he made haste to seize the seaports of Phoenicia. These cities had always been Persia's staunchest naval allies. They had often served in the past as naval bases for Persian offensives against Greece. Now, all of them surrendered to the advancing Macedonians—all except Tyre, which tried to maintain its neutrality. Perhaps the Tyrians were betting on a Persian revival. Alexander could not allow Tyre to serve as a symbol of resistance and a potential Persian naval base. So he embarked on a massive siege.

Located on an island off the mainland, Tyre was a natural fortress. It was not about to give in without a fight. In fact, Tyre stood firm for eight months, from about January to about August 332, until it finally fell. To take the city, the Macedonians built a huge mole from the mainland and brought up siege engines. The battle was decided at sea, however. When the other Phoenician cities surrendered to Alexander, their navies were off fighting on the side of the Persians. Eventually, they switched sides and returned to Phoenicia to fight against Tyre. That sealed the city's fate. The Macedonians broke into Tyre, killed about six thousand to eight thousand Tyrians, and sold about thirty thousand into slavery. Another fifteen thousand Tyrians were saved by relief ships from other, still-friendly cities. As at Thebes, Alexander showed just how brutal he could be.

By laying siege to Tyre, Alexander once again passed the test of Persia's counterattacks. Bloody, frustrating, expensive, and time-consuming, the siege of Tyre was necessary. The Macedonian knew to protect his flank at sea before turning eastward toward Persia. At Tyre, Alexander's strategy of winning a naval battle on land worked, thanks to the Phoenician navy.

But if Alexander had had a navy of his own, the siege might not have taken eight months. As it was, he was dependent on the Phoenicians for ships, and it took time to win them over.

Meanwhile, Persia was fighting in two other theaters in the west. The fleet, led by Memnon's successor Pharnabazus, took or recaptured several strategic Greek islands including Lesbos (in particular, its main city of Mytilene), Chios, Tenedos, Siphnos, Cos, and parts of Crete as well as the Anatolian mainland cities of Miletus and Halicarnassus. The Persian army, back on its feet after Issus, tried to fight its way into Lydia, a rich and strategic province in central western Anatolia. In a bold move, the Persians struck in winter, usually the off-season for warfare. Taking Lydia would have given the Persians a base in the hinterland to support garrisons in Miletus and—slightly farther afield—Halicarnassus.

The Lydian offensive was a strategic stroke by Persia, but the Macedonians responded by displaying the depth of their military talent. Antigonus "the One-Eyed," a veteran commander of Philip, nicknamed for his war wound, defeated the Persians "in three battles in different regions"— unfortunately, no further details survive. But the result was clear: Lydia would not revert to Persian rule. No wonder that by spring 332, various contingents of the Persian fleet defected to Alexander at Tyre.

Looking back at the war between the Granicus and the fall of Tyre, we can see Alexander's good moves, his mistakes, and his luck. His brilliance as a battlefield commander won victory at Issus. He was smart enough to chip away at the enemy's naval bases, but that wasn't enough. Alexander courted disaster by disbanding his fleet. If Memnon had lived or if Darius had stuck to the naval offensive and avoided battle, the Persians might have stirred up revolt in Greece and forced Alexander back home. Ultimately, Alexander's response to Persia's counterattack was to trust that the enemy would stumble. The gamble paid off, and Persia lost the war for the west. But a wise commander does not give the initiative to the enemy, a lesson that Alexander would eventually learn to his cost.

Having temporarily run out of military options, Darius turned to diplomacy. He had to try negotiation, in any case, because his family was being held hostage. Darius made a series of offers to Alexander: in exchange for an end to the war and the return of the great king's family, Darius offered Alexander a large ransom, a Persian royal princess as his bride, and the western Persian empire. Darius first defined this territory rather stingily as western and central Anatolia and then, more realistically, as everything between the Mediterranean and the Euphrates rivers (in today's Iraq). According to the sources, Alexander's senior general, Parmenio, responded positively, saying, "I would accept if I were you, Alexander." The king is supposed to have replied, "So would I, if I were Parmenio."

Historians have doubted this anecdote, since in later years Alexander's propagandists poisoned Parmenio's reputation. But whether the anecdote is true or not, Parmenio offered pretty good advice. Any advance eastward would be risky. Darius retained huge resources. He could organize a new and bigger army than the one at Issus. Worse still, he might refuse to challenge Alexander in battle. If Darius finally accepted Memnon's strategy of a scorched-earth policy and added sudden, unpredictable cavalry raids, he might bog down the Macedonian army on any advance they made to the east.

And what if the Macedonians won? While we don't know what was in Parmenio's mind, it's easy to imagine him pursuing a different grand strategy from Alexander's. As Parmenio perhaps saw it, the purpose of the war was to add new territory and wealth to Macedon, but Macedon would remain the center of gravity; it would govern the new kingdom. If Alexander continued his conquests, however, the tables would be turned, and Western Asia, with its huge mass, would outweigh little Macedon. And then, who would be governing whom? And how stable would the vast new empire be? Could Alexander and the next king of Macedon maintain control of it, or would it break up into separate parts?

If Parmenio expressed these doubts, Alexander might have replied as follows: continuing the war was risky but so was accepting Darius's offer. Peace would give Darius breathing space to regroup and attack again—at a time of his choosing. Better for Alexander to continue the war now and finish Darius off, a task that Macedon's brilliant, veteran army had a real chance of completing. Besides, to put a stop to unrest in Greece, Alexander must conquer Persia's two capital cities, Susa and Persepolis, because otherwise he could not claim to have fulfilled his promise of avenging Xerxes' conquest of Athens in 480 B.C. Besides, the Persian treasury—the largest in the world—would make Alexander the richest man in the world, and the least vulnerable.

But another, unspoken issue might also have loomed large in Parmenio's mind, a matter of domestic politics and constitutional considerations. The king of Macedon had never been an absolute monarch; the Great King was. Parmenio and his fellow Macedonian aristocrats could hold their own against the king of Macedon, but if Alexander became the king of Asia, he would dwarf them.

Alexander responded to Darius's offer by demanding the Persian recognize that, he, Alexander, was now the "king of Asia." The term was vague but it clearly meant something grand, verging on absolute power. And that, it seems, is what worried Parmenio.

The year after conquering Tyre, from 332 into 331 B.C., Alexander would proceed toward Egypt, taking Gaza by force and Judaea by diplomacy. He then proceeded to a bloodless conquest of the rich and fabled kingdom of the Nile, where he had himself crowned as pharaoh. All the time, though, he was looking eastward toward the heart of the Persian empire in Mesopotamia and Iran.

Alexander now hoped that Darius would challenge him in battle. The alternative, a combination of scorched-earth policy and ambushes, made the Macedonians shudder. Alexander didn't have to worry; in 331, he would get his fight. But winning it would take a supreme effort.

HANNIBAL

As soon as spring came to northern Italy in 217 B.C., Hannibal moved south. His plan was to win battles that would convince Rome's allies that Carthage was now top dog, and so would lead them to defect. Stripped of its supporters, Rome would sue for peace. Or so Hannibal hoped.

Hannibal's biggest worry was, as they said in the 1960s, what if they gave a war and nobody came? Or, more precisely, what if the Romans refused to fight a battle? What if, instead, they burned his food supplies and raided the edge of his army?

Hannibal's other worry was whether Rome's allies would really change sides. Unlike Alexander, who won many cities in Anatolia to his side, Hannibal had yet to find a base of supply. Without food and in a hostile country, how long would his men go on following him? What if the war in Italy turned from a glorious fight on the field of honor to a struggle against hunger and want?

A Crossing, a Trap, and a Road Not Taken

Hannibal had hard luck with crossings. The passage through the Alps in 218 B.C. nearly destroyed his army. The crossing of the Apennines from Emilia into Etruria (Tuscany) in spring 217 (perhaps in May) exacted a lesser price, but a heavy one even so. Several routes led over the Apennines into central Italy. Hannibal chose the shortest and least often used one, in order to surprise the Romans. They didn't expect anyone to risk crossing the marshes of the Arno but Hannibal had the audacity to do just that. In 217, heavy flooding led to swampy and sometimes virtually impassable conditions, probably in the area north and west of Florence. It took four days to get through the miserable terrain.

Hannibal deployed his army so that the best troops would march first, before the tramp of tens of thousands of feet softened the ground. By the time the Celts passed through, the soil was so soggy that many drowned in the marshes. But Celtic soldiers were expendable in Hannibal's mind. So were the pack animals, because he expected to get plenty more of them in the south; most of them died on the trek too. All but one of the few surviving elephants now died as well. So be it, Hannibal might have said. But he couldn't have expected what happened next.

Hannibal came down with an eye infection that he refused to treat during the difficult crossing of the marshes, which left his right eye sightless or virtually sightless (the sources disagree). The damage was permanent.

As a soldier, Hannibal does not seem to have suffered much from the handicap. As a leader of men, he might even have benefited from it. His Celtic troops, like many ancient peoples, believed in the symbolic power of a single eye. The Celts worshiped as one of their chief gods Lugus, who closed one eye when he made war magic. So as a one-eyed man, Hannibal might have seemed to "see" things even better than before his injury. The Barca "brand" had just gotten stronger.

Except for their victories in northern Italy, Hannibal's army had little to cheer about since taking the long road from Spain. Including the Celts, they now numbered about sixty thousand men. They were all bone-tired after the trek through the Arno swamp. Some of them had also suffered through the Alps and were unaccustomed to the cold of winter in northern Italy. Malnourished, most of them suffered from scurvy, which slowly weakened them. But the rich fields of Etruria beckoned, as Hannibal surely told them. Once again, he displayed leadership in a crisis. As they crossed the Apennines, the men might have noticed the vegetation change from continental to Mediterranean: first the pines and then, as they descended into the valley, the olive trees. The sun was stronger here than in the Po Valley. Hannibal had entered some of the wealthiest and most intensely cultivated territory in the Mediterranean. Hungry predators, the Carthaginians plundered the rich countryside between Arretium (Arezzo) and Cortona.

But the Romans were nearby. His scouts told Hannibal that a Roman army was camped at Arretium, with a second one less than a week's march away at Ariminium (Rimini) on the Adriatic coast. Each army had about 25,000 men and each was led by a consul: Gnaeus Servilius at Ariminium and Gaius Flaminius at Arretium. Flaminius, a prominent general and politician, had played a key role in conquering northern Italy a decade earlier. Now his troops carried chains for imprisoning the enemies they were confident of defeating. Knowing this, Hannibal marched his men right past Flaminius in order to lure him into battle. It worked.

On the morning of June 21, 217 B.C., Flaminius followed Hannibal along the northern shore of Lake Trasimene, a large body of water in central Italy. The Roman may have felt triumphant. He probably thought that he had Hannibal trapped between his army and Servilius's off to the northeast. A few years earlier, Flaminius had sprung a similar trap on a Celtic force. But as he entered a narrow pass on this misty morning, it was Flaminius who walked into a snare.

The northern shore of Lake Trasimene consists of a series of valleys, each surrounded by mountains ending at the water. It is lush and green territory, heavily planted today with olives as well as grass and alfalfa for hay. Camouflaged and hilly, it was, as the historian Livy writes, a land made for ambushes. Still, it was not easy to hide sixty thousand men, and it is a tribute to Hannibal that he did. At a signal, they descended from the surrounding heights. The Romans were shocked and unprepared.

It took only about three hours for the Carthaginians to cut down the Roman army. With few of the Romans able to line up in order, it was less a battle than a massacre. Some of the Romans sought safety in the marshes that still line the lakeshore, only to be slaughtered in the water. Hannibal's men killed fifteen thousand Roman soldiers and captured ten thousand to fifteen thousand more. Flaminius was among the fallen; one account says that a Celt got his revenge by killing and decapitating the conqueror of northern Italy. Hannibal's army suffered only one thousand five hundred losses, mainly Celts. When the other consul, Servilius, sent his four thousand cavalry from Ariminium to reconnoiter, Hannibal dispatched a mixed force of infantry and cavalry against them, led by his brilliant lieutenant Maharbal. The Carthaginians killed or captured all of Servilius's cavalry.

In short order, Hannibal had destroyed one of Rome's two consular armies and left the other virtually immobilized. It was a complete and utter humiliation for the Roman army. For Hannibal, it was a stunning display of good judgment on the part of a commander.

Rome now feared the worst. The road to the capital lay open, and yet Hannibal declined to take it. Why? Rome was only eighty-five miles away, a four days' march down the via Flaminia, a road recently built by none other than Flaminius. Rome's garrison probably numbered no more than ten thousand men. In addition to his army, Hannibal knew that a Carthaginian fleet lay off the coast at nearby Pisae (Pisa), where he had prearranged a rendezvous. Why not attack Rome by land and cut it off by sea?

The sources hint at a debate in the Carthaginian high command on this very question. But Hannibal's forces were simply not up to it. They still hadn't recovered from their exertions. Ringed by a massive wall, Rome might have required a long siege. Unless Rome fell quickly, there would be time enough for Servilius's men and the legions in Sicily and Sardinia to come to Rome's aid. Rome still had substantial manpower resources. Hannibal had achieved a great deal with small numbers, but he needed reinforcements.

He might have looked for them in Rome's allied cities. South of Lake Trasimene lay the cities of the Etruscans. They included many opponents of Roman rule. By marching up to their walls, Hannibal might have emboldened them to open the gates and let him in.

But, like Rome, the Etruscan towns probably seemed like too big a challenge for Hannibal's weakened army. So, instead, he turned east and marched toward the Adriatic coast. Along the way, he acquired so much booty "that his army could not drive or carry it all off." About two weeks after the battle at Lake Trasimene, Hannibal's army reached the Adriatic. There, "in a country abounding in all kinds of produce," Hannibal finally gave his men and horses the rest they needed. Hannibal's leadership style was to drive his men hard but then reward them generously.

Hannibal now sent a message to Carthage announcing his success; amazingly, this was the first word the city received from Hannibal since he had reached Italy. They were thrilled by his success but the Carthaginians wondered when their general would go for the enemy's jugular.

Fabius the Delayer

Faced with disaster, the Romans did what people have done throughout the ages: they elected a dictator. The Romans originated our term "dictator"; to them, he was a special public official chosen to govern in an emergency. A dictator held supreme authority but only for six months at most. A dictator's power wasn't quite dictatorial: it could be challenged by his second-in-command, who was called the master of the horse. The Romans hadn't elected a dictator for two generations, but now the time had come. For their dictator, the Romans turned in July 217 to an experienced leader, an aristocrat who had been consul and had conquered the Ligurian tribes of the northwest Apennines: Quintus Fabius Maximus. The ex-consul Marcus Minucius served as Fabius's master of the horse.

Like Memnon of Rhodes, Fabius was a general worthy of his opponent. At the age of fifty-eight, he remained vigorous; he had a veteran commander's cunning and the strategic insight and grandeur of vision to match Hannibal's. Unlike his predecessors, Fabius decided not to go on the offensive. Instead, he followed a policy of attrition, aimed at wearing Hannibal down. It was a scorched-earth policy, much like the one that Memnon had called for and the Persians rejected. Fabius understood that Hannibal's strength was his army and its forte was pitched battle. Hannibal's weakness was the need to replenish supplies and numbers of men, both of which he lacked. Rome, by contrast, enjoyed "inexhaustible supplies of provisions and men."

Fabius refused to fight another pitched battle with Hannibal. Instead, he ordered the Romans to follow and harass the Carthaginian while cutting his army off from potential sources of food. Fabius took various steps to protect his forces, such as always camping on high ground, where he was safe from Hannibal's cavalry, and never letting his men go out foraging, where they might face danger. At the same time, he killed or captured numerous Carthaginian foragers.

Fabius threatened to starve out Hannibal. His plan, according to Plutarch, was "to send aid to their allies, to keep their subject cities well in hand, and to suffer the culminating vigor of Hannibal to sink and expire of itself, like a flame that flares up from scant and slight material." He ordered civilians in Hannibal's path to destroy their crops and buildings and to move to the safety of a fortified town.

Hannibal understood Fabius's strategy very well. "He therefore made up his mind," writes Plutarch, "that by every possible device and constraint his foe must be induced to fight. . . ." At first Hannibal led out his army and approached the Roman camp in battle order. Later he marched from Apulia into Campania, hoping the Romans would fight for this fertile and strategic region. But Fabius refused to take the bait. He allowed Hannibal to raid Campania's fields and farms.

The Carthaginians gathered a load of plunder, but to their frustration, not a single Italian city south of the Po Valley opened its gates to the self-proclaimed liberators. One more victory was all it would take, Hannibal hoped, to panic the allies into bolting from Rome. But Fabius frustrated him and the allies remained loyal.

Like Memnon, Fabius had strategic insight. Unfortunately for Rome, Fabius resembled Memnon in another way too: he had limited authority, as events showed. Fabius's way of war made such a mark that, even today, we label a scorched-earth policy "Fabian strategy." But in 217 B.C., Fabius was not popular. Roman culture worshiped the military offensive and looked down on defense. Fabius's soldiers bristled at their commander's passivity, and the Roman public nicknamed him "Hannibal's manservant." The final straw came at the end of Hannibal's raids in Campania.

Loaded with loot, Hannibal hoped to retreat eastward to Apulia, but Fabius blocked off the mountain pass that Hannibal had to take. At the same time, Fabius threatened to attack if Hannibal tried to continue in Campania. It was a trap, but Hannibal wriggled free.

One night Hannibal had his men tie torches to two thousand oxen and drove them over a ridge to lure the Romans after them. The Romans guarding the pass followed on what amounted to a wild-goose chase, thinking they were chasing Hannibal's army. Meanwhile, Hannibal and most of his army escaped with their loot into Apulia. To the Romans, it was humiliating—and bloody; the Carthaginians killed about one thousand Roman soldiers as a parting shot.

It was a prime example of Hannibal's agility. A frustrated Roman author, Florus, called it the "art of Punic fraud." Every time they took a step forward, the Romans found themselves tripping over one of Hannibal's stratagems.

Fabius's deputy, the Master of the Horse Marcus Minucius, opposed the dictator's strategy of attrition. Minucius wanted to fight. The Carthaginian had captured the small city of Gerunium in northern Apulia, slaughtered the population, and used it to house his troops and supplies. When Fabius was temporarily back in Rome, Minucius used the opportunity to attack Hannibal's men when they were out foraging. Minucius won a minor victory, which he trumpeted as a major success, but Hannibal struck back. He lured Minucius into an ambush. Only the last-minute arrival of Fabius with relief forces saved the day.

Spain: Rome's Counterattack

By the end of 217 B.C. Hannibal faced frustration in Italy. But even worse news came from Spain. The Romans had sent an army there in spite of Hannibal's threat to Italy. They defeated Hannibal's brother Hasdrubal on both land and sea. The Romans conquered Spain's eastern seaboard and destroyed Carthaginian naval power off the Spanish coast.

What Memnon had wanted but failed to do in Greece, Rome pulled off in Spain. That is, the Romans sent substantial forces to attack the enemy's base. Rome's offensive began in fall 218. The ex-consul Gnaeus Scipio (uncle of Scipio Africanus) and his army landed in northeastern Spain. Unlike Hannibal, they had a friendly base, the coastal city of Emporiae (northeast of Barcelona). Hannibal had left Spain under the command of his younger brother. Hasdrubal was renowned for bravery, grit, and dignity, but not for strategic acumen. By the time he marched northward to fight the Romans, Gnaeus Scipio had defeated Carthaginian forces near Tarraco and captured the Carthaginian commander Hanno. Rome now controlled most of north-eastern Spain.

The following year, 217, Hasdrubal made a bad situation worse. That summer, he fought a naval battle with Gnaeus Scipio off the mouth of the Ebro—and lost. The Senate was so encouraged that it sent twenty more warships and eight thousand soldiers to Spain under Gnaeus's brother Publius Scipio—the consul of 218 who fought Hannibal at the Ticinus and Trebbia. Together, the two brothers crossed the Ebro and marched as far as Saguntum, where they freed hostages taken by Hannibal. Various Spanish tribes cast aside their allegiance to Carthage and switched to Rome—or so Roman sources claim.

One thing is certain: the Scipio brothers' offensive had hemmed in Hasdrubal south of the Ebro. Worse still, from Hannibal's point of view, Hasdrubal was in no position to send reinforcements. Hannibal's army was too small to conquer Italy. His plan had always foreseen the need for reinforcements, either from winning new allies in Italy or by getting help from Spain or even Carthage. Except for his Celtic troops from the Po Valley, Hannibal had made no progress in solving his manpower problem.

All in all, Hannibal responded to resistance with mixed results. He was able to brush off the rough crossing of the Apennines with a smashing victory at Trasimene. He humiliated a Roman army and lifted his status among his Celtic allies. When a window of opportunity opened for him to attack the city of Rome, Hannibal knew that his army was too tired and hungry to exploit it. He solved the crisis of his men's suffering, but only temporarily. Ominously, he had no solution at all to the challenge of the Scipios in Spain. That, in turn, left him without the reinforcements that he desperately needed.

Hasdrubal personified another of Hannibal's problems: he had no general good enough to entrust with control of another front. Hannibal had no Parmenio, whom Alexander had sent off to Gordium, and no Antigonus, who had skillfully defeated the Persians' counteroffensive in Anatolia. The Carthaginians lacked bench strength, to use a sports analogy. Hannibal could not be in two places at once, and that problem would bedevil their armies throughout the war.

The lack of a first-rate subordinate in Spain was, so to speak, a weakness in Hannibal's infrastructure, and it wasn't the only one. At the end of 217, after more than a year in Italy, Hannibal didn't have a base. Small and depopulated, Gerunium was no solution. Unless Hannibal got a major city to welcome him, his army would break apart soon enough. But no city would accept Hannibal unless he won another victory.

Hannibal had not broken Rome and he remained far from his goal of bringing Rome to the negotiating table.

We might argue that with the Scipios advancing in Spain and Fabius blunting the edge of Hannibal's offensive in Italy, Rome was winning. Yet Carthage would strike back in Spain and Fabius left office in Rome by the end of 217. Luckily for Hannibal, Minucius represented Rome better than did Fabius.

CAESAR

Unlike Darius, Pompey had no intention of giving his enemy pitched battle. Pompey had no illusions about his chances against Caesar's veteran legions. Instead, he would make Caesar dance to his tune. At least, he would try.

The Dunkirk of Italy

For Pompey, Brundisium was where the real war began. Brundisium was his Dunkirk. Dunkirk, of course, symbolizes British resistance to Nazi Germany. When the Germans invaded France in May 1940, they cut off Britain's huge army and threatened to destroy it. But the British retreated to a French city on the English Channel: Dunkirk. From there the British evacuated most of their army by ship to England. It was a brilliant operation, the first step on the road back to victory.

Brundisium (modern Brindisi) was an Italian city on the Adriatic Sea to which Pompey's men retreated from Caesar. Located at the southern end of the Appian Way, Brundisium was the main port for sailing to Greece. From there, in March 49 (by the Roman calendar, January 49 by the solar calendar), Pompey evacuated about 27,000 men in two sailings. It was the nucleus of the new army that he was building in Greece.

Pompey was a first-class strategist. He implemented a variant of Fabius's strategy: refusing to fight. Each man withdrew his army from the battlefield, if in a different manner. Fabius didn't have a strategy for victory, however, merely for avoiding defeat. Pompey had a strategy for victory, but some questioned whether he would be fast or aggressive enough to employ it against Caesar—or whether his rivals in the Senate would trip him up, as they had at Corfinium. Brundisium would be a big test.

Caesar arrived at Brundisium on March 9 with six legions, three veteran and three new. Pompey's fleet had already left, ferrying off about half of his army as well as the two consuls and a large number of senators, though not Pompey himself. The ships would land at the major port city of Dyrrachium (modern Durrës, Albania), disembark the men, and pivot back to Brundisium to pick up the other half of the army. Pompey was still there, waiting to direct their final escape.

Caesar sent two high-ranking officers to negotiate with Pompey: Pompey's chief engineer, captured by Caesar, and one of Caesar's commanders who was friends with a leading Pompeian officer. Caesar asked Pompey for a face-to-face meeting; surely they could iron out their differences. Pompey sent his regrets that, with the consuls already gone, his hands were tied. It made a good show. Neither man wanted the blame for war but neither intended to give an inch.

The real action was taking place in and around the port. Like Alexander, Caesar wanted to defeat his enemy's navy on land. Brundisium's harbor was shaped something like an inverted letter Y. The fortified city was located between the two oblique arms of the letter. The harbor emptied out into the Adriatic through the letter's perpendicular leg. Outside the city walls, and at the spot where the arms met the leg, the mouth of the port was at its narrowest.

It was here that Caesar had his engineers try to block off the harbor. They built a barrier, starting at each shore with breakwaters and earth banks that were joined, in the deep water, by a series of anchored rafts to close the gap. Then they erected screens and towers to defend the barrier against attack by ships or fire.

Caesar was audacious, but so was Pompey. He seized large merchant ships, outfitted them with three-story towers, armed them with catapults, slingers, and archers, and launched them against Caesar's rafts. The two sides thrusted and parried for over a week, which kept Caesar from completing his barrier.

By then, Pompey's ships had returned from Dyrrachium and picked up the rest of his forces. He left behind only a few light-armed veterans to mount the walls. When the signal came to go, they would have to retreat quickly to the harbor, with Caesar's men coming over the walls after them. But Pompey's troops knew the way, while the enemy would have to contend with walls and stake-filled trenches left to slow them down.

Pompey timed his ships' departure to take place at nightfall. The gathering darkness put Caesar's men at greater risk of falling into the Pompeians' traps. The townspeople helped Caesar's soldiers make their way to the harbor, either because they were pro-Caesar or just pro-survival. Still, they had to wind their way around the barriers and by the time they reached the harbor, all of Pompey's ships had escaped except for two that had caught on Caesar's breakwaters. It was March 17, 49 B.C.

For Pompey, Brundisium was a great success. Some people, wrote Plutarch, consider the evacuation "among his best stratagems." Caesar feigned surprise that Pompey had given up Italy without more of a fight, but he knew better. Yet "wars are not won by evacuations," as Churchill said after Dunkirk.

Caesar held Italy, which he had conquered in less than two months. The masses showed no sign of opposition; on the contrary, they prized both the cash he had sent from Gaul and the mildness of his men since crossing the Rubicon. The few senators left in Italy were less impressed. Caesar won little new support when he finally entered Rome soon after leaving Brundisium. What he did get was money—a king's ransom, in fact, from the treasury. But to get it, Caesar had been forced to threaten to kill Lucius Metellus, a tribune of the people who had blocked his way. For once he dropped the mask of clemency.

Thunder in the West

The conquest of Italy did not put Caesar in control. On the contrary, it made him a target. Pompey flanked him on either side. In the west, Pompey's stronghold was Spain. He had close to 100,000 men there. His main force consisted of 5 legions, 80 cohorts of Spanish auxiliaries, and 5,000 cavalry:

a total of 70,000 men. Another army, consisting of two legions as well as auxiliaries, was stationed in western Spain.

In the east, Pompey had five legions or about 27,000 men, with the potential of more to come from new recruits. He could train them while gathering support from the eastern provinces that he had conquered and organized for Rome in the 60s B.C. Meanwhile, Pompey controlled the sea. He could use his ships to prevent the shipment of grain to Italy. Since Italy could not grow enough food for its own needs, the result would be to starve out Caesar.

Caesar, then, couldn't afford to rest in Italy. He had to go on the attack and he had to do so immediately—but not recklessly. He might have been itching to go after Pompey, who was just a short trip away across the Adriatic, but Caesar was as shrewd as he was aggressive. Caesar could not afford to leave those Spanish armies in his rear when he turned eastward because they might join Pompey. But unless Pompey sailed to Spain to join them, they lacked good leadership. So he attacked Spain first. In spite of his famous boldness in battle, Caesar's strategy was methodical, even cautious. He would take out the enemy's strengths piecemeal, one by one.

Caesar had another, less complicated reason to begin with Spain: he could get there. He had enough ships to send three legions, commanded by Curio, on an expedition to Sicily, Sardinia, and North Africa (modern Tunisia), all key sources of Italy's food supply. But that was it for his fleet; Caesar could reach other places only by land. Excellent roads linked Italy and Spain via Gaul. Poor roads and hostile tribes lined the land route to Greece. For Caesar, therefore, all signs pointed to Spain.

Although he was an invader, like Alexander, in attacking Spain, Caesar behaved more like Memnon. Just as Memnon went after Alexander's "soft underbelly" in Greece, so Caesar went after Pompey's "soft underbelly" in Spain.

As he left for Spain, Caesar is supposed to have told his friends that he was going against an army without a leader and that he would return and fight a leader without an army. He meant that the enemy had many troops in Spain but not Pompey, while Pompey had far fewer troops with him in the east.

On the way to Spain, Caesar ran into an obstacle at Massilia (Marseille), an important city that closed its gates to him. Caesar's old enemy Lucius

Domitius Ahenobarbus, last seen at Corfinium, was there; Pompey had sent him to take charge of the defense of Massilia. Caesar moved on and left a force behind to besiege the city, but he dearly felt the absence of Masillia's rich supplies. Yet in spite of these setbacks, Caesar conducted another lightning campaign. How did he do it—and do it against Pompey's hardened and veteran Spanish troops?

It helped, of course, that Pompey was passive. Pompey was the opposite of Caesar, because Pompey joined a bold strategy with operational timidity. On the strategic level, Pompey risked everything on giving up Italy and building a new army in the east. But when it came to actual military operations, Pompey handed over the initiative to Caesar. Alexander had made a similar mistake with Memnon and the Persian navy, but Divine Providence stepped in and saved Alexander. Pompey was not as fortunate. He learned a harsh lesson in the cost of letting the enemy decide when and where to fight.

Spain is a good example. Instead of waiting for Caesar to invade Spain, Pompey could have seized the reins by marching his men from Spain to attack Caesar in Italy. Better yet, he could have gone to Spain himself to take command. Instead, he left everything to his generals in Spain, Lucius Afranius and Marcus Petreius. They were good and experienced commanders, but Caesar was already a living legend. Only Pompey himself could keep his men's morale up if the going got rough—as it surely would against Caesar.

The conqueror of Gaul was dangerous beyond measure once he got near the combat zone. Spain was no exception. As soon as he arrived, Caesar displayed the qualities for which he is famous: audacity, agility, good judgment, a strategy that mixed military force with political persuasion, and the leadership skill to hold his men together despite defeat. He turned his weaknesses into strengths and pressed his advantages to the hilt.

Caesar found the Pompeians west of modern Barcelona, near the town of Ilerda (Lérida) on the Sicoris (modern Segre) River. He went rapidly on the attack. Caesar's forces had more cavalry but the two armies were evenly matched in infantry, and the Pompeians held their own, so the attack failed. Caesar planned to go back on the offensive, but first he needed access to food and supplies. The situation was difficult, though, because Pompey's men held the best ground, and the collapse of a bridge over the river further cut off Caesar.

As usual, failure only made Caesar try harder. What he did was both resourceful and energetic. He had his men build small boats, carried them on wagons about twenty miles to a good crossing point, ferried a legion across, and had them build a new bridge. It proved to be a war-winning operation. Caesar could now harass the enemy with his superior cavalry. In addition, he brought his diplomatic skills to bear and began to win over local tribes that had long hated Pompey. They furnished supplies for Caesar's army.

Afranius and Petreius saw the tide turning so they chose to move to safer territory. It would not be easy to outrun Caesar, especially not when he had more horses. He not only followed the enemy but headed them off, which he was able to do by another bold operation: he had thousands of his soldiers wade through the freezing water of the Sicoris. Caesar and his men, now well supplied themselves, trapped the Pompeians without supplies. They merely had to wait for the enemy to give up. To hasten that, Caesar encouraged his men to mix and mingle with the soldiers in the enemy army. This was not difficult to do, as the two forces were camped near each other, and they both, after all, were Roman. The plan worked and the Pompeians surrendered. Caesar pardoned them and some of them joined his ranks. Meanwhile, Pompey's other forces, in western Spain, quickly surrendered as well.

It took Caesar only three months to conquer Spain and disarm Pompey's best troops, and he did it with little or no bloodshed. It was a triumph of maneuver warfare. Caesar could now turn eastward to Pompey without worrying about an attack from Spain on Gaul or Italy. Meanwhile, Masillia finally fell to him, after a months-long siege, in spite of reinforcements sent by Pompey. Domitius escaped.

Not everything had gone well for Caesar, though. After taking Sardinia and Sicily, Curio had met with disaster in North Africa. The Numidian king Juba, a Pompeian ally who loathed Caesar, sprang a trap for Curio. The Romans lost virtually all ten thousand to fifteen thousand men in their three legions and Curio himself was killed. The loss cut off the people of Italy from a major source of grain. Another setback came in the Adriatic Sea, where Pompey's navy put one small Caesarian fleet out of action and captured another, adding an additional five thousand to seven thousand men to their forces.

In fact, no fewer than three of Caesar's generals had gone down in death or defeat in recent months. Never mind: Caesar himself still strode, magnificent and conquering. Pompey still remained on the defensive. He might have sent a fleet across the Adriatic to bottle Caesar's forces up in Brundisium. He did not, though, and that left Caesar free to move east when he was ready.

Still, there was the enemy within. Caesar's own troops mutinied in Placentia (modern Piacenza) in northern Italy. Civil war frustrated them. The war in Gaul had left them awash in loot, but this time, they had to show clemency and restraint when they wanted more loot. Caesar took a hard line in response. Instead of negotiating, he called an assembly of the entire army. When he rose to speak, Caesar defended the principles of discipline and patriotism. He insisted that Italy must not be sacked. Then, he followed the old Roman strategy of divide and conquer, by singling out one legion. The ninth legion had led the mutiny, and now Caesar promised to decimate it. Decimation was an old-fashioned punishment in which every tenth man was executed. The rest of the army begged for mercy, and Caesar agreed to be satisfied with the heads of a dozen ringleaders. Caesar had won, as one source says, "not through lenience but by the authority of the leader."

The mutiny was over and the army was bound even closer to its commander than before. Rebellion and repression: a ritual dance, no doubt, but Caesar's mastery of the steps might have made his enemy shiver.

Bring Me the Head of Julius Caesar

After grabbing Spain and its armies from Pompey, Caesar deserved a break, especially in the wake of mutiny and defeats elsewhere. But, being Caesar, he plunged into another offensive instead. After returning to Italy at the end of 49 B.C., he spent only eleven days in Rome. It was time enough to have himself elected consul and to impress the public with his moderation. Standard behavior in Rome's civil wars was to round up one's enemies for execution; Caesar continued his policy of clemency instead. Once again, Caesar distinguished his brand.

Caesar now began a very risky military operation, which he had a real chance of losing. Strategically, however, it was a sober choice. It would have been suicide to stay in Italy and wait for Pompey to invade in the spring— with a grand fleet, an ever-growing army, and a limitless supply of money. While Caesar had conquered Spain and lost North Africa, Pompey had gathered a massive army, which he had begun training vigorously. He had 9 legions, with 2 more on the way, as well as 5,000 light infantry and 7,000 cavalry, a total of roughly 55,000 men. Caesar had 12 legions and 1,000 cavalry, but attrition had cut his legions down to 2,000 to 3,000 men instead of the full complement of 4,800, for a total of roughly 30,000 men.

Pompey's army greatly outnumbered Caesar's, and Pompey threatened to come roaring after him as soon as Pompey was ready. Toward the end of the year 49 B.C., Pompey finally gained the title of supreme commander. It wasn't quite enough to corral the senators and aristocrats who sat in his councils of war, each of them convinced that he knew more than the man who called himself "the Great," but at least Pompey now had legal authority.

Many men admired the supreme commander but few gave Pompey the kind of loyalty that Caesar's troops had rendered him ever since Gaul. They were, as a Roman writer put it, *"et devotissimi . . . et fortissimi"*: both extremely devoted and extremely brave. Caesar had that advantage, and he grabbed another advantage in turn—surprise. As he is said to have told his army around this time, "the most potent thing in war is the unexpected." In short, things had changed little since the Rubicon: if he wanted to stay in power, Caesar had to attack.

He began with a gamble. He shipped his men across the Adriatic Sea from Brundisium in late autumn—January 4, 48 B.C. (early November 49 B.C. by the modern calendar). It was about one year since he had crossed the Rubicon. Because he had no warships, Caesar used merchant ships. Because he lacked enough ships to transport all his men, he took only half of them. Expecting that Pompey's fleet would have its guard down, he hoped to slip by them and land on the Albanian coastline, and he succeeded. Once on the alert, however, the Pompeians prevented Caesar's ships from returning to Italy. It took four months before Caesar's lieutenant, Mark Antony, finally had the chance to evade Pompey's fleet and bring the rest of Caesar's troops across the Adriatic.

Alexander too had moved rapidly and decisively in his day, but Caesar took greater chances. Like Caesar, Alexander set out against his main enemy about one year after first launching his invasion (Alexander crossed the Dardanelles in spring 334 and marched toward Darius in spring 333). But Macedonian troops had invaded Anatolia two years earlier and begun laying the groundwork for victory, giving Alexander a head start compared with Caesar. Nor did Alexander do anything as drastic as ship an army across the sea in late autumn. The truth is, Caesar darted ahead of Alexander.

When he crossed the Adriatic, Caesar landed on the coast of Epirus (roughly, modern Albania). His ultimate target was Dyrrachium, about seventy-five miles to the north as the crow flies. Dyrrachium was a Roman naval base at the head of the via Egnatia, the road that led eastward through Epirus, Macedonia, and Thrace (modern Albania, Greece, and Turkey) to Byzantium (Istanbul), linking the Adriatic and the Bosphorus. Pompey planned to winter in Dyrrachium with his army and to cross to Italy as soon as the spring sailing season began. Then he planned to crush Caesar.

But with so few forces at his disposal, Caesar was in no position to attack Dyrrachium. The most he could do was make threatening moves in its direction by taking a few towns that lay on the way. As it happens, Pompey and his army were to the east of Dyrrachium at the time, but they hurried there at the news of Caesar's arrival and beat him to the city.

Then one of those little things happened, one of those rare moments of enlightenment in the fog of wartime. It took place during one of the stabs at negotiation that Caesar made from time to time. He was, after all, a great politician as well as a great general, and he knew how much the average Roman yearned for peace. So, as he had done earlier outside Brundisium, Caesar now called for talks.

Pompey said no. He was ahead in the military game and he had no intention of throwing away his advantage. Still, refusing the offer made him seem unreasonable. Even some of his men thought so: since the two armies were camped close to each other, Caesar sent a negotiator to Pompey's troops, and they welcomed him. But Pompey's officers firmly opposed talks and one of them came forward and started arguing with Caesar's representative. Suddenly, Pompey's soldiers began to throw javelins and wounded a number of Caesar's men.

The peace talks collapsed but not before one of Pompey's lieutenants laid things on the line: "There can be no peace for us," he said, "until Caesar's head is brought in." The Latin rings with power: *nam nobis nisi Caesaris capite relato pax esse nulla potest.*

It boiled the war down to its essentials—one man. As long as Caesar was alive, peace was impossible. He would never back down. If he died, no one else could hold his army together. But Pompey's death would have been a different story, engendering among his supporters an equal measure of mourning and relief. His goal was power but theirs was a republican government, and they would be glad to go on fighting for it without him. Without Caesar, though, there would be no Caesarians, as the followers of Caesar were called.

If Pompey thought he could win a direct assault on Caesar, he would have made one. He preferred instead to starve out the enemy. It was Pompey's by-now-familiar caution, but it made sense, as the enemy had limited food and supplies and no way to return to Italy.

The situation drove Caesar to distraction. At one point, he made the improbable move of slipping out of camp and hiring the captain of a small boat to bring him back to Brundisium. The weather turned rough and the captain wanted to turn back, but Caesar insisted on continuing because of "Caesar's good fortune." Luckily, Caesar came to his senses before the boat was swamped and returned to shore. Was it just a stunt to boost morale? Back at his camp, Caesar's men hailed his safety and vowed to beat Pompey without reinforcements, all on their own.

They didn't have to. Three months after their arrival, in April 48 B.C. (February 48, by the modern calendar), Antony finally managed to show up with the rest of Caesar's legions. Once again, Pompey's blockade had failed. In fact, the fault looks even greater when we consider that a Pompeian squadron of fifty ships raided Antony's base at Brundisium. Antony fought them off, but just think what a full-scale attack could have achieved. As so often, Pompey gave up the initiative to the enemy.

Antony had actually been driven off course and landed forty miles north of Caesar. Caesar marched north to meet him, and Pompey tried to block him. Pompey failed in that, although his navy did manage to capture all of Antony's ships, leaving Caesar's forces cut off from Italy. Ever wily, though, Caesar beat Pompey back to Dyrrachium and cut him off from his supplies in the city. Pompey made camp on Petra, a fortified hill near the sea and a harbor, with Dyrrachium to his north and Caesar's camp in between.

And there, the two sides sat and dug in. After more than a year of mobile warfare from Spain to the Adriatic, the struggle to control the Roman empire settled down to a rumble over a twenty-mile-square strip of hills and sand on the coast of Albania.

Pompey's Game

Caesar had cut Pompey off from Dyrrachium but only by land. Since Pompey held command of the sea, he could ferry supplies to Petra. Caesar couldn't stop that, but he could prevent Pompey from sending his cavalry into the hills in search of the fodder they needed for their horses.

It was a small victory but Caesar wanted to turn it into a big one. He decided to have his men build a wall, punctuated by forts, to blockade Pompey's army. The wall eventually stretched for seventeen miles over hilly terrain. Pompey answered by building a fifteen-mile long "counterwall" to keep Caesar's army away from his troops. There now followed the strangest battle of the war. For more than three months, the two sides were locked in a kind of armed wrestling match of raids and counter-raids.

It was a war of attrition, and attrition was Pompey's element. He was a great organizer who liked nothing better than to twist the noose slowly around another army's neck. Caesar was all speed. He jabbed brilliantly, looking for an opening against the foe, but Pompey ground him down.

Caesar made the mistake of playing Pompey's game at Dyrrachium, although he tried to play it differently. As soon as he linked up with Antony, Caesar challenged Pompey to a pitched battle against his reunited forces. But Pompey was too smart to fall for that, knowing that his men were not ready to take on Caesar's veterans in deadly combat. Later, on another occasion, Caesar led an assault on the city of Dyrrachium, but it nearly cost him his life, and the attempt failed. So Caesar put his hopes in his wall.

As a military strategy, it could hardly succeed. The wall would reduce Pompey's supplies but not destroy them. Cut off from the city and the sea, Caesar's men would suffer more. It was nearly a year since the last harvest, and there was little food to be found by foraging. In fact, Caesar's troops were reduced to eating roots, which left Pompey to dub them animals and not men.

But the wall's purpose was as much political as military. It meant to humiliate Pompey by showing that a smaller army could cut him off—an army that he feared to face in conventional battle. Dolabella, who was with Caesar at Dyrrachium as an officer—apparently forgiven for earlier losing a fleet in the Adriatic—wrote to Cicero, his famous father-in-law, to tell him to dump

Pompey and switch to Caesar's side, because only losers allow themselves to be blockaded.

"So what?" Pompey might have responded, and rightly so. (Cicero stayed loyal to Pompey, by the way). Pompey figured that eventually Caesar's men would crack, and they did. After three months of siege, two of Caesar's Gallic cavalry officers defected to Pompey because Caesar had caught them stealing money. They brought key intelligence about weak points in Caesar's defenses. In early July (early May by our calendar), Pompey launched a series of joint land-sea attacks. Although Caesar's forces managed to drive them back, it was not easy, and they took heavy casualties. Caesar himself had to jump in at the head of the reserves.

Not long afterward, Caesar led a counterattack. At first it went well, but then, to quote Caesar, "fortune . . . produces great changes out of little movements, as it happened then." Caesar's men mistakenly entered a kind of maze of abandoned walls and ditches. They paid for their error— Pompey attacked them and they panicked. Caesar now risked his life—and almost lost it—in an effort to stop them: the incident with which this book began.

But not even Caesar could stem the tide of panic. The result was a major disaster: about a thousand of his men, including thirty-two officers, were killed and others taken prisoner. Also lost were thirty-two battle standards, a sign of shame to a Roman army.

Caesar's position looked grim, but then a surprising thing happened: nothing. Caesar expected Pompey to close in for the kill but Pompey held back. He suspected an ambush and he thought it was an unnecessary risk to attack. As far as he was concerned, he had won the war. He expected that Caesar's hungry and defeated army would simply break up. If they managed to hang on, they could no longer do real damage.

Pompey's soldiers now saluted him as *"Imperator!"*—that is, "victorious general." Jubilant, Pompey accepted the tribute, but he didn't repeat it. Calling himself *"Imperator"* would offend many, because in this case, the title came from a battle in which he had killed fellow Romans, not foreign enemies.

Anyway, Pompey had a bigger problem to worry about. Caesar was unbeaten. Caesar had expected Pompey to follow up his success and deliver the crowning blow, but he never came. Caesar felt surprise and contempt. He said to his friends, "Today the enemy would have won, if they had a commander who was a winner."

Looking back later, Caesar accused Pompey of overconfidence, and of forgetting that the victory was due more to Caesar's men's bad luck than to any prowess on Pompey's part. By not finishing the job, Pompey gave Caesar breathing space to come up with a new plan, while not bothering to do the same himself, as Caesar later sneered.

Caesar had no intention of giving up. Success spoiled Pompey, but failure stiffened Caesar's spine. He realized that he was finished at Dyrrachium. Better withdraw eastward, over the mountains into central Greece, specifically into the rich and fertile region of Thessaly. By now, it was mid-July (mid-May by our calendar) and the winter wheat would be ripening in the fields. Caesar's men could harvest it and eat. He also recognized that he needed to rebuild his men's morale before risking another fight. He gathered the army, told the troops to take heart, and punished a few of his standard-bearers for good measure. Then, after sending the baggage train ahead at night, he withdrew his army at dawn.

In private, Caesar is supposed to have confessed that he was wrong to blockade Dyrrachium. In public, he admitted nothing. He told the troops that they should blame their loss on anyone but him. It was arrogant but shrewd. Caesar considered the army to be like a child that would be lost without faith in its father—himself. Shake that trust and he would orphan them.

As he retreated to Thessaly, Caesar did nothing less than save his army. It was an inspired display of leadership. No surprise, for, aside from the strategic blunder of blockading Dyrrachium, Caesar had offered brilliant leadership throughout the winter—spring campaign of 48 B.C. He led at every level, from the front line to intermediate-sized units to the strategist's tent. He led directly and indirectly, by example and by mental agility. He showed an extraordinary knowledge of his men and clearheadedness about their strengths and weaknesses. He accepted setbacks but never defeat. Caesar proved himself to be a man without illusions but also without gloom.

When it came to cunning and strategic insight, Pompey was Caesar's equal. In organizational skill, Pompey was his superior. His strategic withdrawal from Italy was masterful. His defense of Dyrrachium was shrewd. But he lacked Caesar's audacity and speed. His army could not compete in pitched battle. He failed to destroy Caesar when he had him at his mercy at Dyrrachium. Worst of all, Pompey was capable of self-delusion. Eventually, Caesar too would fall prey to this weakness, but in 48 B.C., his mind was still as cold as the snows of Gaul and as sharp as a wolf's tooth.

The Essence of Decision

"War is a harsh teacher." After his experience in the first year and a half of war, each of our three generals would have nodded in agreement to this saying of Thucydides. They each faced surprises and reversals.

About a year and a half after the outbreak of war, Hannibal and Caesar had each penetrated to the heart of enemy territory. Although they took great risks to get there, neither succeeded in conquering his opponent's stronghold. Caesar was driven back from Dyrrachium, while Hannibal didn't even try to take Rome. Neither man had taken his last shot yet, however—far from it.

About eighteen months after the start of his war, Alexander had not yet reached the enemy's homeland, but he had conquered its rich, western rim. Like Hannibal, he had defeated the enemy in two pitched battles; Hannibal also won a third battle that was effectively a massacre. Caesar hadn't found an enemy willing to fight him in a pitched battle, but he had conquered Italy and Spain as well as Sicily and Sardinia even so, with seemingly little effort.

Alexander, Hannibal, and Caesar each found himself challenged by the enemy's game. Each man began the war with the hope that the enemy would honor the standard protocols of warfare in the Greek, Carthaginian, and Roman worlds: decision by pitched battle. The enemy had other options, though, and he chose to exercise them, and none of the three would-be conquerors found it easy going.

Take Alexander. When he crossed the Hellespont, he thought that he had a viable fleet. He quickly came to the conclusion that he didn't, and sent most of his ships home. But he was hasty, as the fleet would have come in handy in later operations. Alexander thought that he could shut down the Persian navy by making war on it by land and taking its naval bases. He turned out to be too optimistic. The siege of Halicarnassus was costly and left the harbor in Persia's hands. Some of Persia's ports on the mainland proved too difficult to take, and Persia easily reconquered the islands that had gone over to Alexander. In Memnon of Rhodes, Alexander had a frighteningly competent opponent. In fact, a year after he invaded Anatolia, Alexander faced the real threat of a Persian invasion of Greece.

Two things saved him. First and foremost, Divine Providence intervened. Memnon died of a sudden illness in spring 333. Second, Alexander had superb strategic intuition, which let him guess Persia's default mode correctly. As soon as Memnon died, Darius called off the invasion of Greece and called his Greek mercenaries into service in a land battle against Alexander instead. For Persia, it was strategic suicide. For the Macedonians, it was confirmation of the enemy's fatal flaws.

Hannibal too learned hard lessons. Losing the sight in one eye was the least of them for a tough soldier. He faced the frustration of leading an army that was too tired to make more of its victory than to eat and rest. He got the first glimpse of an enemy that, no matter the size of its defeat, had no intention of surrendering. And he learned that Rome knew how to fight back, not merely with power but cunning.

By its attack on Spain, Rome threatened Hannibal's base. It demonstrated as well a strategic tenacity that Persia lacked. In order to respond, Hannibal needed support and reinforcements. The home government in Carthage could provide those in time, if it agreed. What it could not provide, however, was another general as good as Hannibal. The great man had no peer.

Fabius's strategy in Italy might have troubled Hannibal even more than the battle for Spain. If the Romans avoided pitched battle, he could not win but at best survive. Hannibal needed big victories to attract allies away from Rome and toward him. Otherwise, his small army could harass the Romans but not defeat them. His main hope was to lure Rome back into the arena of pitched battle. It was a good hope, as things turned out, because the Romans did not stick to Fabius's strategy.

As for Caesar; he had the most serious trouble of all with an enemy who refused to play by his rules. That reflected both Pompey's clearheadedness and Caesar's philosophy of the offensive. Had Caesar been less aggressive, he would have evacuated Dyrrachium when Pompey's refusal to fight a pitched battle there became clear. Instead, Caesar could have gone to Thessaly and either tempted Pompey into battle there or at least wintered in easier conditions. But Caesar risked everything on a battle of attrition at Dyrrachium, where he stood at a distinct disadvantage. Like Fabius, Pompey preferred attrition to pitched battle. At Dyrrachium, Caesar lost not only the battle but nearly the entire war. Only Pompey's overconfidence allowed Caesar to live to fight another day.

Like Hannibal, Caesar suffered from a subordinate who was not up to his level of competence: Curio lost North Africa for Caesar as Hasdrubal had cost Carthage major setbacks in Spain. Alexander did better with Antigonus in Anatolia.

After eighteen months of war, all three men had suffered setbacks. Alexander had responded most effectively, but he faced the least competent enemy. Caesar was in the most serious trouble, Hannibal somewhere in between.

But the period of coping with the enemy's initial resistance was over. Each of our generals was about to face a crisis that could decide the war.

4

CLASH

O N THE MORNING OF OCTOBER 1, 331 B.C., ON A BROAD AND TREELESS PLAIN beneath the Zagros Mountains in what is today Iraqi Kurdistan, the cavalry charged. Once the trumpet sounded, thousands of horsemen from out of the Eurasian steppe, all heavily armed—some to the point that even their horses wore armor—came hurtling out of the Persian lines. They aimed at outflanking and outfighting the Macedonians and driving the enemy's lines into chaos. It was the start of Gaugamela, the greatest battle that Alexander and Darius would ever fight.

A little more than a century later and three thousand miles to the west, on an August morning in 216 B.C., the harsh and mournful sound of the Celtic war horn rang out in the valley of the Aufidus River in southern Italy. The Celts were fighting for a large Carthaginian army that was about to clash with an even more massive Roman force. The Carthaginian cavalry charged up a lane between the river and the left flank of the Roman infantry. The Celts attacked with a hail of javelins, followed by lances and long swords. Alongside them rode squadrons of Spanish cavalry armed with spears and *falcatas*, curved swords with a deadly eighteen-inch blade. The sixty-five hundred Celts and Spaniards outnumbered the twenty-four hundred Roman horsemen by more than two to one. In the narrow space between the river and the Roman infantry, there was no room to maneuver, so the cavalrymen on both sides dismounted and fought on foot. It was an old-fashioned, blood-and-guts, hand-to-hand fight. The worst day in the history of the Roman army—the battle of Cannae—had begun.

A little more than 150 years later and three hundred miles to the east, on a hot, steamy summer day in 48 B.C., six thousand cavalrymen advanced across the central Greek plain to the rumble of the commander's horn and the cry of the trumpet. Well armed, well fed, well led, they were the sons of aristocrats and kings, making up a mosaic of nationalities from Gaul to Italy to Greece. Wearing chain-mail armor or tunics, plumed helmets or felt caps, brandishing javelins and lances, long swords and scimitars, they galloped over the gap separating them from their enemy. Only a thousand cavalrymen, most of them Gauls and Germans, rode on the other side. The attackers planned to roll them up, charge into the flank of the enemy's infantry, and plunge his army into chaos. In spite of the international cast of cavalrymen, this was a Roman conflict. It was the great civil war between Caesar and Pompey and its bloodiest battle—the battle of Pharsalus—was under way.

Three great battles, three dramatic charges: Hollywood couldn't have done it better. But screenwriters have it easier than conquerors. They don't have to argue with their audience in order to write a climax into the script; the audience demands it. Moviegoers love a crisis; military strategists are less predictable. Having overcome initial setbacks, each of our three great commanders now wanted to force a decision via pitched battle, but he had to get the enemy to oblige. If the enemy respects the conqueror's reputation as a giant of the battlefield, the enemy might prefer an indirect strategy such as a war of attrition or a counteroffensive in another theater.

Bringing their opponents to the battlefield, then, was a challenge for Alexander, Hannibal, and Caesar alike. After Issus, Alexander hoped that Darius would agree to a rematch, but Alexander had no way to know what Darius was thinking. After Fabius's strategy, Hannibal adjusted his plans to try to lure the Romans back into battle, but the decision was up to them. After Dyrracchium, Caesar hoped to breathe life back into his army and tempt Pompey into fighting a pitched battle, but Pompey resisted—at first.

In the end, the enemy obliged, and the three generals each got the battle they had hoped for. The result was each man's finest hour. At Gaugamela (331), Cannae (216), and Pharsalus (48), Alexander, Hannibal, and Caesar respectively won three of the great pitched battles of military history. Here, we examine how they did it. What they made of the results is a subject for the next chapter.

GAUGAMELA

From Egypt to Babylon was about 750 miles by the caravan routes through Syria. It was just off this historic road, on the hot and dusty Assyrian plain, south of the foothills of the Zagros Mountains, that the armies of Macedon and Persia met for their greatest battle.

Eclipse

October 1, 331 B.C., was a day of destiny. Even Babylon's famous astrologers took note. They recorded a battle that morning in which an invading army inflicted a heavy defeat on the great king's troops. The stars, they say, had predicted it. A week and a half earlier, on September 20, a lunar eclipse—at nighttime, with Saturn present, Jupiter absent, and a west wind blowing—foretold ruin for the king at the hands of an intruder from the west. And so it happened at the battle of Gaugamela (pronounced "gaw-guh-MEE-lah") on October 1, when Alexander defeated the last army that Darius would ever raise against him.

Alexander was eager for this battle. He hoped to beat Darius again, and to finish what he had started at Issus, making Alexander in fact what he already claimed to be: the king of Asia. But Darius was eager to fight as well, and the question is why. Wouldn't Darius have been better off by avoiding battle?

Darius might have followed a scorched-earth policy instead, which would have worked simply: deny food to Alexander's army as it marched eastward. Meanwhile, Persian cavalry units could attack in sudden, unpredictable, hit-and-run raids, especially dangerous if the Macedonians split up in small groups to look for supplies. Bleeding, hungry, and off balance from Persian attacks, the army might force Alexander to turn back. True, he would still control Darius's lost provinces west of the Euphrates, but Darius would hold the east.

But this strategy too was risky. Many towns might prefer opening their storehouses to Alexander rather than go hungry for Darius. In the end, they could very well decide that one king was as good as another. Darius, therefore, had his reasons to choose to fight another battle. If anyone could make the third time a charm, it was he.

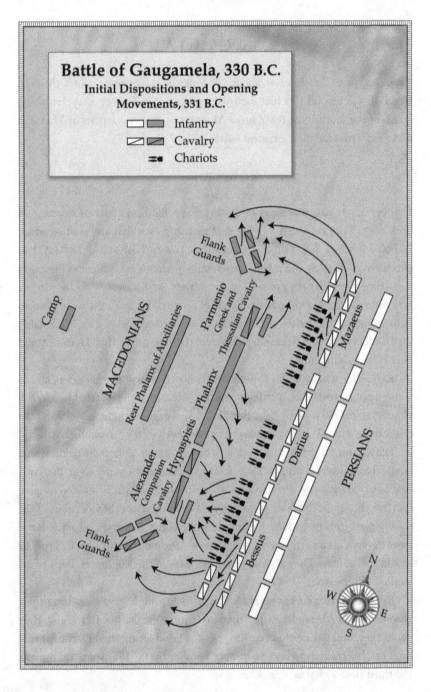

Battle of Gaugamela, 330 B.C.

Initial Dispositions and Opening
Movements, 331 B.C.

Infantry
Cavalry
Chariots

Flank Guards

Camp

MACEDONIANS

Rear Phalanx of Auxiliaries

Parmenio
Greek and
Thessalian Cavalry

Phalanx

Alexander
Companion
Cavalry   Hypaspists

Flank
Guards

Bessus

Darius

Mazaeus

PERSIANS

N
W   E
S

He had spent the eighteen months since Issus wisely: he showed good judgment by building a new army. Unlike his earlier armies, it was almost entirely a cavalry force—and an excellent one. Despite Alexander's victories, Darius still controlled a gigantic empire, and it held untapped resources. Then as later, Central Asia was famous for its horsemen, and Darius assembled a superb group.

They came thundering out of the vast Eurasian steppe. Descendants of nomads, they were renowned for horse breeding and cavalry tactics. Darius's best cavalry were the riders of Bactria and Sogdiana (modern Afghanistan, Tajikistan, and Uzbekistan), supplemented by cavalry from western India and by the knights of the Saca peoples (who lived north of Sogdiana, in the eastern tip of modern Uzbekistan). The Saca were so heavily armed that even their horses wore armor, but the horses of Central Asia were and are known for great stamina.

They had weapons as good as the Macedonian army and better armor. Some had a well-deserved reputation as archers. Others received Macedonian-style pikes, long swords, and shields. Darius provided them, because he had learned the hard way just how effective they were.

These magnificent, terrifying, and deadly horsemen also enjoyed an excellent commander in Bessus. A prominent nobleman, Bessus was satrap of Bactria and Darius's relative. He molded an elite force that could stand comparison with Alexander's Companion Cavalry.

Darius's problem was infantry. A state-of-the-art military in 331 B.C. required a balanced mix of cavalry and infantry. Alexander's heavy infantry, for example, protected his cavalry from a frontal attack while adding weight to the cavalry's offensive punch. At Gaugamela, Alexander had about forty thousand infantrymen. But Darius had to do without effective infantry: Alexander had cut off the supply of Greek mercenaries, the traditional source of Persia's heavy infantry. Darius would have to make do with the two thousand Greek mercenaries he had left and two thousand elite Persian infantrymen, who were no match for Alexander's numbers.

To slow down Alexander's deadly cavalry charge, Darius had two other hopes: elephants and scythed chariots. Neither was very promising. Darius had fifteen elephants at Gaugamela. They could have protected him from an attack by Alexander's cavalry, but Darius's own troops probably lacked the training necessary to handle the beasts, and the elephants likely stayed in camp. Then there were Darius's scythed chariots. These fierce-looking machines bristled on either side with spikes, spearheads, sword blades, and scythes. Yet past experience showed that disciplined units of soldiers could parry any threat from them.

It came down to Darius's cavalry. So he gave them an edge in numbers. Alexander had seven thousand cavalrymen. Darius's cavalry numbers are unknown, but they greatly outnumbered Alexander's, probably by at least three to one if not more: twenty-five thousand Persian cavalrymen is an educated guess.

Finally, Darius carefully chose a suitable battlefield and did everything he could to lure the enemy to fight there. He picked a wide-open plain, with few or no shrubs or bushes, and had his engineers flatten the few low hills: now his chariots and cavalry would have the space to maneuver that had been lacking at Issus. He chose Assyria (Iraqi Kurdistan) as the place to make his stand. The region offered plains and plenty of food and it stood on Alexander's likely marching route south and east: to Babylon (near modern Baghdad), now Darius's western capital, and to Persia beyond it.

Darius gave his cavalry the tools to carry out a double envelopment of the enemy. They would surround Alexander's army on both sides and overwhelm it. That was the plan: the question was, how well could the Persians execute it? And could Alexander make a set of countermoves to stop it?

For his part, the Macedonian King fielded the largest army he had ever commanded. They were veteran forces and they enjoyed the morale boost of past victories.

In early spring 331, Alexander and his men headed northeast from Egypt. After stopping at Tyre, they marched inland. Around August 1 a Persian regiment watched the Macedonians cross the Euphrates River at Thapascus (today, in north-central Syria) but it did nothing to stop them. Indeed, it looks as if the Persians were pointing Alexander toward Darius, who was waiting about three hundred miles to the east in Assyria with his army. As Alexander marched eastward, Persian scouts, captured by the Macedonians, gave the false news that Darius planned to block Alexander from crossing the Tigris. Alexander hurried to the Tigris but found no one there. The river was fordable but just barely; a rough current tired out Alexander's men by the time they reached the other shore. Still, the Persians did nothing to oppose them other than burning crops to deny the enemy food. It was mid-September.

Roughly seventy-five miles away, the Persians were waiting on Darius's chosen battlefield. They were probably somewhere between the Gomel River and the Jabal Maqlub Hills, which rise three thousand feet above the plain: either north of the hills, near the small town of Tell Gomel, or south of the hills, near the city of Qaraqosh (modern Al Hamdaniya). In either case, the terrain was similar, a large expense of fairly flat land among eroded hills.

After crossing the Tigris, Alexander rested his army for two days. Then, on the night of September 20, came the eclipse. Alexander had planned to start the march again the next morning, but his men were too frightened. Instead, he sacrificed animals and called in a soothsayer to reassure the troops that this was an ill omen for the Persians, not them. As a good leader, Alexander attended to his men's mood.

And yet, the coming days reawakened their fears. Nine days of marching and resting brought the Macedonians to the Jabal Maqlub, from whose heights they could see Darius's army clearly, about three and a half miles away, filling the plain in its battle order. That huge force gave Alexander and his senior commanders enough pause that he delayed the battle for a day.

Defense with a Sting

Alexander rode around the entire battlefield the next day on a scouting mission with his light-armed troops and Companion Cavalry. He then put his mind to work on refining his battle tactics. Not that he planned to change a winning formula. Alexander left the heart of the Macedonian battle order in place, but he needed to protect it from the danger of being outflanked by Darius's big and powerful cavalry. Masterful tactician that he was, Alexander figured out Darius's plans and came up with a way to counter them.

The Persian line stretched for several miles across the plain. Darius held the great king's traditional position in the center, guarded by his elite Persian infantry and Greek mercenaries. Fifty scythed chariots and fifteen elephants (which would not take part in the actual battle) were posted in front of him. The right wing, commanded by Mazaeus, former satrap of Syria, was made up of cavalry from Syria, Mesopotamia (Iraq), and parts of Iran—which produced excellent horsemen. Mazaeus also had fifty scythed chariots. The left wing, commanded by Bessus, satrap of Bactria, contained the great cavalry contingents of the east as well as one hundred scythed chariots. This wing was Persia's stronger arm, and it would face Alexander's best troops on his right wing. The bulk of Persia's infantry stood in the rear, which was appropriate, since they were too weak to play much of a role in battle.

As Alexander could see, his opponent had a bigger army than at Issus, rich in cavalry but poor in infantry. Alexander understood that, in strategic terms, Darius stood on the defensive; he had challenged the enemy to come to him. In tactical terms, though, Darius needed to go on the offensive: Darius had to attack first.

Cavalry was the Persian's strong suit. Fresh and motivated at the start of battle, his horsemen might overwhelm the enemy. But if Darius let Alexander attack first, he risked cracks in his shiny military machine—if not worse. Darius had enough heavy infantry to absorb a frontal attack by Alexander but not enough to turn around and go on the counteroffensive.

Darius's superiority in numbers allowed him to outflank Alexander on either side. His best move in battle was to envelop Alexander's two wings with his powerful cavalry. If they did their job well, they would leave the rest of the Macedonian army defenseless—and certainly unable to attack. Alexander had to come up with a plan that would parry the Persians' cavalry strike and allow him to counterattack in turn. He also had to protect his flanks without thinning out his line to the point where it left his center weak. His solution was a novel, flexible formation.

At first glance, Alexander arranged his army in a familiar pattern. The Macedonian infantry phalanx took its usual position in the center, linked to the Companion Cavalry on their right by the hypaspists, the elite corps that made sure no gap opened up in the line. On the left stood two sets of cavalry units—those of the Thessalians and those of the other Greek allies. As usual, Alexander took command of the right wing of his army and put Parmenio in charge of the left.

What made this army different, however, was a series of additional formations that created what was more or less a rectangle. The sides of the rectangle were made up of a flank guard on each wing. Each of these two flank guards was thrown back at about a forty-five-degree angle from the front line. Each flank guard was made up of several infantry units, arranged like a set of steps, and guarded by a screen of cavalry. Finally, the back of the rectangle was made up of a second set of infantry, positioned behind the front line and parallel to it. Their job was to turn and meet the threat from the rear—the Persian horsemen might ride all the way around the rectangle.

It was on the sides of the rectangle, though, and not the rear, that Alexander planned to fight. He wanted to draw the Persian cavalry into a fight with the flank guards on his army's two wings. Those guards' mix of cavalry and infantry represented defense with a sting. Hidden behind their own horsemen, the infantry would emerge during the battle and dash into action. Light-armed troops, including archers and javelin-men, they offered a quick and deadly counterweight to the Persian's superiority in cavalry numbers—especially on Alexander's right wing, where he was stationed and where he put his best troops.

Alexander predicted that the charge of the Persian cavalry on either wing would leave a gap in the enemy's line. He planned to rip right through that gap by a combined charge of his elite Companion Cavalry and the Macedonian phalanx. Meanwhile, however, his weaker wing, the left wing under Parmenio, would bend under a Persian onslaught. Alexander knew that he might find himself in a race against time, hurrying to win on his right and then turning to help Parmenio before the Persians overwhelmed him.

In short, Alexander displayed his extraordinary judgment as a commander. He took his superb, combined-arms force and—on the spot—made it better. He displayed agility as well as insight. Above all, it was an exercise in audacity.

Having figured out his battle plan, Alexander called a conference of his top officers. He told them that they were fighting not for a province or a country but for the control of all "Asia"—that is, for the Persian empire. He emphasized the importance of strict discipline; of keeping silent on the advance but marking the charge with shouts and battle cries. Then, ever the good leader, he attended to morale by giving the men a meal and a good night's sleep. He himself rested as well, but not before he sacrificed to the god Fear, according to one source.

Darius, for his part, feared a Macedonian nighttime attack, so he kept his men at their posts all night long. Not knowing when or where the enemy might attack, he couldn't rely on just a small force of guards to protect the army. The Persians faced the morning fatigued, which hardly helped them in battle.

At dawn, Alexander appeared in his best armor and rode up and down the ranks. He held his lance in his left hand, raised his right hand, and called on the gods. In Anatolia and Egypt, oracles had proclaimed him to be the son of Zeus. Alexander did nothing to discourage the idea, as it strengthened his brand. Some Greeks had already hailed previous conquerors as demigods, and Alexander had outdone them.

As he rode along the ranks, Alexander asked the gods, if he really was the son of Zeus, to guard and help strengthen the Greeks. As if on cue, an eagle supposedly appeared above Alexander and flew straight toward the Persians.

The battle was about to begin.

The Eagle Pounces

Gaugamela is hard to reconstruct. The battle lines stretched for miles, so no one man was in a position to see the whole thing. The flat and featureless landscape offered no landmarks to aid memory. Both sides engaged in complex tactics. Each side's cavalry charges raised clouds of dust. Even with perfect sources, the battle would be a challenge to describe, and our sources are flawed.

Alexander began the battle by marching toward the right, moving at an oblique angle to the Persian front. As he drew near the end of the Persian line, Darius began to worry that Alexander would move off the ground that had been smoothed for his scythed chariots. So he sent the Bactrian and Saca cavalry under Bessus to ride around Alexander's right and stop his march.

The trumpets and battle cries sounded. Alexander, in turn, ordered the leading edge of his right flank guard to charge—just a small squadron, which the Persians easily pushed back, but it served as bait. The rest of Bessus's cavalry now joined in, a terrifying sight as they charged. But the fight was developing exactly where Alexander wanted it, on his right flank guard. His defense with a sting was up to the challenge. He did not destroy Bessus's cavalry but he stopped it.

Meanwhile, Darius ordered his scythed chariots to plow into the enemy. But the Macedonians were prepared. On the Macedonian right and center, a screen of archers and javelin-men fired; in some cases they actually grabbed the reins and pulled down the drivers. Some chariots got through, but the men had been trained to part ranks and let them pass. The chariots accomplished little or nothing, at least on the Macedonian right. Perhaps they did more damage on the Macedonians' weaker, left wing, where another Persian cavalry charge, led by Mazaeus, hammered Parmenio's Thessalian cavalry.

Around this time a gap appeared in the Persian line, between the left and the center, caused by the departure of Bessus's horsemen. Alexander seized the moment. He formed his elite Companion Cavalry into a wedge, ordered the Macedonian phalanx to advance beside them, raised the battle cry, and charged. They cut through the opening in the enemy line and ripped apart his exposed flank. The sources describe the scene vividly: "For a short time the battle became a hand-to-hand fight. The cavalrymen around Alexander and Alexander himself pressed the enemy hard and robustly, shoving and using their lances against their faces. They pounded the Persians, and the Macedonian phalanx, thickly massed and bristling with pikes, struck them as well."

As at Issus, Darius was the target. Kill or capture the king and win the war: that was Alexander's plan. It would have worked too, thanks to his men's unstoppable advance, but Darius turned and fled. He was no coward; he hoped to fight again another day.

Besides, the battle wasn't over, and for a while, it looked as though events elsewhere on the field might give Darius his chance. Just as Bessus's charge opened a gap in the Persian line, so Alexander's charge left one or more holes in the Macedonian center and left. Now, Persian and Indian cavalry poured through them. They had a golden opportunity to join Mazaeus's fight against Parmenio's already struggling troops.

Parmenio, meanwhile, sent a message to Alexander asking for help, but the message probably never reached him. The battlefield was chaos, and in all likelihood, Alexander had already taken off in pursuit of Darius. Darius's flight filled "the air . . . with the groans of the fallen, the hoofbeats of the horses, and the constant noise of the whips," according to one source. It also raised a thick cloud of dust that hampered the Macedonians' pursuit. Alexander turned back toward his left wing.

If Alexander had gambled on Parmenio muddling through, he was correct. The old man had a history of hanging on in a tough fight, and his

Thessalians were intrepid. Meanwhile, instead of helping Mazaeus against the Macedonian left, the Persian and Indian horsemen plundered Alexander's camp far behind the lines. They wasted their opportunity to aid Mazaeus, only to be driven back by Macedonian infantry in the rear.

In any case, once the Persian cavalry learned about Darius's flight from the field, they halted the struggle. Not that they were broken: as they rode off, they ran smack into Alexander's Companion Cavalry, who were finally heading toward Parmenio. The result was the most hard-fought cavalry encounter of the day. There was none of the usual spear throwing or turning movements that were the rule in cavalry fights. This was a brawl, with every man trying to break through and save his life. Sixty of Alexander's Companions fell, and three senior officers were wounded, including Hephaestion, Alexander's closest friend.

It did nothing to change the outcome of the battle. Alexander had delivered Darius a decisive defeat. The Persian did not fail from want of trying. He maneuvered the enemy onto his chosen battlefield, where he forced him to face an overwhelming array of power on horseback. But the Macedonians brought the most versatile army in the ancient world to the field, at the height of its self-confidence and experience. They had outstanding commanders: Parmenio, for example, was an unsung hero for absorbing the enemy's battering and holding the Macedonian left together. They had a marked advantage in infrastructure.

But the main difference between the two armies—the decisive advantage—was Alexander's superiority as a general. Both in preparation for the battle and in the heat of combat, Alexander showed himself to be Darius's master. Displaying strategic intuition, he scrutinized the enemy's battle order with an expert eye and rearranged his tactics handily. He kept his cool in the heat of battle and aimed the decisive blow at the right place and time. True, not everything went according to plan: Darius escaped, the Macedonian line was broken, and casualties were not small. But the result crowned Alexander's achievements. Darius was a good general but Alexander was a military genius.

There are no accurate casualty figures for the battle. The sources probably minimize Alexander's losses and inflate Darius's: their estimates range from 100 to 500 Macedonian dead, and from a sky-high 40,000 to a silly 300,000 Persian dead. Although Gaugamela saw ferocious fighting, many

Persians escaped, some of them in units that maintained good order. Persian casualties were not light but they were not huge either.

Gaugamela was Alexander's greatest battlefield victory. It marked the end of pitched battle against the Persian empire. Mesopotamia and, for that matter, Iran too now lay at his feet.

Darius fled first to the nearest city, Arbela (modern Irbil), about sixty miles to the southeast. He then headed into the mountains of western Iran, with the remnants of his royal guard and his mercenaries, as well as Bessus's cavalry, which had survived in good order. Mazaeus and his surviving men fled to Babylon.

Alexander too went to Arbela after the battle. There, his men acclaimed him as "king of Asia." Alexander had first claimed that title in a letter to Darius after the battle of Issus. Now, it seemed no mere claim: it was real. At Arbela he also took the diadem—a ceremonial cloth headband—as his royal insignia. Three weeks later, after hammering out a settlement with Mazaeus, Alexander entered Babylon, where he was again acclaimed as king, this time officially.

But the war was not over. Darius still controlled Iran and Central Asia. Not only did Alexander have to catch him, he had to win his surrender to Alexander's new royal title as king of Asia. And he wanted to get Darius to bring the remaining Persian elite along with him. Otherwise, Alexander would have to conquer another million square miles of territory the hard way, hill and valley by bloody hill and valley. Either that, or he would have to accept that the "king of Asia" did not control eastern Iran or the provinces beyond it.

Nor could Alexander count on the support of his army. As far as many of his commanders and men were concerned, the war was all but over—only the capture of Persia's royal capital was left. They had no interest in the remote east. They wanted only as much of Persia's former empire as they could govern from Macedon.

Alexander would have to solve these problems if he was to enjoy the fruits of his victory at Gaugamela.

CANNAE

The "table land," or *Tavoliere*, is a sweeping plain, rich in farmland, and stretching across twelve hundred square miles in Apulia (Puglia) in southeastern Italy. Once, in prehistoric times, it was part of the ocean, but the land was dry as dust when, on a summer day in 216, Hannibal and the Romans met on the region's southern edge, at Cannae.

The Greatest Land Battle

August 2, 216 B.C., the day of the battle of Cannae, was one of the most terrible days in human history. Nearly as many men died on that August day at Cannae as on an August day in Hiroshima, two thousand years later—and without gunpowder, let alone an atomic bomb. (Hiroshima's casualties rose much higher over time because of radiation sickness.) Swords, spears, sling stones, horses' hoofs, the weight of thousands of marching feet on the fallen, heatstroke, exhaustion, terror, and even despair: these were death's tools at Cannae.

Cannae was to Hannibal what the lever was to Archimedes. The Romans outnumbered Hannibal at Cannae by nearly two to one and they got to fight the battle when and where they wanted. And yet Hannibal annihilated them.

Hannibal, the victor, killed about 48,000 Romans and took about 20,000 prisoners; only about 15,000 Romans escaped. The Romans killed between 6,000 and 8,000 of Hannibal's approximately 50,000 men. The Romans lost about 75 percent of their army: a little more than half of the Roman army was killed and another fourth was captured. The Carthaginians lost about 10 to 15 percent of their army. It was one of the most lopsided victories of all time.

Skeptics then and now have downplayed Hannibal's genius. They argue that he didn't win the battle, but rather, the Romans lost it. There is some truth in this. Without Roman errors, Cannae would have been a Roman defeat but not a disaster. Yet without Hannibal's brilliance, Cannae might have been a Roman victory.

How did this explosive battle come about? Both the Romans and Hannibal wanted it. Hannibal was confident of his ability to win yet

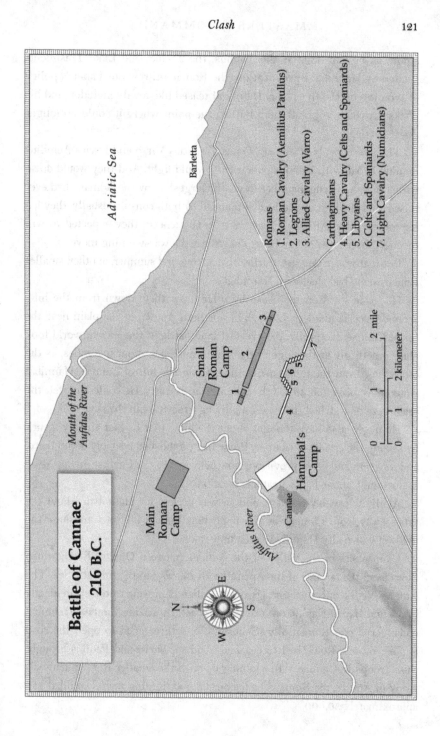

**Battle of Cannae
216 B.C.**

N
E
S
W

Adriatic Sea

Barletta

Main Roman Camp

Mouth of the Aufidus River

Small Roman Camp

Aufidus River

Cannae

Hannibal's Camp

1
2
3

4
5
5
6
7

0   1   2 mile
0   1   2 kilometer

Romans
1. Roman Cavalry (Aemilius Paullus)
2. Legions
3. Allied Cavalry (Varro)

Carthaginians
4. Heavy Cavalry (Celts and Spaniards)
5. Libyans
6. Celts and Spaniards
7. Light Cavalry (Numidians)

again, as he had done at the Ticinus, the Trebia, and Lake Trasimene. Incited by Hannibal's provocation, the Romans threw out Fabius's policy of avoiding battle. In 217 B.C. Hannibal teased like a wily matador, and his tricks drove an angry Roman bull to the point where it could no longer resist battle.

The new consuls of 216 B.C., Gaius Terentius Varro and Lucius Aemilius Paullus, broke with Fabius's policy; they would fight. And they would do so with a massive, sledgehammer force, the largest army the Romans had ever raised, and the first one to be commanded by both consuls; usually, they led separate armies. Although they were inexperienced, they expected to win through sheer force of numbers. They wanted a war-winning move.

But that was in August. Earlier that spring and summer, another, smaller Roman army had shadowed Hannibal.

He made the Romans chase him. He drew them down from the hills around Luceria (modern Lucera), in northern Apulia, to the plain near the sea at Cannae. Ironically, the greatest land battle in the ancient world took place practically at the edge of the sea. Cannae lies about five miles, as the crow flies, from the modern coastline. From the hill of Cannae, Hannibal would have been able to see the blue Adriatic clearly. He could have felt the sea breeze or watched the swallows diving gracefully in the sky.

He might also have thought about the blow that he had already struck by seizing the citadel of Cannae. Rome had established a supply dump there, and its grain and other provisions now belonged to the Carthaginians. More important, Cannae had a strategic location.

Apulia is cavalry country, and so was perfect for Hannibal. About ten miles away from Cannae lay the important Roman ally of Canusium, the fields of which city Hannibal's men now raided.

Cannae sits in the valley of the Aufidus (modern Ofanto) River, which flows from the far side of the Apennine all the way to the Adriatic Sea. The Aufidus Valley offers access across the Italian peninsula to the strategically important Bay of Naples, on Italy's west coast. By seizing Cannae, Hannibal endangered one Roman ally (Canusium) and threatened to open the road against others. Rome had to respond. And so, Varro and Paullus brought their troops to Cannae. After joining up with the smaller Roman army already in Apulia, the Romans had about 86,000 fighting men. Hannibal had approximately 50,000.

In its last stretch, in the area around Cannae, the Aufidus River sweeps between two ranges of hills and then, northeast of the citadel of Cannae, the hills drop away, the valley opens up, and there is a broad, slightly sloping plain that would have served well for the battle. Most historians locate the battlefield there, although a case can also be made for a site in the hollow between the hills.

Before the day of battle, the two sides maneuvered. When they reached the vicinity of Cannae, the Romans probably camped on the left bank (north side) of the river Aufidus. Hannibal was camped on the right bank, at the foot of the citadel of Cannae. The Romans threatened Hannibal with a small camp on his side of the river, and then Hannibal responded by moving his camp across the river to the Roman side on the left bank. On August 1, Hannibal challenged the Romans to fight but they refused. Then, the next day, the Romans crossed the river again and took up Hannibal's challenge.

What explains this elaborate game of chicken? One possible explanation is the Roman system of command, by which the two consuls alternated the supreme command daily. The ancient sources say that Paullus, who commanded on August 1, had decided not to risk a pitched battle against Hannibal, but Varro took command on August 2—and took the plunge. More likely, the Romans wanted to fight on the right bank, where the terrain was slightly less favorable to cavalry. Parts of it lay on a gentle gradient and parts offered less room to maneuver than on the left bank.

In either case, shortly before dawn on August 2—that is, shortly before 4:30 A.M. (daylight time)—Varro raised the red flag outside his tent, the traditional Roman signal for battle. Despite claims of tension in the sources, the other consul, Paullus, is likely to have cooperated fully. Rome had sent out its legions and they had found the enemy. The day of glory had arrived. Immediately after sunrise—6:00 A.M. (daylight time), Varro began leading the men out of both camps. He led the troops from the main camp across the River Aufidus to the right bank, where the troops from the smaller Roman camp joined them. Hannibal climbed a low hill and watched the Romans arrange for battle, as his own forces prepared.

The Romans left ten thousand men behind to garrison the main Roman camp and to threaten the Carthaginian camp, thereby forcing Hannibal to subtract guard troops from his already smaller numbers. So 76,000 troops took the field for Rome: 70,000 infantry and 6,000 cavalry. Of those 70,000, an estimated 50,000 were heavy infantry while 20,000 were light armed. Of the cavalry, an estimated 2,400 were Roman citizens and 3,600 Italian allies of Rome.

To turn to the other side, Hannibal brought 50,000 fighting men to Cannae: 40,000 infantrymen and 10,000 cavalrymen. The estimated breakdown of those numbers is as follows: the 10,000 cavalrymen consisted of 2,000 Spaniards, 4,000 Celts, and 4,000 Numidians. The 40,000 infantry consisted of 32,000 heavy armed and 8,000 light armed troops. The heavy infantry comprised 8,000 Libyans, 4,000 to 6,000 Spaniards, and 18,000 to 20,000 Celts.

Each side had been at Cannae long enough to reconnoiter the ground and make its plans for battle. Each side fought according to its way of war. Brutal simplicity marked the Roman plan. Hannibal's army moved with the cunning of a wrestler who, with a feigned glance or a misleading hand movement, tricks his opponent into mistaking the true direction of his attack.

The Romans drew up their infantry in a conventional parallel formation. The Roman army faced south, with the Roman heavy cavalry anchored next to the river, on the right wing; allied heavy cavalry held the left wing. The infantry was placed in the center, drawn up in a conventional parallel formation, but with one important and unusual detail. The Romans grouped the companies (maniples) tightly together, to make an infantry formation that was especially deep and narrow. The result was to create a virtual human battering ram, aimed at the center of Hannibal's line.

The condensed order of the troops also spoke to the Roman soldiers' inexperience. Because the Romans had raised such a huge army, much of it consisted of raw recruits. Perhaps the only way to keep order on the battlefield was to bunch them close together. The more experienced men were grouped in the center, providing a solid core, while the less experienced soldiers stood on the wings. The consul Varro commanded the left wing while the other consul, Paullus, commanded the right; the two ex-consuls of the previous year commanded the center.

The Roman infantry at Cannae was drawn up to a depth of between fifty and seventy-five ranks. The width of the infantry was about one to one and one-fourth miles, with the cavalry covering about another half mile, for a total of about one and one-half to one and three-fourths miles. Hannibal had far fewer men, but he had to cover the same frontage or risk having the enemy attack his flanks.

The Roman generals were still thinking about the previous battle instead of focusing on new conditions, as they should have. They knew what had worked at the Trebia and they wanted to try it again but to do it better. That is, they had broken through the Carthaginian center with their infantry at the Trebia, so they decided to stake everything at Cannae on breaking through the center with their infantry again. Against an ordinary opponent, that might have worked.

But Hannibal had not let his understanding of tactics stand still. Unlike the Romans, he *had* learned something from history. At the Trebia, Hannibal had been willing to sacrifice his center in order to win on the wings. At Cannae, he would also sacrifice his center but not to win on the wings. Instead, he held his wings in reserve and then had them turn inward to strike the advancing Romans on their flanks. It was a complicated and risky maneuver that only a professional army with veteran soldiers and a solid network of subordinate officers could carry out.

Unlike the Romans, Hannibal worked almost entirely with veterans. No new Africans or Spaniards had joined his army since the start of the war; only the Celts could have provided new recruits, as they probably did.

At Cannae, Hannibal came up with a brilliant variation of past tactics. He organized his center in a crescent, billowing out toward the enemy. He manned the center with infantrymen, Spaniards and the Celts. They made, Polybius says, "a strange and terrifying appearance," brandishing great swords and drawn up in alternate companies, the Celts bare-chested and the Spaniards wearing short, purple-bordered linen tunics. But they were not Hannibal's best troops—that honor went to the Libyans, who stood on the two wings. Experienced, loyal, and hard as stone, the Libyans also had the advantage of bearing state-of-the-art arms and armor, selected from among the loot from the fifty thousand Roman troops killed or captured since Hannibal had crossed the Alps.

The cavalry played a crucial role in Hannibal's plan. His heavy cavalry, who were Spaniards and Celts, stood on his left flank, near the river and opposite the Roman cavalry. His light cavalry, the Numidians, held his right flank. Hannibal and his brother Mago commanded the infantry center. Hasdrubal (not Hannibal's brother) commanded the heavy cavalry on the left, while Hanno led the light cavalry on the right. Maharbal commanded a reserve force of cavalry. Hannibal's army faced north.

Bloody Morning

Probably around 9:00 or 10:00 A.M., the battle began. Ancient battles usually started with skirmishing by the light troops, and Cannae was no exception. The experienced Carthaginian slingers and javelin-men got the better of the Romans. Then, the survivors on either side withdrew into the ranks of the infantrymen, leaving a stunning sight: about 100,000 men on foot or horseback, poised to fight to the death. The most massive army of citizen-soldiers that the world had ever seen was about to march into one of antiquity's two or three best professional armies. In the summer, the Apulian plain is hot and dry, and the marching of the men no doubt stirred up an enormous cloud of dust.

The cavalry clashed first. Hasdrubal's heavy cavalry on the Carthaginian left wing charged the Roman cavalry. Cavalry battles in this period usually consisted of a series of charges and pursuits, with reserves pouring in to allow each side to re-form and charge again, until finally the loser turned and fled. Not Cannae. Hemmed into a narrow space beside the river, the Roman cavalry tried to hold its ground, but the Carthaginians were more numerous, more experienced, better trained, and more confident. Many of the Roman horsemen dismounted and tried to fight on foot. It was a desperate move, leading Hannibal to comment that they might as well have handed themselves over to his men in chains. What was left of the Roman cavalry fled.

On the Carthaginian right, the light cavalry under Hanno held its own against the Roman-allied heavy cavalry. Suddenly, Hasdrubal's heavy cavalry appeared to help them. It seems that, after defeating the Roman heavy cavalry, they actually rode around the rear of the Roman army until they reached their comrades on the opposite wing. It was a prodigy of coordination and command. The Roman-allied cavalry broke and fled. The Roman army no longer had any cavalry. For them, Cannae was now entirely an infantry battle—and it was well under way.

While the cavalry clashed, the Roman legions had advanced. The Roman infantry pushed against the Celts and Spaniards in the center of the Carthaginian line. Vastly outnumbered, the Celts and Spaniards in turn retreated backward carefully, changing their position from one of billowing outward to curving inward. As stated in chapter 1, Hannibal's entire battle plan depended on the infantry line bending without breaking. The Celts and Spaniards had to hold on long enough for his cavalry to neutralize Rome's horsemen, at which point the Libyan troops on the wings would spring into action. The Celts and Spaniards had to maintain an orderly, fighting retreat while observing fellow-soldiers dying all around them. Hannibal's casualty figures show just how heavy a burden the center of his line bore: 4,000 of his 5,500 fallen infantrymen were Celts.

The Celts' famous love of battle might have kept them on the field, but only professional training and seasoned officers could have maintained their order—that, and the presence of Hannibal himself among them, on horse-back, and protected by a ring of bodyguards, but close enough to the front that he ran a risk.

Nine out of ten armies would never have been able to execute the ma-neuver. Most forces would have folded under a blow as hard as the one the Romans struck. Yet Hannibal's army not only bent without breaking, it then executed a series of countermaneuvers that were as breathtaking as they were devastating.

The Romans advanced so far against the enemy center that they marched alongside the two contingents of Libyans on their flanks. When that happened, and when the signal came that the Carthaginians had demol-ished the Roman cavalry, the Libyans got their order to spring into battle. They turned inward and marched against the enemy. With the Libyan front pressed against the Roman flank (and with no cavalry to protect that flank), the Romans were at their most vulnerable. On top of that, the Romans were tired; the Libyans were fresh.

Bloody Symphony

Still, what happened next was not preordained. If the Roman flanks had consisted of veteran troops and if they had been well commanded, then at least some units might have been able to turn and punch their way through the Libyans. But the flanks were Rome's newest and least experienced le-gions. They probably panicked and fled toward the center, tripping up the more experienced troops there in turn. That best explains why the Roman push against the Carthaginian center ran out of steam, even though the Roman consul Paullus rode there from his place on the right wing, in a vain attempt to rally his men.

For the Libyans what followed was, as Livy says, "slaughter rather than battle." For the Romans trapped in Hannibal's vise, it was a foretaste of hell. Every sense was tormented. Sounds included horns and trumpets, war cries in a half dozen languages, the thud of tens of thousands of marching feet, the thunder of hoof beats, the clash of iron, and the screams of the dying. Smells ranged from the slaughterhouse stink of bloody entrails or the more ordinary stench of sweat, vomit, urine, and feces. The scorching heat of a midsummer day in southern Italy, under the weight of arms and armor, touched everyone and left a dry taste in the mouth. The dust churned up by the local south wind blinded some; others had a clear sight of the field so covered with blood and slippery corpses that just standing was difficult.

And then there was Hasdrubal's cavalry. After coming to the aid of Hanno's men against the allied cavalry, they left the light cavalry to polish off what was left of the enemy horsemen. Now, in a move of extraordinary generalship, Hasdrubal had his men ride against the rear of the Roman infantry. Hasdrubal's horsemen charged the Romans again and again from several different directions. It was another blow to the enemy's morale. Had the Romans been more experienced and better led, they might have fought their way out of here too. But they did not.

With this move, the Carthaginians closed the ring. Between Celt and Spaniard infantrymen in front, Libyans on the wings, and Hasdrubal's cavalrymen in the rear, the Romans were surrounded. It was a complete envelopment, which makes Cannae a classic of the military art. Many have admired it, most famously the German general Alfred Graf von Schlieffen, who designed a new Cannae on a vast scale to surround the entire French army across hundreds of miles in 1914—but when his plan was tried, it failed.

There were so many Roman dead: about 48,000, if not more, or more than half of the Roman army. Some of them were still alive the next morning, when Carthaginian soldiers roamed the battlefield and slaughtered the wounded. Few battles in human history have produced anything like that amount of carnage.

The roll call of the dead was a who's who of the Roman elite. It included eighty senators or men eligible for membership in the Senate; twenty-nine colonels (to give the equivalent rank of the military tribunes); numerous ex-consuls, including one of the consuls of the previous year; and the consul Paullus, one of the two commanding officers of the Roman army. No names of Carthaginian casualties are recorded, but they may have included senior commanders—for, if they were any good, senior officers would have risked their lives to lead their men, as many still do today.

Cannae was a triumph for Hannibal. It demonstrates the many facets of his supremacy in battle: his agility and good judgment, his tactical sophistication and refinement, his timing and rhythm, his mastery of deception, his superiority in infrastructure, his knack of choosing the right officers and of holding them on the proper leash—loose enough to leave them the initiative but tight enough so they followed his plan—and his skill as a morale builder for his entire army. Divine Providence played a role as well. Hannibal conducted the battle like a symphony; as it turned out, not a note was out of tune.

Cannae was Hannibal's greatest victory. It was also the bloodiest defeat in Roman history. Inexperienced citizen-soldiers had turned out to be no match for hardened professionals led by a brilliant general. Amateur Roman armies had led a tiny city-state to the mastery of Italy and the central Mediterranean. Now, though, the Roman way of war was dead. As the sun went down on August 2, 216 B.C., many might have wondered: Was Rome itself finished?

Not Publius Cornelius Scipio. This young military tribune (colonel) was one of the few Roman soldiers—about 15,000 out of 86,000 men—to survive. Another 19,000 men were captured, which leaves about 4,000 soldiers whose fate is unknown. Like many of the Roman escapees from Cannae, Scipio sought refuge at Canusium—it was nearby, on a defensible hill, and loyal to Rome. There, he rallied the wavering and faint of heart, promising them that Rome would rise again.

Fate would give Scipio the chance to make good on that promise.

PHARSALUS

Ancient Thessaly was known for witches and war. The witches were supposed to have harnessed the power of the moon. The warriors took advantage of the earth. A region in central Greece, Thessaly, features a plain
that was made for the clash of armies: wide and flat, with rivers running
through it for anchoring one's flank. A ring of mountains closes the region in, as if to accentuate the drama. It was here that Caesar and Pompey
settled their feud.

Days of Decision

The thirty days from early July to early August 48 B.C. (early May to early
June by the solar calendar) decided the contest between Pompey and Caesar.
Pompey counted on hunger and misery to soften up the enemy to the point
where his army could deliver the final blow—if his opponents didn't collapse on their own. What he didn't count on was Caesar's ability to do the
impossible.

Having rallied his beaten troops at Dyrrachium, Caesar next marched
them rapidly over miserable terrain, including two hundred miles through
the Pindus Mountains, and into Thessaly. He then proceeded to secure food
for his hungry men in a rough, brutal, and effective manner. The word had
got out about Caesar's defeat at Dyrrachium and most cities, even those allied to Caesar, now feared Pompey too much to open their gates. So Caesar
opened them himself.

He chose the small city of Gomphi, strategically located on the main
pass into Thessaly from the west. Gomphi was rich and full of supplies. The
authorities begged Pompey for help, but he had not reached Thessaly yet,
which gave Caesar a free hand. It took only an afternoon for his army to
storm the walls. For once, they had their commander's permission to plunder, and they did. The soldiers ate and drank themselves silly and took out
their frustrations on the population. Twenty of the town's leading men were
found dead in an apothecary shop; they preferred to take poison rather than
face Caesar's men. As soon as the news spread, the people of all the cities of
Thessaly opened their gates, except Larissa, which had a substantial Pom-

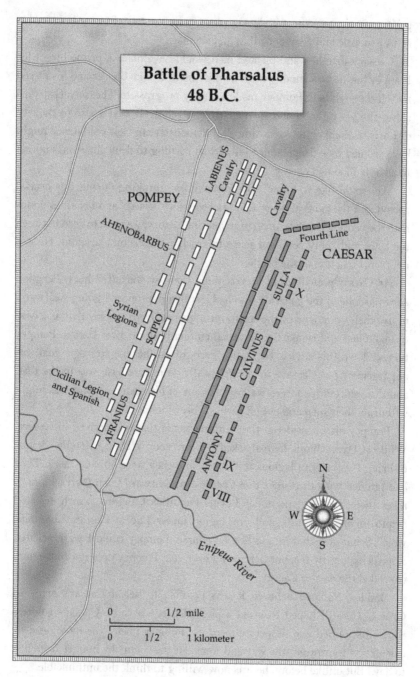

Battle of Pharsalus
48 B.C.

peian garrison to protect it. At a stroke, Caesar's policy of terror boosted his army's morale and provided allies and supplies.

Caesar's drunken and bloated men would have made a prime target for Pompey but he was about a week behind them. Unlike Caesar and his forced march through hell, Pompey made a stately progress to Thessaly, eastward along the via Egnatia and then south by a relatively easy route to the city of Larissa. Pompey took his time, but demonstrating self-confidence might have seemed more important to him than rushing to deny a few days of rest to a badly bloodied enemy.

We would like to know what Pompey was thinking during this crucial period, but the general never told his own story. Caesar and his allies dominate the written record. As often in ancient history, we have to read between the lines and apply common sense to reach a satisfactory account. Here is my reconstruction of the battle.

As Caesar pulled out of Dyrrachium, Pompey consulted his colleagues. Afranius, one of the generals who had lost Spain, proposed going westward: to use their command of the sea to reconquer Italy, to employ that as a base to take Gaul and retake Spain, and then finally to go after Caesar. Pompey turned down this advice. He rightly recognized that his strategic goal was not territory but Caesar's army. Politically, Pompey's base was in the east, and if he shifted his forces westward, some of his eastern supporters might withdraw their men and cut off their supply of money.

Pompey also considered the reinforcements that had arrived in Greece. While at Dyrrachium, he had asked the governor of Syria, Metellus Scipio, to bring two veteran legions to Greece, and they were already there. They had tangled with the forces that Caesar sent eastward from Dyrrachium to meet them: two legions under Lucius Domitius Calvinus, which defeated Scipio in one skirmish, and one legion under Lucius Cassius Longinus, which Scipio defeated in another. Of course, Pompey could have evacuated Scipio's legions by sea, but that would have cost Pompey prestige and, again, conceded the east to Caesar.

Besides, Pompey believed it was possible to defeat Caesar's army in Greece. He still hoped to avoid a pitched battle because Caesar's soldiers were "disciplined and desperate men." So Pompey made "the most prudent calculation to protract the war and wear out the enemy by hunger from day to day." But unlike before, he was now willing to think the unthinkable.

The sources tend to blame Pompey's advisers and his own weakness for listening to them. Hotheaded and ignorant of war, they thought Caesar was finished, if only Pompey would give the final push. Some had lost their fortunes and were eager to get their hands on the property of Caesar's supporters. Many distrusted Pompey and his ego: he was "more reserved, not better" than other tyrants and would-be tyrants, as Tacitus put it. Caesar's lieutenants fought for Caesar; Pompey's fought for senatorial government. There was talk of getting rid of Pompey once they had finished off Caesar.

Also, they accused Pompey of dragging the war on longer than necessary. Domitius Ahenobarbus, the man who lost Corfinium a year before, sneered that Pompey was a second Agamemnon, referring to the pompous supreme commander in Homer whose power lasted only as long as the war against Troy. Another senator, Marcus Favonius, complained that, thanks to Pompey's sluggishness, they would never get back to Italy in time for this year's figs. Some of Pompey's eastern allies joined the chorus and demanded a pitched battle.

At last, Pompey gave in, like a ship's captain surrendering the rudder in a strong storm—as Lucan later put it. Pompey agreed to fight a pitched battle. The question is, was it out of weakness of character or was it a considered decision? If the latter, was his reasoning military or political? The sources offer various motives. One writer says that Pompey saw the danger of battle, but his men forced him into it. A second disagrees, and concludes the problem was Pompey's need to please as well as his thirst for glory. Another author says simply that some god misled Pompey.

It is hard to believe that the man who stood up to Caesar at Dyrrachium caved in to Favonius and his figs now that the army was in Thessaly. More likely, Pompey changed his mind, half out of hope and half out of fear. In his assessment, Cicero says that Pompey had finally begun to have confidence in his troops after their recent success; he forgot that they were merely an inexperienced and hastily collected assortment of men. But Cicero wrote in hindsight, two years later.

At the time, Pompey might have felt that it was now or never. By giving Caesar breathing space in Thessaly, Pompey had made a mistake. Caesar's army was, obviously, not starving, but they had to keep moving to find new supplies. With the harvest about to come in, they would soon be able to feed themselves for months, and then, they could unleash ruin. Pompey knew that as long as Caesar was alive, he was dangerous and unpredictable.

Meanwhile, his own army was not likely to improve. It had just gained two veteran legions under Metellus Scipio. That and the wind at its back after Dyrrachium had made it strong—for now. With the commanders pulling in opposite directions, Pompey probably wondered how long its present strength would last. He could comfort himself with what the defector Titus Labienus, Caesar's former lieutenant, maintained: that Caesar's army was no longer the fierce force that had conquered Gaul. Military and political logic alike now said to Pompey that fighting a pitched battle was the best of several bad alternatives. Pompey's judgment was intelligent, reasonable, and wrong.

Indeed, it's difficult to convince a proud, well-fed, and well-supplied army *not* to fight. Memnon tried and failed to make the case before the Granicus; Fabius met the same fate before Cannae; now it was Pompey's turn.

And so, in the end, Pompey allowed himself the luxury of hope. The classical writers on war would have bristled. "Hope is a pacifier to danger," wrote Thucydides. War, as he knew, rewards realism and punishes dreams. The dark 3:00 A.M. of the soul looked Pompey and Caesar in the face. Caesar stared back; Pompey flinched.

The Crisis of the Chiefs

Pharsalus lies in the heart of Thessaly, at the southern edge of the central Thessalian plain, astride both east-west and north-south roads. The mountains sit just south of the town, while the river Enipeus flows north of it, and the foothills of other mountains rise north of that: the valley is about five miles wide at Pharsalus, while it narrows to the east and opens up to the west. It was in the vicinity of Pharsalus that Pompey and Caesar met in pitched battle. The battle probably took place north of the river: between the Enipeus and the hills lying between the modern village of Krini and Mount Dogandzis. The date was August 9, 48 B.C., by the Roman calendar; June 6, 48 B.C., by today's solar calendar. It was a hot, steamy, summer day.

To understand the battle, first turn the calendar back a few pages to each army's separate arrival in the area. Caesar got there first. About seven days after Gomphi, Caesar made his camp outside Pharsalus in the fertile plain.

Found in Pergamum, Turkey, this bust of Alexander is a reproduction from the third century B.C. of an original from Alexander's lifetime. *(Erich Lessing/Art Resource, NY)*

This section of a large mosaic from Pompeii shows Alexander the Great, armed and on horseback, about to confront Darius in battle, probably at Issus in 333 B.C. *(Erich Lessing/Art Resource, NY)*

The same mosaic shows King Darius III of Persia in his chariot, with a look of terror in his eyes, about to face Alexander. *(Erich Lessing/Art Resource, NY)*

This silver tetradrachm coin from the era of Alexander the Great shows the king in profile, wearing the lion skin of Heracles (Hercules). *(Berlin/Art Resource, NY)*

A carved relief in the royal palace of Persia's capital city, Persepolis, depicts soldiers of the Persian king. Alexander burned the palace in 330 B.C. *(Serhan Güngör)*

A Carthaginian silver double shekel issued by the Barcas in Spain, probably around 230 B.C. It advertises their power by showing the Punic god Melqart as Heracles, with a club over his shoulder, on the front and a war elephant on the rear. *(British Museum)*

This marble bust from Capua may possibly represent Hannibal, the great Carthaginian commander. *(Alinari/Art Resource, NY)*

A bronze bust from Herculaneum said to represent Scipio Africanus, the man who defeated Hannibal. *(Scala/Art Resource, NY)*

Foundations of Punic houses line the slope of Byrsa Hill, the acropolis of ancient Carthage. In the distance lies the great city's harbor. *(Barry Strauss)*

This marble bust shows Julius Caesar with a strong, weather-beaten face and a receding hair-line. *(Vanni/Art Resource, NY)*

A silver denarius coin, struck in 44 B.C., depicting Caesar wearing a victory wreath. He bears the title of DICT PERPETUO, that is, dictator for life. *(Yale University Art Gallery/Art Resource, NY)*

A marble bust of Caesar's great opponent Pompey, who was defeated at the Battle of Pharsalus. *(Bildarchiv Preussischer Kulturbesitz/Art Resource, NY)*

The ruined columned bases of the Basilica Julia march across the center of this photo of the Roman Forum. The basilica was a large public building originally dedicated by Caesar in 46 B.C. and funded by spoils from Gaul. *(Barry Strauss)*

It was flat and open farm country, where his men could easily harvest the grain that was about to ripen. Perhaps he placed his headquarters on a low hillock with a good view of the countryside. He was near the road that went north to Larissa, Pompey's headquarters in Thessaly, and just north of the crossing of the Enipeus River. This strategic spot gave Caesar control of the terrain: not only Pharsalus and the southern half of the plain but also the way south to Boeotia and its rich farm country. It was an apt place to wait for Pompey. He arrived a few days later and camped in the foothills several miles to the north.

For several days, Caesar tried to tempt Pompey down from the hills to fight on the plain. Caesar lined up his men for battle on the low ground, while Pompey lined up his men in the foothills. Pompey refused to descend, perhaps because he was hoping that Caesar's men were hungry and desperate enough to attack an enemy on the high ground. When they declined, Pompey finally sent his men down to the plain to fight on August 9.

It was early morning. Caesar had given up on fighting a battle here. He decided to move his camp to a hill town ten miles to the northeast, where he expected to find more food. The men were already taking down their tents when suddenly, scouts reported the enemy's deployment. Caesar made a quick decision and addressed his men: they would have to change plans and prepare for battle. One source reports that Caesar told his soldiers that they would finally be able to fight other men instead of having to fight want and hunger. Caesar himself states his words as "Let us be ready in our hearts for a fight. We won't easily find a chance like this again." He ordered a purple tunic to be hung from the commander's tent, the Roman sign for battle, and at the sight his men supposedly shouted for joy. They were no ordinary army—they were Caesar's men. Rarely in history has one man's leadership tied his soldiers more closely to him.

It was the moment Caesar had been waiting for. It was the supreme battle. It was, as the poet Lucan puts it, *discrimina ducum:* "the crisis of the chiefs."

The two armies lined up on roughly a north-south axis, bounded by the foothills to the north and by marshy ground around the Enipeus to the south. The battle lines stretched for about two and a half miles. The Caesarians were in the east, the Pompeians in the west. Caesar deployed about twenty-two thousand heavy infantrymen from eight legions and one thousand cavalrymen. There were also light-armed troops from northern Greece.

Caesar arranged his men in the standard Roman formation: three lines, with the best units on the flanks. The battered Legions VIII and IX were combined into a single unit on the left flank, commanded by Mark Antony. Caesar's best legion, the Tenth, held the right flank, under the command of Publius Sulla. Domitius Calvinus commanded the center. Caesar massed his cavalry on the right flank. He left another two thousand heavy infantrymen to guard his camp.

Pompey deployed a much bigger army, of about seven thousand cavalry and perhaps as many as forty-five thousand heavy infantrymen: nine Roman legions and the best of his Greek allied contingents. Pompey too deployed his infantrymen in three lines. He placed his best legions strategically: on the left flank, the two legions that had previously served with Caesar, commanded by Domitius Ahenobarbus; in the middle, the two Syrian legions under Scipio and, on the right flank, a legion from Cilicia (southern Turkey) along with cohorts brought over from Spain, all commanded by Afranius. In between the best units Pompey deployed the rest of his heavy infantrymen, including two thousand "beneficiaries," junior officers whom he had personally promoted. He placed perhaps four thousand heavy infantrymen on garrison duty in his camp and the forts nearby.

The two commanders, each on horseback, spent most of the battle opposite each other: Pompey on his left flank, Caesar on his right.

Most of the legionaries in the two armies were Roman citizens, Italians by origin if not current residence, since many had settled in the east. The two cavalries were each a mixed lot. Caesar's horsemen were in large part Gauls and Germans. Pompey's cavalry included a large contingent of Roman aristocrats, the sons of senators and knights. But it also contained thousands of men from the east, representing a diverse group of peoples from Greece to Egypt, a few of them even kings and princes. It was a coat of many colors.

Ever the tactician, Pompey planned no ordinary battle. He knew that his infantry couldn't beat Caesar's veterans, but he reckoned that it wouldn't have to. Having missed an opportunity to use the cavalry at Dyrrachium, Pompey decided to stake everything on them now. He would leverage his cavalry's superiority in numbers, equipment, and supply. Add to that his light-armed infantry troops: slingers and archers, most of them Greeks, Syrians, or other easterners.

Pompey's plan was to mass most of his cavalry on his left flank: about six thousand men, commanded by Titus Labienus. The rest of Pompey's cavalry, a small force of six hundred, guarded his right flank. At the start of the battle, Labienus and his six thousand cavalry would charge Caesar's right flank and then circle around to his rear. At the same time, several thousand slingers and archers—the artillery of the time—would strike from a distance and soften up the enemy lines. Labienus's horsemen would drive off Caesar's insignificant cavalry, charge into the flank of the enemy infantry, and cause a panic. It would take a series of attacks, withdrawals, and renewed attacks, but eventually the cavalry would fold up the enemy's right wing and drive it toward his center.

Pompey gave his legions a simpler task: hold the enemy. Normally, Roman infantrymen began a battle by throwing their javelins and advancing, and then closing in with their swords. But at Pharsalus, Pompey issued an unusual order: he told the legions to stand still. A regular advance might cause Pompey's inexperienced lines to fall into disorder. He hoped that, by standing in place, they might break the impetus of Caesar's attack while maintaining their own good order. They would force Caesar's men to march further to reach them, which might tire the enemy. Meanwhile, his men's immobility might make it easier for them to wield their shields against enemy javelins. They might even be able to counterattack, but the main thing was to provide a strong wall while Pompey's cavalry and light-armed troops hammered Caesar's men.

It would have been a good plan if carried out by Alexander's or Hannibal's seasoned horsemen. Or, rather, it would have been a good plan but it lacked the element of deception. One wonders what Labienus thought of it, because back in Gaul, he had been a master at tricking the enemy. No tricks now. Caesar, who could see what Pompey was up to with his cavalry, knew how to respond. He withdrew individual cohorts from the third line of each of his legions and formed an unusual fourth line, which he positioned behind the cavalry, probably at an oblique angle. This weakened the third line but, as usual, Caesar was willing to take a risk. The enemy could not see this fourth line, which meant that Caesar could add surprise to the advantages of his terrible new weapon. The matchless professionalism of his troops allowed Caesar to take chances, but this was a move of supreme audacity, something that only an exceptional commander would have dared.

About eighty thousand men had now lined up against each other, with more guarding the camps nearby. Pompey and Caesar, each on horseback, rode down the lines with their final words to incite fellow Romans to kill each other. The men's shouts and cries rang out in answer across the valley.

Once the trumpets sounded the start of battle, little worked out as Pompey had planned. Caesar's legionaries ran forward against the Pompeians to throw their javelins, but when they noticed that the enemy standing still, they stopped. A dazzling display of discipline, the halt let them catch their breath and then start up again, full of energy for the attack. Even so, Pompey's men managed to hold their ground. Locked in combat, each side soon drew its second line into the fight. The roar of battle, as the poet Lucan imagined it, included the weight of groans as if from one immense voice, the clanging of armor against crashing bodies, and the sound of sword breaking against sword.

The decisive action took place on Caesar's right flank. Pompey's cavalry, six thousand strong, "its wings deployed across the entire plain," as the poet says, thundered toward the enemy. Archers and slingers followed on foot behind them, firing so many missiles so rapidly that you could almost imagine them melting in the heat. Just as planned, the assault forced Caesar's cavalry from the field. Led by Labienus, Pompey's cavalry redeployed in squadrons and began to surround the infantry lines on Caesar's exposed flank. It was the high-water mark of Pompey's effort. Then Caesar ordered his fourth line to advance. Suddenly, the Pompeian cavalry faced not an infantry's flank but its front, with a wall of iron-tipped spears in its path. It was an obstacle that ancient cavalries never succeeded in overcoming.

"No circumstance contributed more than this to Caesar's victory on that day," writes Frontinus, "for as soon as Pompey's cavalry poured forth, these cohorts routed it by an unexpected onset, and delivered it up to the rest of the troops for slaughter."

The key to victory, according to some sources, is what Caesar told his infantrymen: aim for the enemy's face, on the principle that vanity would make an elite horseman turn and flee. But that was nothing new; Alexander's men too aimed for the enemy's face. More likely, the real cause of Pompey's defeat was panic. When the cavalry piled up against the unexpected obstacle of Caesar's fourth line, it probably lost its nerve. Experienced men might have coolly retreated, re-formed, and attacked again, once the enemy gave them an opening. Not Pompey's rookies. Discipline and formation were gone; all that was left was a mad dash back to safety. If Labienus tried to get the cavalry back into formation, to strike Caesar's fourth line in its rear in turn, it was a vain attempt.

And that was that. Caesar's fourth line massacred the archers and slingers who had been left in the lurch. Then, the model of discipline, they turned and crashed into the left flank of Pompey's infantry line, attacking it in the rear. Caesar meanwhile ordered his third line of legionaries out of reserve and into action. Pompey's infantry was now under attack from two sides, and, on one of them, pounded by fresh troops. It was too much: after a slow retreat at first, the Pompeians ran.

As he surveyed the ruin of his enemy, Caesar is said to have remarked, "They wanted this. In spite of all my achievements, I, Gaius Caesar, would have been condemned if I hadn't asked my army for help."

Pompey had already left the field and returned to camp. The battle of Pharsalus, as he well knew, was over. The war, however, would go on. It was his job now to try to salvage as much of his army as he could.

Brilliant strategist, masterful tactician, tireless organizer, cunning diplomat, Pompey lacked only one thing: he wasn't Caesar. Pompey understood neither Caesar's audacity nor his agility. Knowing that Caesar's army was strained to the breaking point, he could not conceive of the magic of Caesar's leadership. The worse things got, the stronger Caesar made his men. Pompey couldn't imagine Caesar coming back from the defeat of Dyrrachium and beating him in pitched battle. It took nearly superhuman effort, and that is precisely what Caesar brought to bear.

Flight

The sources paint a picture of Pompey in despair, but it is hard to trust them. In all likelihood, he tried to organize the defense of his camp. Legionaries, Thracians, and other non-Roman soldiers manned the ramparts, but few of the soldiers who streamed back from the battlefield joined them: most of them kept running. The midday sun was blazing and even the victors were exhausted, but Caesar urged them to attack. The Caesarians stormed the camp. Pompey's officers led as many defenders as they could into the hills.

As soon as the fate of his camp was sealed, Pompey rode off through the back gate with a bodyguard of thirty cavalrymen. They headed toward Larissa.

Meanwhile, Caesar's men were itching to gorge themselves on the luxurious food and to loot the silver plate laid out under ivy-covered bowers in Pompey's camp. Caesar, however, drove them forward in pursuit—another sign of their discipline. They found the Pompeians on a nearby hill that lacked water, and immediately began to surround it with an earthwork. But the enemy fled and took to the ridges in the direction of Larissa. Caesar would not let them escape. He divided his forces and left most of them to defend his camp and Pompey's. Taking four legions, he tracked down the enemy to another hill a few miles away, and had his weary men immediately begin building a wall to cut them off. As night began falling, the Pompeians finally sent representatives to negotiate surrender. Caesar offered lenient terms and the enemy surrendered the next morning. Only a few senators had escaped during the night.

The results of Pharsalus were, as often in great battles, lopsided. Caesar lost only 230 men (including 30 officers), according to his claims, but other writers raised the figure to 1,200 men. Caesar says his men killed 15,000 Pompeians and accepted surrender from another 24,000; another eyewitness source estimated Pompey's losses at only 6,000 men. One thing is certain: the dead included Domitius Ahenobarbus, Caesar's archenemy, who was killed by Caesar's cavalry as he fled from Pompey's camp to the nearby hill. Caesar claimed the honors of victory: 180 military standards and 9 legionary eagles.

The same day that the last Pompeians surrendered, Caesar hurried to Larissa, but Pompey had already escaped. He was fleeing to the coast, ready to board a ship to go east. Pompey had no intention of giving up. Why should he have? He still claimed the title of supreme commander of the Roman state, and he was not without the means of backing it up. He still had about seven thousand soldiers at Dyrrachium. He still commanded a fleet of six hundred warships. He still knew more powerful people who owed him favors than most Romans could ever dream of meeting.

So Pompey slipped out of Caesar's hands and prepared to continue the struggle. Caesar followed, eager to end the war.

THE ESSENCE OF DECISION

Gaugamela, Cannae, and Pharsalus: these killing fields saw too much skill not to impress and too much blood not to appall. Six thousand to seven thousand men were killed at Pharsalus, on a conservative estimate. Gaugamela could hardly have been less bloody, but Cannae wins the prize. With roughly 55,000 men killed—most of them Romans—it was one of the bloodiest days in human history. It gives one pause to think that most of the damage was inflicted by professional killers.

The three winning armies moved with grace and precision. Alexander's men adopted a new battle formation as easily as a new pair of shoes. Hannibal's Africans turned on the legionaries with parade ground exactness. Caesar's legionaries stopped in midcharge as if doing a favorite dance step. Alexander's and Hannibal's army each blended cavalry and infantry as smoothly as liquid oxygen and hydrogen in rocket fuel—and as explosively. What Caesar's force, with its inadequate cavalry, lacked in versatility, it made up for in suppleness.

The genius of the winning generals is equally impressive. Each man correctly analyzed his opponent's strengths and weaknesses and responded with ingenuity and pluck. By forcing the enemy into a slugging match on the Macedonian right wing Alexander bogged down the Persians' best cavalry and opened a path toward Darius. By neutralizing Rome's cavalry, Hannibal cleared the field for a choreographed massacre of the Roman legions. By surprising Pompey's cavalry with a solid front of fresh infantrymen, Caesar destroyed his opponent's offensive capability.

Each of the winning commanders displayed a healthy mix of respect and contempt for his foe. Through spying or intuition, each of them guessed his enemy's plan. Caesar knew that Pompey's cavalry had the numbers to destroy him but he was confident that it lacked the backbone. Hannibal sized up the legionaries' power and their clumsiness. Alexander knew what a Persian cavalry charge could do, but he had faith that his light-armed troops, specialists in darting between horsemen, could stop the enemy in his track.

Each of the winners took operational and tactical risks. Alexander and Hannibal had bodyguards but fought in the front; Caesar held farther back but was on the battlefield. Caesar took the chance of thinning out his third infantry line in order to form a fourth line to throw at Pompey's cavalry. Hannibal knew that his Celts were hard to discipline, but he counted on his ability to keep their battle line bending in retreat without breaking. Alexander bet that his left flank under Parmenio could hold out long enough against the enemy's charge for him to destroy Darius.

We must also salute the winners' ability to hold their armies together. Although Alexander's army had a relatively easy time of things on the road to Gaugamela, they still faced fear, as shown by their responses first to an eclipse and then the sight of Darius's huge force. Alexander had to reassure them.

Hannibal's force had just faced six difficult months against Fabius. But those deprivations were nothing compared with what they had suffered crossing the Apennines, and that, in turn, paled next to the problems of crossing the Alps. So, by the time they faced an enormous enemy army at Cannae, Hannibal's men were ready.

Caesar's army probably wins the prize for deprivation. Between January 49 and August 48 they covered more territory than even Hannibal's men. They had no victories in pitched battle to buoy them, and they suffered heavy casualties in the siege of Dyrrachium. They were rarely permitted to loot and were often late in being paid. Within a month of enduring death, hunger, and exhaustion, they turned everything around and won a smashing victory.

Each of the three winning armies was part band of brothers, part gangland family. They fought for honor and loot. Principles were optional. Alexander claimed to be waging a war of revenge and a preventive war, but neither claim was convincing; he wanted to conquer an empire. Caesar declared that he was fighting for freedom and status, but the future dictator's defense of popular power rings hollow, and his preoccupation with rank attracts few supporters today. Hannibal's claim of self-defense against Roman aggression is more persuasive but it is hard to separate it from his lust for conquest.

It is easier today to sympathize with the defenders. The Persians and the Romans were each defending an empire, but it included their homeland. Pompey was as selfish as Caesar but his supporters truly believed in liberty, at least as narrowly defined: the freedom of the few to guide Rome toward the public good, as they saw it.

Each battle saw such a one-sided outcome that it begs the question of what the loser was thinking by ever agreeing to a pitched battle in the first place. In hindsight, Darius, Paullus and Varro, and Pompey each accepted a fight that he should have avoided. A Fabian strategy of refusing battle might have worked as well for them as it had for its namesake. The strategy might have played out quite differently in each battle.

Instead of leading Alexander to Darius, the Persians might have contested his crossing of the Euphrates and the Tigris. They could have burned crops and emptied granaries. With their horsemen and archers tailor-made for raids, they could have harassed Macedonian foraging parties. Meanwhile, they could have forced Alexander to fight for every city he wanted instead of allowing him to negotiate surrenders. In short, if the Persians had used the Fabian strategy, they would have made Mesopotamia a desert. If Alexander still managed to cross it, they could have blocked the Zagros Mountain passes into Iran. They could have removed the treasures of Susa and Persepolis and brought them eastward for safekeeping.

If the Persians had made conditions harsh enough, the Macedonians might have had enough. They might have forced Alexander to accept Darius's offer of the western provinces and turn back.

The Romans who faced Hannibal had to do only what they did before Cannae: not fight in Italy. They should have remained on the defensive while harassing Hannibal and denying him supplies. At the same time, they should have pressed their Spanish offensive. Eventually, they would have forced him to leave Italy and defend Spain. That would not have ended the war, but by sparing Rome the defeat of Cannae, it would have kept Rome's allies from defecting and increased Rome's resources for the struggle ahead.

In Pompey's case, things might have gone differently if he had refused battle. At the time of Pharsalus, he had launched a naval offensive in the west. One fleet had attacked Sicily, another was blockading Caesar's remaining troops in Brundisium. If successful, as they probably would have been, they would have cut off Italy from its food supply and kicked the props out from under Caesar's supporters in Italy. Spain was already showing signs of unrest against Caesar's governor, and these would have grown with Pompey's success.

Meanwhile, Pompey might have frustrated Caesar in Greece. Imagine a continual series of raids by Pompey's cavalry on Caesar's troops trying to cut down ripe grain in the fields. Caesar would no doubt have struck back, but with hungry and tired men. Imagine the news from the west seeping into Caesar's camp. If Pompey held his army together, he might have tempted traitors in Caesar's ranks to join him, just as he had done at Dyrrachium. That might have given Pompey an opening, if only for an assassin, but a dagger could have ended Caesar's quest.

If avoiding pitched battle would have worked out well, why then did the commanders agree to fight? For one thing, hindsight isn't history, and there is no guarantee that a Fabian strategy would have worked. For another, pitched battle had its own rewards. Ancient culture put a higher premium on honor than on cunning. To turn down battle was to risk losing face, which might have led waverers to switch sides. Battle was risky but making a decision was easy and quick. A Fabian strategy meant a long war and more chances for a bronco like Caesar to buck.

The losing generals did not go into battle without preparing to meet a dangerous enemy. All of them put together big armies that greatly outnumbered their opponents'. Darius recruited excellent horsemen, made plans to compensate for his lack of heavy infantry, and chose his battlefield carefully. Paullus and Varro massed their legionaries tightly in order to compensate for the men's inexperience and to increase the odds of breaking through the enemy line. Pompey did not seriously consider a pitched battle before first bruising Caesar's army in siege warfare. Still, he recognized the weakness of his infantry and rested his plans on his cavalry. In short, the losing generals tried to exercise due diligence, but they failed.

The victors would never have won, of course, unless Divine Providence had convinced their enemies to fight. That same providence gave them the resources to win. They owed some of their success to a general's willingness to engage in terror or to brand himself as a god's son. A more important factor was the superior professionalism—the better infrastructure—of the victorious army. The ability to feed their men in hostile country was also a matter of infrastructure. Then there was the leadership by which a commander bound his officers and soldiers to him. Next came the agility to come up with new tactics and the audacity to carry them out. Finally, there was the good judgment of the commander, the combination of intuition and expertise that had him do just the right thing at just the right time. Nothing played a greater role in making Gaugamela, Cannae, and Pharsalus into virtuoso pieces.

The day after battle, the question was what each of the participants would do to justify the terrible carnage. Could the winners translate success on the battlefield into victory in the war? Could the losers rally their societies in defeat and continue the war? We turn to those questions.

5

CLOSING THE NET

FOR SEVENTY DAYS IT RAINED. ALEXANDER'S MEN HAD NEVER EXPERIENCED anything like the Indian monsoon. The heavy rain was constantly slapping on their tents, with thunder and lightning often accompanying the downpour. Everywhere the men stepped, there seemed to be mud. Their Greek clothes were gone and they had to dress in Indian dhotis, white cotton cloths wrapped around their legs. Between the weather and the foreign garments, the men had never felt so far from home.

Their morale was already low when the monsoon finished it off. Their weapons were worn out. Even their horse's shoes had worn thin from all the marching. The men had suffered casualties and they were exhausted. They were about three thousand miles from Macedonia as the crow flies—much farther, if you consider the rough terrain they had crossed and the circuitous route they had marched. Now they wanted to pack up the loot that they had won at such a heavy price and go home. In the summer of 325 B.C., nine years after Alexander had launched his expedition, it looked like the end of the campaign.

About a hundred years later and three thousand miles away, Hannibal's younger brother, Mago, was listening to the sound of another kind of water—the Mediterranean. He was riding on his flagship in a flotilla sailing from Genoa to Carthage, and he was lying in a sickbed. It was autumn 203 B.C. Two years earlier, Mago had sailed from the island of Minorca, off Spain, to Italy, with fifteen thousand men, in a bold move to reinforce Hannibal. After he conquered Genoa and raised a local alliance, Mago received reinforcements from Carthage: men, money, and seven elephants. But in 203, a Roman army defeated Mago in a battle near Milan and he suffered a deep wound in his thigh. He was recalled home to defend Carthage from a threat from a Roman army.

Mago hoped that a ship's rocking motion would be easier on his wound than Italy's bumpy roads. He looked forward as well to the standard of medical care available in Carthage. But he died of his wound just south of Sardinia. Mago's fate foretold a bad end awaiting Hannibal in his war with Rome. It was a far cry from the glory days of Cannae.

A little more than 150 years later and five hundred miles to the southwest, in Roman Africa (modern Tunisia), another rainstorm came thundering down. At midnight, in a November sky, a teeming rainfall, with pebble-sized hailstones, struck Caesar's legionary camp. As usual, Caesar had made his men travel fast and light. Leather tents would have been a luxury—most men had rigged lean-tos from reeds, twigs, and clothing. The storm washed away everything and put out the campfires. Soldiers were reduced to wandering the camp with their shields held over their heads for protection. An enemy army was camped nearby but they did not push. Caesar, as usual, was lucky, but he had pressed his luck.

The battle of Pharsalus seemed long ago: it was January 46 B.C. (November 47, by our calendar), about a year and a half later. But the Roman civil war was far from over. The Pompeians had regrouped after their defeat. Caesar had given them breathing space, because other matters required his attention. He had to find funding—and Cleopatra had found him. Caesar had finally turned back to the Pompeians only a month before the rainstorm. He could shrug off a storm; the enemy's armies were another matter.

As these three anecdotes remind us, it takes more to win a war than victory in pitched battle—even a big victory. Winning takes the ability to reap strategic advantage afterward. The victories of Gaugamela, Cannae, and Pharsalus did not guarantee that Alexander, Hannibal, and Caesar would end their war well. Darius, the Roman republic, and Pompey all still had the resources to bounce back.

The challengers had to close the net.

Closing the net is where things started to get messy, messy because they were complicated. The clarity that victory in pitched battle offered was gone. Instead, the great commanders had to meet a truly bewildering array of challenges to close the net. These challenges entailed a number of military and political changes, from refining troop organization and tactics to reevaluating grand strategy, and from knowing the political workings of the enemy to shoring up support at home. Changes were required at every level of planning. Alexander, Hannibal, and Caesar showed their greatness by keeping their armies together and achieving more victories (if with varying degrees of success) during this crucial stage. But without their knowing where to stop, the enormity of the challenges would soon prove too great, even for them.

ALEXANDER

Even after Gaugamela, Darius still had access to a wealth of money and manpower. Given time and space, he might have mobilized them. To keep that from happening, Alexander needed to be fast and deadly, but there was also something to be said for a light touch. If he let the Persians maintain their dignity, they might bow to his authority and accept him as king, bringing a quick end to the war. The alternative might be a long and bloody slog in Central Asia and beyond. A war there would demand yet more resources and mobility, while it might call forth new excesses in terror. If doing too little risked danger, doing too much threatened a quagmire.

Yet Alexander relished the challenge. A long war in Asia would drain Macedon but invigorate Alexander. With every passing day the old country interested him less. There were new worlds to conquer! No more merely king of Macedon, he was now king of Asia—and lord of battle. The East was a gigantic school of war and Alexander was an eager student.

The Reckoning: Darius's Revenge

Alexander made warfare look easy. His march into Iran after Gaugamela is a case in point. After accepting Babylon's surrender, Alexander rested his army for a month and then marched his forces into the mountains of western Iran. As usual, he pressed the enemy quickly and hard.

His first goals were the enemy's two capital cities, Susa and Persepolis. Susa lacked defenses and its commander was quick to surrender, but deep mountain passes protected Persepolis: the Persians intended to fight. It was December; snow posed a real risk for the Macedonians, but Alexander did not want to give the enemy a chance to regroup, and so he forged ahead.

To reach Persepolis, Alexander had to defeat three separate stands against him in the rugged Zagros Mountains. The enemy knew the terrain and chose his ground carefully, in mountain passes and gorges, but Alexander's forces were fast, mobile, and cagey. Again and again they turned the defender's position and surprised him with an attack from the rear. The Macedonians inflicted heavy losses and killed the enemy commander. Persepolis surrendered.

Once again, Alexander had handled his forces like a virtuoso; his soldiers demonstrated their skill and versatility; and he and his troops showed that audacity pays back dividends tenfold.

Susa and Persepolis were treasuries as well as capitals. Between them, they housed the world's largest collection of gold and silver, and now it belonged to Alexander. He was the proud owner of 180,000 talents of gold and silver—312 tons of gold and 2,000 tons of silver. The young king had become the richest man on earth—a stunning reversal for someone who had started his invasion broke.

When Alexander entered Persepolis, he showed his contempt for it: he let his men loot the town, except for the royal palace. This was harsher treatment than elsewhere, but Alexander recognized Persepolis's status as the center of Persian religion. He wanted to deny the enemy any sacred ground to strike back at him. At the end of his four-month stay in Persepolis, Alexander finished what his policy of looting had begun—he burned the royal palace to the ground. If Alexander was king of Asia, it was not by grace of Persia's gods—that was the message that he sent to the people of Persia.

The Greeks got a different message—payback. Years before, when they first raised the subject of invading Persia, Philip and Alexander had sold the expedition to their Greek allies as a war of revenge for Persia's invasion of Greece under King Xerxes in 480 b.c. The Greeks bought it. Now, with Greeks and Macedonians in Iran, the circle was nearly complete. What Athens had been to Xerxes, Persepolis was to Alexander: the symbol of enemy resistance. Just as Xerxes once burned down Athens, so Alexander burned Persepolis.

The burning also signaled that the war was coming to an end. Not only

Greeks but Macedonians too reached that conclusion. With revenge, riches, and an empire that stretched from Egypt to Iran, they thought it was time to go home and enjoy life. But Alexander disagreed. Having been proclaimed king of Asia, he had no intention of settling for less than the entire Persian empire. But he did not need to press the point yet, because another issue was on the agenda: Darius was still at large. Not even the most homesick soldier could ignore that, because as long as Darius was free, he was trouble for them all. Darius could still raise an army from Persia's rich and unconquered eastern provinces.

While Alexander spent the winter of 331 to 330 in Persepolis, Darius was about five hundred miles to the northwest, in the city of Ecbatana (modern Hamadan). He had a small army, including the remaining Greek mercenaries—still loyal to their chief—and was trying to raise new troops from the east. But there was no sign of them when, in May 330, Alexander marched on Ecbatana; Darius fled eastward with his troops and his closest advisors, the still-loyal satraps of the eastern empire.

Alexander hurried after them, traveling hundreds of miles through Iran until he reached its treacherous northeastern desert. To speed the way, Alexander divided his forces and left a portion with Parmenio. Then, several weeks later, the news came that the satraps had mutinied and deposed Darius. His loyalists fled into the mountains with the remaining Greek mercenaries. Alexander stripped his forces down to cavalry and raced after Darius. Even so, they were too late. The eastern satraps had assassinated the king and left the body for Alexander to find. Meanwhile, they fled homeward. It was summer 330.

If Alexander had captured Darius alive, he might have reaped a political and military bonanza. With luck, Darius would have accepted Alexander as the rightful king. With a little more luck, the rest of the Persian nobility would have followed him and admitted that the game was up. That, after all, would have spared Persia further bloodshed and—a Persian patriot might have said—given it time to recover and to plot Alexander's eventual overthrow. As for Alexander, he would have the loyalty of the eastern satraps without having to fight for it.

But it was not to be. It is even possible that the other satraps saw this coming and bristled at it as a dishonorable policy: that may be why they overthrew Darius and killed him.

The greatest of the eastern satraps was Bessus, satrap of Bactria. He had fought well as a cavalry commander at Gaugamela. Now, the other satraps proclaimed him as Artaxerxes V, rightful king of the Persian empire. Bessus returned to Bactria to prepare an army to fight the invaders.

This left Alexander with a dilemma. The Persian empire stretched eastward another thousand miles. If he invaded the east in pursuit of Bessus, Alexander would face tough fighting, far from his home base. If he stayed in the west and consolidated the rule of his new empire, Alexander would have to prepare for raids if not a major invasion from Bessus's territory.

Security concerns, therefore, dictated that Alexander go after Bessus. But security was not what moved Alexander. I wonder if Alexander ever put things as bluntly as one of the sources claims: he didn't want Darius's corpse; he wanted his kingdom. But that was the truth.

He knew that the Persian empire included rich lands in the east: Aria (today's Afghan province of Herat), famous for its agriculture and especially its wine; Arachosia (centered on Kandahar in southeastern Afghanistan); and Bactria (roughly, northern Afghanistan), known for its fertile farmland. There was also northwestern India (today's Pakistan and the Punjab). This last, wealthy region had probably slipped from the Persians' grasp years before, but they still exercised some influence there.

Alexander wanted to conquer these lands not only as a security zone but also for their riches and for the glory. In his own mind, Alexander now belonged to a very select club: Achilles, Heracles, Dionysus (not just god of wine but conqueror of the East), Cyrus the Great, and Semiramis (the mythical Assyrian queen) were its other members. Alexander would settle for nothing less than the entire Persian empire. Besides, Alexander was first, last, and always a warrior king. He excelled at war and he loved it more than any other activity.

Alexander's heart and head told him to go east. The other Macedonians saw things differently, as they made clear when they heard the news that the Greeks were going home but they had to stay. It happened like this.

In spite of all his victories, Alexander had always been vulnerable in Greece. His many enemies there had long threatened to open a second front against him, and in 331, they finally did. Led by Sparta, a coalition of city-states challenged the Macedonians under Antipater. In his sixties, Antipater was a veteran general and ambassador who had served Philip and befriended young prince Alexander. As king, Alexander had appointed Antipater to govern Macedon in his absence.

If the rebel Greeks had won, they might have forced Alexander to turn back. Memnon's ghost was surely smiling, but not for long. Alexander sent enough money to Antipater for him to hire massive numbers of mercenaries. They crushed the enemy and killed the Spartan king. In 330, while still at Persepolis or just shortly after leaving, Alexander learned the good news: he no longer had to worry about Greece.

No longer did he need to keep his Greek troops; they had done little fighting and served as virtual hostages. Previously it was too dangerous to send them home, where they could stir up trouble. That had changed now. So Alexander released his Greek "allies" and gave them generous bonuses. He also gave them the choice of staying and reenlisting as mercenaries, which some did.

Unfortunately for Alexander, Greek enthusiasm for home proved infectious and the Macedonians began to complain. Why not put down their arms and enjoy the loot that they had amassed? Alexander's officers advised him to call an assembly and address the men. He gave a speech that touched on three themes: security, honor, and royal favor. The Persians were currently in a stupor, he said, but if the Macedonians withdrew, the enemy would wake up and attack them as if they were women. Anyone who wanted to leave was free to do so, but Alexander would go on acquiring the inhabited world with his "friends" and "those willing to fight." In other words, any Macedonian who wasn't with Alexander was against him. The rhetoric worked; the soldiers roared their approval of following Alexander wherever he would lead them. No doubt it helped if, as one source claims, he grossly underestimated the distance to Bactria.

Alexander's points seem strong until we consider the counterarguments. The eastern provinces had never proved easy for the Persians to hold. Even if conquered, those provinces would probably rise in rebellion one day. In the meantime, they would require garrisons of thousands of men. Most important of all, Alexander had pressing business in the west—consolidating his rule—and an eastern campaign would be a long and dangerous distraction.

Then there were the objections that we earlier imagined Parmenio holding. Alexander could be king of Macedon or king of Asia but not both. As king of Asia, Alexander would force the freewheeling Macedonian nobility to bow down to tyranny.

Parmenio's voice would no longer be heard: Alexander had left him behind. The grand old man of the Macedonian army was now seventy years old; the young king now felt confident enough to go into battle without him. He left Parmenio in the rear, in Ecbatana. Armed with a division, Parmenio's job was to guard communications and to protect the treasury. Parmenio didn't pull the purse strings, however: those belonged to Harpalus. Like Parmenio, Harpalus was a Macedonian noble, but he was much younger. And he was Alexander's man—one of the king's boyhood friends. Harpalus was now imperial treasurer. Parmenio had been shut out of the eastern campaign. Only his sons took part, Philotas, commander of the Companion Cavalry, and Nicanor, commander of the elite infantry corps known as the *hypaspists*. But they were weak reeds.

Cleaning House with Blood and Iron

Alexander and his army plunged eastward, in pursuit of Bessus. For the next three years, Alexander would be fighting on two fronts, against rebels both without and within. Being king of Asia was no longer just a title—it was the experience that Alexander lived every day. Just what the title meant would have to be worked out. Alexander had no intention of being a Persian king, but he had to be more than a Macedonian king. He had millions of new subjects, after all, and he had to offer them something more than a conqueror's spear.

What Alexander came up with was a compromise between the freewheeling ways of the Macedonian court and the pomp of the Persian autocracy. He also tried to widen his court circle markedly. But Alexander was too Persian for the Macedonians and too Macedonian for the Persians. The Macedonians resented his decision to wear Persian dress, such as the diadem and the girdle, and to adopt Persian court ceremony, including *proskynesis*, that is, throwing oneself flat on the ground before the king in a gesture of submission. They bristled at Alexander's order that his closest advisors wear Persian scarlet robes. They disapproved of the admission of Persian nobles into his retinue, including Darius's brother Oxyathres. They despised the introduction of eunuchs and the royal harem and they felt threatened by Alexander's new Persian royal guard.

The Persians, for their part, were not fooled by the title "king of Asia," which they rightly saw as a far cry from their royal title of "great king,

king of kings, king of lands"; it was, in fact, a Greek invention, signaling a new kind of royal absolutism. From the defeat of Darius to the burning of Persepolis to the new Macedonian military governors in every province, the Persian elite resented the conquest.

Unhappy Persians continued to fight—for four more long years of war. As for Alexander's own men, Macedonians and Greeks in his entourage responded to the compromise with rage, grumbling, and conspiracy. Alexander responded too—with murder.

It would be easy to accuse him of unique savagery, but bloodshed was as Macedonian as hunting, the national sport. Every Macedonian king had secured his royal title by having other claimants to the throne murdered—at least, every successful Macedonian king. Alexander went further than most in the sheer number of alleged plotters, conspirators, and grumblers that he had executed. Then again, none of his predecessors had ever done anything as radical as Alexander. When a king changes his policies as dramatically as Alexander did, he fires those who refuse to support him. In this case, these "firings" proved fatal.

Macedonian kings also had reason to worry about assassination. Alexander's father, Philip II, was murdered in office, as had been Philip's older brother, Alexander II (r. 369–366). No wonder Alexander was nervous about plots and conspiracies. Between 330 and 327, Alexander executed a dozen generals, courtiers, and advisors, including one he killed with his own hands.

Rebellion beset Alexander from both sides. In 330 he faced a near mutiny by his own army, which did not want to continue eastward. Then his discovery of a plot ended with the execution of two of his chief generals: the great Parmenio and his son Philotas (a convenient excuse for Alexander to rid himself of rivals; neither played an active role in the conspiracy). In 328 Alexander murdered the general Cleitus "the Black" after a drunken quarrel that included Cleitus's angry condemnation of Alexander's Persian habits. It happened at a party in the palace at Maracanda (modern Samarkand). Macedonians had a reputation as hard drinkers and on this occasion, they consumed herculean amounts—enough for Alexander to grab a spear and run Cleitus through.

In 327 a group of royal pages was tried and executed for conspiring to kill Alexander. Their tutor, Callisthenes, a Greek philosopher and Alexander's court historian, was also tried and probably killed. Earlier, he had publicly refused to engage in *proskynesis*.

Although Alexander appointed many Persians as satraps, they had to turn real power over to Macedonian commanders and treasurers. Many of the Persian satraps rose in revolt. Few of them lasted in office.

Alexander never found his balance between Macedonians and Persians. No wonder, because integrating a conquering elite with a defeated but still proud aristocracy is monumentally difficult. Success would have required every ounce of a master statesman's skill, but Alexander rarely focused his attention on domestic politics. His passions were war and conquest; everything else was a distraction.

In one area alone did Alexander show the political touch of a master—in the politics of the army. Over the ten years of his expedition, he transformed the Macedonian army into a personal possession. He purged his rivals ruthlessly in the officer corps and replaced them with his friends and comrades. They included talented soldiers, like Craterus and Perdiccas, and less talented ones, like Hephaestion. Alexander had an intimate friendship with Hephaestion that might have included a physical element. Meanwhile, Alexander reorganized units to weaken private and regional ties. He wanted only one focus of loyalty—himself.

The Macedonians never formed a majority in Alexander's army, but for a long time they were a military and political elite. Although Alexander had other excellent troops, the Macedonians were the army's two fists and its backbone. In 334, they made up around 17,000 out of a total of more than 40,000 troops. Between 333 and 330, another 15,000 Macedonian reinforcements came from the homeland to join Alexander, for a total of more than 30,000 Macedonians. But Macedon had no more manpower to spare, and attrition began to reduce the number of Macedonians. By 324 there were only 18,000 Macedonians in Alexander's army.

The character of their comrades changed radically as well, from allies to mercenaries and from European to Asian. In 334, the rest of Alexander's army consisted of allies from Greece and from Macedon's Balkan neighbors such as Thrace. After the Greek allies returned home, Alexander replaced them with two groups of soldiers: mercenaries—mostly Greeks—and Easterners. The latter were a mixed group of Iranians and Central and South Asians. No longer did a majority of Alexander's troops speak Greek.

Meanwhile, Alexander moved shrewdly and sharply to weaken the Macedonians' power in the military. They had always been a minority in the army, but now they lost their privileges. They stood on an equal footing with new Iranian heavy infantrymen and cavalrymen, who were trained to fight in the Macedonian style or at least an approximation of it.

Blood and Snow

It was "mission creep" on a monumental scale. Alexander stayed in the East for five years, until summer 325. What began as a hunt for Bessus turned into the conquest of the Persian Far East: Aria, Arachosia, Bactria, Sogdiana (modern Tajikistan and Uzbekistan), and northwestern India. It was a region of about one million square miles, roughly 40 percent of the Persian empire. It included desert, steppe, and some of the world's toughest mountain terrain. Its extremes of climate ranged from snow to heat to monsoon rains.

The war against Bessus quickly became a tale of three rebels, as first Satibarzanes, satrap of Aria, and then Spitamenes, warlord of Sogdiana, either joined or replaced Bessus as military opponents.

Satibarzanes specialized in treachery. He fought for Darius at Gaugamela and then, less than a year later, joined Bessus in assassinating him. He surrendered to Alexander when the Macedonians reached Aria and then rebelled once they moved east on the way to fight Bessus in Bactria. Alexander turned back and forced Satibarzanes to decamp with two thousand cavalry for Bactria.

But in spring 329 Satibarzanes went back to Aria with more troops and raised the flag of rebellion again. This time, Alexander sent his lieutenants to polish him off. For once, the backstabbing satrap took on a fair fight. In fact, he opted for the manliest form of warfare, hand-to-hand combat. Satibarzanes challenged Erigyius of Mytilene, one of Alexander's most loyal Greek commanders. Erigyius killed the insurgent leader and sent his head to Alexander, who was several hundred miles to the east.

Meanwhile, Bessus proved no match for Alexander's audacity. Unable to organize a large army in Bactria, Bessus retreated northward, hoping first that the spring snows in the mountains, then the desert, and finally a hard-to-cross river—he had burned all the boats—would stop Alexander from following him. But Bessus was wrong. Alexander pushed his men over the passes of the Hindu Kush mountains and across the desert to the Oxus River (modern Amu Dar'ya), where he had his men build rafts to cross into Sogdiana. That did it for the followers of Bessus.

Spitamenes and another Sogdian noble arrested Bessus and handed him over to Alexander. To emphasize his position as king of Asia, Alexander punished Bessus for murdering Darius, and he imposed the penalty that Persians thought fit for a regicide—first Bessus had his ears and nose cut off, then he was crucified.

But Spitamenes turned on Alexander, and he proved the toughest opponent of all. Alexander drove northward to Maracanda and the river Jaxartes (in Tajikistan), which ancient geographers considered the northern boundary of Asia. Meanwhile Spitamenes and his followers launched a general rebellion in Alexander's rear, in hopes of driving out the invader. They put up such a fight that it took Alexander two years to beat them—and at a huge cost.

The war brought out the best and worst in Alexander. The terrain was difficult, the climate hostile, the allies not to be trusted; every victory seemed to be followed by a defeat. The enemy employed unconventional tactics that shocked and bloodied the Macedonians but Alexander responded masterfully.

Spitamenes's best troops were archers on horseback, and at first they wreaked havoc with Alexander's forces, penning in and slaughtering his heavy-armed troops. But Alexander adapted with javelin-men on horseback and archers on foot. By late 328, the Macedonians had crushed the enemies' forces, and Spitamenes's head too was delivered to Alexander. Unrepentant Sogdian barons took refuge in impregnable-looking rock fortresses, but in spring 327 Alexander's men found a way to climb them and force surrender.

The cost of victory was high. The toll of dead and wounded soldiers climbed well past anything that Alexander's men had seen before, perhaps seven thousand dead. On just one day at the Polytimetus River (in modern Uzbekistan), a force of about 2,500 men was massacred by Spitamenes; supposedly only 350 survived. Luckily for Alexander, the overwhelming majority of the soldiers were mercenaries and not Macedonians. Still, it was the bloodiest day of his reign for his army; he lost almost as many troops on that one day as in all the fighting against Darius. The campaign was hard on Alexander too—he was wounded twice, suffering a concussion and a minor fracture of the tibia.

But the biggest losers were civilians. The Macedonians massacred and enslaved them by the thousands. It was part revenge, part deterrent, and part recreation—a gruesome but effective way for the tired and frustrated troops to blow off steam.

Monsoon and Mutiny

India was wealthy but hard to conquer, much less hold. Some Indian rulers invited Alexander in, hoping to use him against their enemies, but those enemies could fight. The strategic balance sheet argued against invasion. But perhaps Alexander was thinking only of the mythical balance sheet: he wanted to invade India because that's what heroes of legend did. Since he had executed most of his officers who weren't yes-men, there was hardly anyone to stop him. So in spring 327, Alexander invaded India.

He followed the Kabul River Valley and the Khyber Pass into what is today Pakistan, unleashing terror and massacres against centers of resistance in the hills. In spring 326, when the Macedonians reached the Indus River, their local allies helped them build a bridge. King Ambhi welcomed Alexander into the great city of Taxila (near modern Islamabad). All the other local rulers bowed to Alexander except for Porus. He controlled a rich kingdom to the east and he refused to submit. The stage was set for battle.

The battle of the Hydaspes (Jhelum) River in May 326 was Alexander's last pitched battle. Compared with earlier fights, Alexander's numbers were small, but there wasn't an ounce less drama.

Greatly outnumbered in cavalry by Alexander and outclassed in infantry by the Macedonian phalanx, Porus pinned his hopes on two weapons—his elephants and the river. The Macedonians had never fought large numbers of elephants before, and Porus had eighty-five of them if not more (the sources disagree). But if Porus had his way, he wouldn't have to put the animals to the test. He planned to make a stand on the Hydaspes and keep Alexander from crossing it.

The Hydaspes was a wide river in ancient times, although changes in the landscape keep us from knowing just how wide. In May, it overflows with melting snow from the Himalayas, and in 326 an early rainy season added to the river's width. So Porus could hope for success.

But Alexander was wily. After he moved up to the riverbank, he kept Porus guessing by constantly moving units of his army from place to place. He brought up huge supplies of grain, to give the impression that he was prepared to wait until the river dropped in September. He had boats transported from the Indus River, nearly two hundred miles away, to threaten a crossing sooner. Meanwhile, Porus lined the opposite shore with his elephants to intimidate Alexander, while his scouts scoured the enemy's camp to guess his intentions. Porus marched his men here and there to stop possible crossings.

In this atmosphere of suspense and frustration, Alexander made his move. He took a small part of his forces—six thousand infantrymen and five thousand cavalry—and snuck upstream one rainy night. He had already chosen his crossing point, which had a convenient, midstream island, and had hidden a small fleet of boats there. Meanwhile, he ordered the main Macedonian army to stay in its camp and distract Porus. Alexander's men crossed safely.

Word quickly reached Porus that an enemy force was over the river, but he didn't know who they were or how many. So he sent a cavalry unit under his son to challenge them, but the Macedonians were ready. They stunned the Indians and killed large numbers, including Porus's son. The survivors reported to Porus that Alexander himself had crossed the river. Clearly, Porus had to stop him, so he moved against Alexander with the bulk of his army. The Indian chose a sandy plain for the battlefield.

And so, for Porus it all came down to his elephants. He lined the beasts up at regular intervals in front of his phalanx. His cavalry protected the two flanks. But Alexander and the Companion Cavalry launched a devastating charge against the cavalry on Porus's left flank and wheeled into the flank of his infantry. Porus tried to transfer cavalry from his right wing as reinforcements but a detachment of Macedonian cavalrymen under Coenus rode them down.

Now came the turn of the Macedonian phalanx. The men marched relentlessly forward against the enemy's soldiers—and his elephants. The Macedonians attacked the great beasts with their sarissas and drove them into a rampage. The pachyderms turned both on the Macedonians and on their own men. The key to survival against elephants was to stay disciplined. It took steady nerves and drill-ground precision to open up spaces in the lines to let the beasts pass through. The Macedonians were masters of self-control and made way for the elephants, but the Indians got stuck and were trampled on. Once the elephants were gone, the phalanx regained its momentum against the Indians' front lines. Meanwhile the Macedonian cavalry rode around to the enemy's rear. Squeezed on both sides, the Indians were slaughtered.

Their king survived. Porus was a tall man and he rode on a large elephant, which made him a target. In fact, he suffered multiple wounds, but Porus lived—and kept his dignity. When taken prisoner and brought to Alexander, he was asked how he wished to be treated. "Like a king," Porus replied. Alexander granted his wish. Strong men always recognize each other. No doubt realizing that it was better to have Porus guarding the empire's Indian flank than to leave a power vacuum in his place, Alexander spared his life and his kingdom. He made Porus swear allegiance and even increased the territory under Porus's control.

Victory at the Hydaspes marked the high point of Alexander's Indian campaign. He marched about one hundred miles further eastward, to the Hyphasis (Beas) River, conquering as he went, but traveled no farther. From summer 326 until he reached southeastern Iran in December 325, Alexander undertook a long and very violent march home—much against his will.

After defeating Porus, Alexander set his sights on the Ganges River Valley. This was the heartland of the Nanda dynasty, a large and wealthy state that covered most of northern India. It had a lot more military manpower—and elephants—than Porus did. That shouldn't have bothered Alexander's army, not after its record of victory, but the men were in no mood for new adventures. After seventy days of monsoon rains, after Porus's elephants, after the horrors of Bactria and Sogdiana—indeed, after everything that had followed the death of Darius in 330—the Macedonians had had enough. The Ganges was just two hundred miles away, but they were done advancing—and they told Alexander so. In late July 326, the Macedonians mutinied.

By this point, the Macedonians no longer made up the majority of his troops, but Alexander had no intention of relying on an assortment of mercenaries and Iranians, Bactrians, Sogdianans, and Indians. He didn't trust them without having Macedonian soldiers to keep them in line. Alexander tried to pressure the Macedonians by taking to his tent until they gave in. It was the tactic used by Achilles in Homer's *Iliad*. But Alexander's troops wouldn't budge. Coenus, hero of the Hydaspes, spoke to Alexander on their behalf.

If even his officers supported the mutineers, Alexander had no choice but to submit. But he left the decision to the gods; he had his priests offer sacrifices to continue the march, but the sacrifices proved unfavorable. That allowed the king to say that since the gods opposed a further advance, he would take the army home. But Alexander neither forgave nor forgot. Coenus died suddenly a few days later. Some modern scholars suspect poison but the ancient sources say Coenus died of disease. In his anger over the mutiny, perhaps Alexander wished a similar fate for the rest of his men, but he needed them. Still, two years later, he finally got a chance to take revenge.

The fastest and easiest way to go home was for Alexander and his men to go back the way they came, through the Khyber Pass and Bactria. But that would be admitting defeat. Alexander still had new worlds to explore, even if they did not lie in his preferred direction, to the east. He would travel down the river valleys of the Punjab to the southern Indus Valley and the Indian Ocean, a distance of more than a thousand miles. Then he would turn westward toward southern Iran, with some of the men marching overland and the rest traveling by sea.

Alexander began by having his men return to Porus's realm and build a vast fleet on the Hydaspes—eight hundred or more ships. The fleet sailed in November 326, accompanied by an army marching on either shore. It is estimated that Alexander had a total of 100,000 men by now.

The Macedonians had to fight all the way to the sea. The Indian kingdoms put up a spirited resistance but rarely posed much of a threat to the invaders. The Macedonians responded with terror. They massacred unarmed people, charged the cavalry into columns of refugees, and killed civilians who were trying to cross a river or hid in the woods.

There was regular fighting as well. Things went very badly for the Macedonians during an engagement near the modern city of Multan in January 325. To inspire his weary men, Alexander personally led the attack on a strong city and received an arrow wound in his chest. He nearly died because of the blood loss required to remove the arrow, leading his men to bewail their fate, leaderless in a hostile land very far from home. But Alexander recovered.

In July 325, after putting down two major rebellions, the Macedonians reached the sea not far from the modern city of Karachi, Pakistan. A month later, Alexander was ready to depart. He had already taken the Macedonian old and wounded, along with all his elephants and a few battle-ready troops for protection, and sent them back through the Khyber Pass and Bactria. Now he dismissed his Indian troops and divided the rest of his forces in two. He marched westward along the coast with perhaps about thirty thousand men, while the rest sailed with the fleet. Alexander started out in August but the fleet waited for the monsoon to end in November. The commander of the fleet was another of Alexander's boyhood friends, Nearchus of Crete.

The launching of Alexander's Indian Ocean armada was an extraordinary moment. Nearchus was a trailblazer. If Alexander had lived to old age and held his empire together, the fleet's success could have opened a new chapter in the history of the relationship between East and West. Contact between India and Greece might have become a central theme of ancient history. But even within the limits of fact, even though Alexander's successors turned their backs on India, the fleet was remarkable.

The fleet speaks to Alexander's ambition, his leadership, and his ability to grow as a military strategist. In 334, at Miletus, he dismissed his navy. Nine years later, in India in 325, he built a fleet and gave it an audacious mission, which it carried out smartly. As a result, the scales now dropped from Alexander's eyes when it came to sea power and its potential. By 323, he was ready to entrust his navy with the future of his army.

Meanwhile, the march overland to Iran was painful. Alexander's route took him through the Gedrosian Desert (roughly, the Baluchistan region of Pakistan). Cyrus the Great had once lost an army in this harsh terrain and Alexander wanted to outdo him by making it across the Gedrosian Desert. Alexander succeeded, but those around him paid the price. He spent two months crossing the desert, taking an inland route, which left food supplies on the coast for the Macedonian fleet but forced Alexander on a more difficult journey. Although the soldiers suffered, almost all of them survived. But many camp followers—women and traders—died and all the animals were slaughtered. The natives, meanwhile, faced famine after the invaders devoured their meager food stores.

By December 325 the Macedonians had crossed the desert and reached southeastern Iran. The rainy season had begun and they were back in contact with the heartland of Alexander's empire. The fleet arrived soon afterward, as did the men who had marched back via Bactria. The war in the East was over. Now what?

HANNIBAL

After Cannae, two roads to victory lay ahead for Hannibal. One called for marching on the city of Rome and storming it, as Alexander had stormed his enemy's capitals. But Rome wasn't Persepolis and it wouldn't fall easily. The other called for Hannibal to rest his army and skip a hopeless attack on Rome. Instead Hannibal would pick off Rome's allies one by one, the way Alexander had picked off cities like Miletus and Tyre. But Italy wasn't Anatolia and, unlike the Macedonians, the Carthaginians hadn't mastered the art of besieging cities. There had to be another way out for Hannibal, but what was it?

Maybe not storming Rome, but *frightening* it. The sight of Hannibal's army outside the walls would panic the city and unnerve its friends nearby. Meanwhile, there were other possibilities. Finding new allies outside Italy, getting new resources from home, using dirty tricks or diplomacy to pry away Rome's Italian allies, opening a second front in Sicily or Sardinia, getting Rome to the negotiating table—any of these or a combination of them might work, but Hannibal would have to decide. He might even decide to cut his losses in Italy and move on. Whatever the choice, it would challenge every inch of his strategic judgment and leadership.

Mago's Rings

Hannibal had passed eighteen dramatic months. From the time he entered Italy in late 218 to his victory at Cannae in summer 216, the Carthaginian had won four battles against Rome and so frustrated the enemy that they gave up on Fabius's strategy just when it was starting to work. If Hannibal had then marched on Rome and shocked the city into coming to the peace table, he would have won the war.

But the war dragged on. Rome did not agree to negotiate; Hannibal did not march on Rome. His strategy was, rather, to surround Rome with a web of enemy alliances and slowly squeeze it to the point of surrender. After

Cannae, most of southern Italy defected to Hannibal. The most important recruit was Capua, Italy's second-largest city, and a glittering prize. Capua offered Hannibal prestige, a supply base, and comfortable winter quarters. (Capua was known for the good life, but the story that the city corrupted him is just a story.) Much of Sicily joined Carthage as well, a boon to the Carthaginian navy, which now had way stations on the route to Italy. Farther afield, King Philip V of Macedon, whose country was powerful once again, made an alliance with Hannibal against Rome.

But all was not well. In order to woo his new Italian allies, Hannibal had been forced to promise not to conscript their men, so they did not solve his manpower problems. True, they did supply some soldiers to Hannibal, and they certainly did not contribute men to Rome, as they would have otherwise. But Hannibal had to garrison the cities that had joined him, and that cost him men. He had to protect the cities from Roman reprisals and to prevent them from rejoining Rome. All in all, the allies didn't help Hannibal. They tied him down, as the Lilliputians did to Gulliver.

Another problem was that Hannibal's alliances were incomplete. Not a single city in central Italy joined him. For all his gains in southern Italy, important cities there remained loyal to Rome, which offered the enemy forward posts, control of roads, and, most important of all, seaports. Hannibal did not have enough men to conquer all these places. Though highly effective, his army had never been large. His battle casualties likely included junior officers, essential to future success. In short, Hannibal needed reinforcements—and he naturally turned to Carthage.

Yet Hannibal faced a paradox: he needed to conquer a port in order to open a secure supply route to Carthage, but he couldn't do so without getting the Carthaginian reinforcements he had set his sights on. The temporary, imperfect solution was to land reinforcements on the Italian coast, but first Carthage had to agree to send them.

In 215 B.C., Hannibal sent his brother Mago from Italy to Carthage. Mago brought the Carthaginian senate news of Hannibal's achievements. As a dramatic illustration, he poured out onto the hard Senate House floor hundreds of golden rings, "of that sort worn only by Knights, and only by the first among them," rings that had been taken from killed or captured Romans. Then he asked for reinforcements in money, manpower, and grain. The Senate agreed but not unanimously, and the amount they sent was small compared with the resources that they committed to other fronts.

The Carthaginian senate cheered for Cannae but it was skeptical. Some senators no doubt remembered that it took nearly two years for a single Roman ally to join Hannibal. Those who were well informed about Italy might have noticed the many places that had stayed loyal to Rome. And then, perhaps some senators nervously eyed their own fingers at the sight of Mago's rings.

Meanwhile, Carthage's new alliances faded like spring flowers in its hand. Macedon, for example, promised to send troops to help Hannibal in Italy, but Rome commanded the sea and blocked any Macedonian landing. Rome also threatened Macedon by stirring up a war nearby in Illyria (modern Croatia). Could the Carthaginian navy have broken Rome's naval stranglehold? After a rebuilding phase, Carthage had enough ships and manpower to give the Roman fleet a real fight, but it lacked the one essential for victory: guts. Carthage's admirals refused to risk a battle and so the Macedonians stayed home.

Then there was Sicily. Carthage scored a coup in 215 B.C. with the defection of Syracuse, Sicily's greatest city. This rich, glittering seaport was armed to the teeth. No less a figure than Archimedes, one of antiquity's greatest mathematicians, helped Syracuse devise new weapons. Carthage sent a huge expeditionary force, 28,000 men, to help Syracuse. But Rome laid siege to Syracuse in 213 and captured it in 211, after a two-year struggle. Archimedes was killed during the sack. Meanwhile, a Carthaginian naval expedition tried to retake the island of Sardinia, a former Carthaginian colony, but Rome crushed it.

Carthage frittered away its energies on one new initiative after another, but Rome broke each one in turn. Meanwhile, Rome held fast to its traditional strategy. It kept a firm grip on its oldest allies in central Italy and continued to raise new armies there. But it did not use them in a major pitched battle against Hannibal.

After Cannae, the Senate admitted that Fabius had been right. Instead of accepting Hannibal's challenges to battle, it went back to the strategy of shadowing Hannibal's forces and cutting off his food supplies.

This move was greatly to Rome's credit. It demonstrates the strategic wisdom of Rome's leaders, but it also shows the deep well of popular support they drew from. The Fabian strategy was slow and frustrating. It worked only because the Roman people trusted their government. Indeed, the Roman political system stood on the firmest of foundations.

Rome focused its energies on the area around Capua, Hannibal's major new ally. Capua was only 125 miles from Rome; the Romans did not want Hannibal to get any closer. So Roman generals intervened in still-friendly cities near Capua; they ordered all grain to be harvested early and locked up in fortresses. Meanwhile, Roman raiders cut down Capua's crops in the fields. To feed his men, Hannibal marched to the major Roman supply depots nearby: the cities of Naples and Nola. Rome kept these cities in line by garrisoning and fortifying them as well as by executing any local waverers. Naples was also an important seaport, while Nola was a key road junction. Frustrated and hungry, Hannibal had no choice but to move his army farther south.

But the Carthaginian was hardly out of steam. He captured the major southern Italian port of Tarentum in 213 B.C. by means of a ruse, not by storming or besieging it. After negotiating with disaffected Roman allies in Tarentum, Hannibal arranged for a commando unit to rush to hide outside one of the town's gates one night while his allies pretended to be returning from a hunt. While the guards were admiring a large boar carried by the supposed hunters, Carthaginian soldiers rushed in. They had carefully chosen a night when most of the Roman soldiers were partying and unprepared.

Still, the attack was not a complete success. Hannibal took Tarentum but a Roman garrison held out in the town's citadel, which had access to the sea. This greatly limited Hannibal's ability to use Tarentum as a port, and Tarentum was the port where Philip of Macedon's troops would land, if he ever sent them.

Five years later, in 208, Rome in turn tricked its way into recapturing Tarentum. An Italian serving in Hannibal's garrison fell in love with a local woman whose brother served with the Romans. The brother talked the lovesick Italian into betraying the town to Rome. By then, Rome had successfully starved out Capua after a long siege; the city surrendered in 211. And Hannibal never took a seaport even more strategic than Tarentum—Regium, the gateway to Sicily, stayed stubbornly loyal to Rome.

Hannibal was still in Italy, but even though he was bottled up in the south, he remained dangerous, especially if reinforcements reached him.

Rather than risking a pitched battle to drive him out, Rome attacked Hannibal's base in Spain. In 209 B.C., a Roman army in Spain shocked the Carthaginians by capturing their well-fortified capital city of New Carthage (Cartagena). It was as bold a move as Hannibal's march on Italy and as cunning in its execution as his tactics at Cannae. The Roman commander had taken the trouble to learn about the daily ebb of water from the lagoon north of the city, due to the wind, that left a poorly defended part of the wall accessible—and used the information to take New Carthage in a bloody afternoon. This Roman was none other than Publius Cornelius Scipio (later Africanus), son of the consul of 218, also named Publius Cornelius Scipio, who had lost to Hannibal at the Ticinus.

A brilliant general, Scipio copied Hannibal's tactics in pitched battle as well. At the battle of Baecula in Spain a year later (208), Scipio won a solid if not decisive victory over a Carthaginian army by enveloping its flanks. It was a move out of Hannibal's playbook. Never before had a Roman force maneuvered so well; Scipio had trained his men long and hard.

The Carthaginian general at Baecula was Hannibal's brother Hasdrubal. He had saved most of his men; now he was ordered to transfer them to Italy. Finally, Hannibal would get the reinforcements he was desperate for. Hasdrubal marched in 207. Like his brother, Hasdrubal crossed the Alps. He too found Celtic allies in northern Italy. He too brought elephants with him—ten of them. Including his Italian allies, Hasdrubal had about thirty thousand men. Unlike Hannibal, who crossed the Alps in the snows of late fall, Hasdrubal timed his crossing for warm weather, and he probably chose an easier route. Unlike Hannibal, though, Hasdrubal did not surprise the Romans, who knew that he was coming.

The Romans mobilized two forces, one under each consul: one in the north, to oppose Hasdrubal, the other in the south, to try to keep Hannibal from marching to join his brother. The Romans had reason to be concerned about what would happen if Hasdrubal won a major pitched battle—a likely result if he joined forces with Hannibal. That might have pushed war-weary Roman allies into the Carthaginian camp.

Then, Providence took a hand in events. Hasdrubal was based in Umbria in north-central Italy. He sent four horsemen south to Hannibal with information about his location and with plans for the two generals to join forces. The Romans captured Hasdrubal's messengers and discovered his plan.

This allowed them to detach part of their southern army and send it north to join the forces against Hasdrubal.

The Romans cornered Hasdrubal in north-central Italy, in the vicinity of the modern city of Urbino. The Carthaginians were outnumbered, had no cavalry, and didn't know the countryside. The Romans forced them to fight a battle on the banks of the Metaurus (modern Metauro) River. Once again, a Roman attack on the Carthaginian flank delivered a devastating blow, and the Carthaginian army collapsed.

Hasdrubal died in battle. The Romans decapitated him, sent his head south with a team of riders, and threw it into Hannibal's camp. The story goes that in his distress, Hannibal cried out, "Now I understand the fate of Carthage!" But, if this is true, it doesn't mean that Hannibal had given up. He withdrew his army to Bruttium, the "toe" of the Italian boot, but he held on tenaciously to Italian soil.

What Went Wrong?

In nine years, from 216 to 207 B.C. Hannibal had gone from being Rome's conqueror at Cannae to being its virtual prisoner in a corner of southern Italy. Why?

When he began the Second Punic War in 218 B.C., Hannibal knew that Carthage could not match Rome's manpower or its navy. Its strength was the professionalism of its small but elite army and his own ability as its leading general. Because Carthage could not match Rome's resources, a long war was to its disadvantage. If it were going to win, Carthage would have to win quickly.

Hannibal's actions from the time he left New Carthage (spring 218) to his victory at Cannae (summer 216) followed that strategy. His march on Italy shocked Rome. His victories in four battles left the Romans fearful "for themselves and for their native soil."

At this moment, fresh from victory at Cannae, Hannibal should have opened a new military offensive. He made a diplomatic push. He tried to rebrand himself in Roman eyes as a man of peace. For the first time after winning a battle, he addressed the Roman prisoners and spoke in soothing terms. Then he sent a Carthaginian envoy, one Carthalo, to Rome to negotiate. Hannibal offered to ransom his Roman captives if the Senate would pay a high price for each man. The Romans recognized this as a trick, meant both to transfer money to the enemy and to sap Rome's fighting spirit. If the Senate had agreed, in the future, Roman soldiers might have preferred surrender to fighting to the death, secure in the knowledge that eventually they would be ransomed. The Senate refused.

Hannibal could have offered another olive branch but it is doubtful that the Senate would have taken it. The war often defied expectations. Just as Hannibal surprised the Romans at Trasimene by not fighting fair—by laying a trap instead of coming out in the open—so the Romans surprised Hannibal after Cannae. According to the unwritten rules of the day, if its armies lost battle after battle, a state was supposed to surrender. Instead, Rome fought on.

After the fighting ended at Cannae on August 2, Hannibal's officers surrounded him with congratulations. Most of them called for a well-deserved rest, but not Maharbal, Hannibal's commander of cavalry: he advised an immediate attack on Rome. In five days, he said, Hannibal could be dining on the Capitol, Rome's citadel. Maharbal offered to go first, with his horsemen. Hannibal declined. It was not so easy a thing to do, he said, and besides, he needed time to reflect. Maharbal is supposed to have replied, "Truly, the gods have not given all their gifts to the same man." You know how to be the victor, Hannibal, but not how to use your victory." The famous Latin saying is: *"Vincere scis, Hannibal, victoria uti nescis."*

A Roman writer comments, "It is widely believed that the day's delay was the salvation of the City and the Empire." The story of Maharbal's criticism probably goes all the way back to men who lived through the Second Punic War, which should add weight to it. But today, most historians side with Hannibal. They point out that Rome was located 235 miles (380 kilometers) from Cannae, so marching the army to the Capitol would have taken weeks—not four days. By that time, Rome could have organized its defense.

Rome was protected by thick walls nearly seven miles long and boasted a state-of-the-art system of towers, trenches, and, on the town side, an earth-filled platform for the defenders. The walls enclosed an area of one and a half square miles.

Unless traitors opened Rome's gates, Hannibal would have had to take the city either by storming the walls or by laying siege to the city and starving it out. Storming the walls would have required siege engines, which would have taken weeks or more to construct. Besieging Rome would have meant surrounding it with trenches and a palisade, no small undertaking.

If Hannibal really expected the Romans to negotiate after Cannae, he showed bad judgment. He didn't know his enemy. But by failing to build on the battle's momentum by attacking Rome, he showed poor strategy and weak leadership.

What If?

If Hannibal had decided to go for Rome after Cannae, the cavalry could have pushed ahead. By riding hard, Maharbal and his horsemen could have reached Rome in a week or so—"five days" was an exaggeration. Still, the news of Cannae would barely have arrived and suddenly Rome would have seen the enemy at the gates. Fear and alarm would have followed. And then, Hannibal and his army would have joined the cavalry. A forced march could have gotten them to Rome in as little as two weeks.

It's not likely that Rome would have agreed to negotiate, but fear might have spread to cities in the vicinity. Hannibal might have increased the pressure on the Romans to come out and fight. And he might have tipped some of Rome's allies in central Italy over the edge and into his arms. Some of those cities did waver as the war dragged on, and Hannibal's presence might have made the difference.

Still, it is fair to ask: What if Rome hung on? Hannibal would probably have been unable to take the city by storm, because Rome's walls were too strong. What if he settled down for a siege?

Hannibal had 45,000 men after Cannae, but that included the wounded, so his effective strength may have been only around forty thousand men. Rome was a large city. Yet a few years later (211 B.C.), with far fewer men in their siege army, the Romans took the great Sicilian city of Syracuse, whose walls were longer than Rome's (18.6 miles)—indeed, they were one of the greatest fortresses of the ancient world. The siege of Syracuse lasted two years. Rome eventually took the outer walls by storm. Shortly afterward, a traitor opened the gate to the inner city. A spree of looting and murder followed.

Besides, in August 216, Rome had no great number of soldiers to man its walls. There were about eight thousand soldiers in the city and about another five thousand nearby, guarding a strategic bridge on the Appian Way, the southern approach to Rome. While waiting for Hannibal, Rome started conscripting new troops, even from the slave population, but they were raw recruits. If the siege had lasted, Rome might well have had to form a relief force by withdrawing legions from its provinces: northern Italy, Sardinia, Sicily, and even Spain. Cannae's fifteen thousand Roman survivors could have been added to the mix.

A strong Roman relief army might have made Hannibal raise his siege of Rome, but not if he received reinforcements as well, from Carthage. If Hannibal laid siege to the city of Rome and if it looked like he had a chance of success, Carthage's home government might have finally agreed to send him more troops.

The problem wasn't that Hannibal couldn't take Rome but that he wouldn't. Maybe Hannibal didn't understand the extent of his victory at Cannae. Maybe he overestimated the strength of the Romans. But the main obstacle to attacking Rome was, it seems, Hannibal's inflexibility. Neither his war aims, nor his philosophy of operations, nor his military strategy, called for attacking Rome. It was time for a leader whose judgment was shrewd enough to change strategy. It was a moment for audacity and agility, but Hannibal had a plan and he stuck to it.

Destroying Rome was never Hannibal's war aim; rather, he wanted to cut its power down to size. He wanted a peace treaty, not a war to the death. He was willing to see Rome continue as a regional power in Italy, as long as it didn't threaten Carthage.

When it came to military operations, Hannibal's entire philosophy was to fight mobile, not static warfare. He could make long marches, outrun or surprise the enemy, fight pitched battles, and conduct raids and ambushes. The one thing he couldn't do was to take a city by siege. In fact, his entire military career consisted of only one major siege and that took place not in Italy but in Spain, at Saguntum (219 B.C.). It was no easy undertaking: the capture of Saguntum took eight months and cost Hannibal a serious leg wound. In the years after Cannae, this inability to take a city by siege turned out to be a major shortcoming. For example, in the aftermath of Cannae, Hannibal could have attacked the several thousand Roman survivors who were huddling in the nearby hill town of Canusium. But Canusium was well defended and Hannibal passed it by. By taking Canusium, Hannibal might have tipped additional Italian cities into his camp. And, unbeknownst to him, he might have removed from the equation the man who would become Carthage's worst enemy. One of the refugees at Canusium was Scipio, who had fought at Cannae.

And then there is the question of Hannibal's ego. During the siege of Saguntum, Hannibal was forced to leave for a few weeks to deal with rebels in another part of Spain. He turned command of the siege over to Maharbal, who did so well that, as Livy cattily put it, "neither the Carthaginians nor their enemies noticed the leader's absence." The same Maharbal later commanded the cavalry at Cannae and then castigated Hannibal for not marching on Rome.

Did jealousy play a role in keeping Hannibal away from Rome? Perhaps he feared that an attack on the city—whether a raid, assault, or full-blown siege—would only play to Maharbal's strengths. Great men like Hannibal should not be reduced to petty motives, but heroes too have egos.

For good or ill, Hannibal's army was set up for battle, not siege. He should, then, have changed his army. Alexander, after all, had managed to do this, after he moved eastward from Iran. He adapted to the new conditions needed to fight in the mountains of Bactria and the steppes of Sogdiana. Alexander carried out daring and successful sieges of supposedly impregnable fortresses. To equal his hero Alexander, Hannibal needed to match his agility and his audacity. Two centuries later, Caesar would do just that. Caesar not only excelled in pitched battle, but he was also a master of siegecraft, as he showed in Gaul at Alesia and in Italy at Corfinium. Hannibal did not reach the same height.

RULES OF WAR

A larger question as to Hannibal's success as a military leader relates not to his operations but to his strategy. It may even go to the core of Hannibal's being. Had Hannibal always set too much store on cunning? Having learned that craftiness was a good way to win battles, perhaps he believed that it was also a good way to win wars. He would have been much better off, in 216 B.C., had he taken advantage of the shock of the moment.

Hannibal's strategy against Rome was flawed. He planned to surround

Rome with a web of enemy alliances in central and southern Italy, which he would weave together with his alliances with the Celts in the Po Valley. Then, he would slowly squeeze Rome to the point of surrender. But Rome was no easy victim. And a long war, a war of attrition, which drained each side's military talent pool, wore down each side's manpower, and shattered each side's political and financial willpower—such a war did not play to Carthage's strengths.

In fact, Hannibal's strategy threatened to be a repeat of the First Punic War (264–241 B.C.). That twenty-three-year-long conflict exhausted both parties, but Carthage threw in the towel first—and so, Rome won. Rome, for its part, had always been able to take a punch.

After Cannae, Rome's allies in southern Italy began defecting to Carthage, but they moved slowly and cautiously. The cities in central Italy never broke with Rome. Meanwhile, Carthage's new friends contributed so little to the war effort and cost so much that Hannibal might have thought, "Be careful what you wish for." In spite of Cannae, all signs pointed to a long war—the last thing Carthage needed.

Meanwhile, the war in Spain had already begun and, in the end, it was devastating. Because of its sea power, Rome could attack Spain at will. Not that the war was easy: it took ten years for Rome to put Carthage on the run in Spain. Yet all the while, Rome tied down Carthaginian troops that could have been sent to reinforce Hannibal. Romans understood that: winning a war sometimes means accepting losses where it hurts in order to win where it matters. That is a fundamental—and crucial—rule of war.

To conquer an enemy who has superior resources in manpower, material, and money, an invader has to move quickly. Let the war drag on, and the enemy may husband his resources, grind down the invader, and even counterattack the invader's home country. To win, the invader has to shock the enemy with lightning attacks that strike at his heart.

Alexander and Caesar understood the principle of shock. Hannibal seems to have understood it at first, but then something happened. Either he lost sight of it, or he failed to receive the necessary support from his home government to carry out a winning strategy, or both.

Hannibal lacked the ability to reach his enemy's heart, but he could deliver a series of body blows. That, he gambled, would be enough to win victory, Hannibal forgot that time was not on his side. By not destroying

Rome, Hannibal gave it the chance to heal its wounds and come roaring back.

Another fundamental rule of war is, if you invade another country, don't let it invade you in return.

Rome displayed a ruthless wisdom about prioritization. Carthage, by contrast, was all over the map. Instead of focusing intensely on winning the war in Italy, it diverted resources all over the western and central Mediterranean: to Spain, Sardinia, and Sicily. Nor did Carthage make good use of its alliances.

Carthage should have accepted its inability to drive Rome from Spain and have settled for neutralizing it. Carthage should have thrown its energies instead into prosecuting the war in Italy. By keeping up the pressure there, Carthage might have finally pried away some of Rome's crucial central Italian allies, for example, cities with Latin rights (limited Roman citizenship) such as Spoletium (Spoleto) and Beneventum (Benevento), peoples whose loyalty was essential for Roman success.

Consider the resources diverted to Spain in spring 215 that might have gone to Hannibal in Italy: 12,000 foot soldiers, 1,500 horsemen, 20 elephants, 60 warships—destined for Italy but diverted to Spain after setbacks there under Mago. And Spain was not the only place to which Carthage sent men and animals that could have been sent to Hannibal in Italy. It sent 17,000 soldiers to Sardinia and 28,000 to Sicily. These numbers dwarfed the reinforcements that Hannibal actually received: 4,000 Numidian cavalry, 40 elephants, plus money and provisions.

We can only guess what Hannibal thought of Carthage's priorities. Certainly he accepted the Spanish and Sicilian expeditions, where the Carthaginian high command included his brothers and other powerful friends. Maybe he even championed these new campaigns out of frustration with the stalemate in Italy. But I doubt it. If Sicily or Spain had become the decisive theater in his mind, it's hard to see why he stayed in Italy. He knew that he was Carthage's best general: that was not just egotism but plain fact. But he did not have the tools to finish the job.

We can only guess as well at the mix of motives that kept Hannibal in Italy. Hope and fear no doubt played a part. Pride in his men and loyalty to their achievements surely did too.

Hannibal asked the Carthaginian senate for reinforcements, but they were too little and too late. Roman history shows what wan enthusiasm the Roman senate had for victorious Roman generals returning to Italy at the head of their army. We might guess that the Carthaginian senate held similar sentiments about Hannibal. So they proved stingy in supporting his war effort in Italy.

If we believe the ancient sources, in later years, Hannibal regretted his decision not to attack Rome after Cannae. Indeed.

CAESAR

The battle of Pharsalus offered Caesar the chance of winning the war, but only if he showed that he had the right skills. Success was still up for grabs. To win, Caesar needed mobility, but he lacked a fleet. He needed manpower, but he lacked money. He needed to divide his enemies, but they remained firm. He needed more battlefield victories, but his troops were tired and his enemy was cautious. The road ahead would test Caesar's good judgment, his strategic wisdom, and his willingness to take risks. And none of it might have availed without the help of Providence.

A Severed Head

As great a victory as Pharsalus was, Pompey was still able to rally huge forces to his side. About eighteen thousand of his soldiers lived to fight again.

Led by men like Cato and Metellus Scipio, Pompey's allies retained their depth and intensity. Headquartered on the Adriatic island of Corcyra (modern Corfu), they had the most powerful navy in the Mediterranean. Pompey's son Cnaeus was a successful naval commander, and a younger son, Sextus, would soon be ready to join him.

Pompey had yet another potent ally in King Juba of Numidia, who had destroyed Curio's army and saved North Africa for the Senate. So Cato and Scipio evacuated Corcyra and Dyrrachium and sailed to North Africa, bringing Pompey's surviving troops with them. Last but not least, war is expensive, and Pompey still had enormous sums of money. Caesar was rich in victory, but not in cash.

In order to win the war, Caesar had to deal with these enemies, either by arms or diplomacy. Negotiations should have been the course of choice, since both sides had suffered setbacks and both sides ultimately wanted the good of Rome. But the opposing sides defined that good differently.

The senators wanted to keep power in their own hands. They were a tiny elite, but they claimed the right to rule an empire because of their noble birth and their devotion to liberty. They defined the good life as freedom of speech and no-holds-barred competition for votes in elections that brought them public office and honors.

Caesar saw things differently. He was a brilliant leader and he knew it—after Pharsalus, he knew it more than ever. He had conquered Gaul, Britain, Italy, Spain, and now, Pompey the Great. In his life, Caesar had been not only a soldier but also a prosecutor, administrator, deal maker, orator, and writer, and excelled at them all. Now, he stood on the verge of power such as only one Roman had ever held before: Sulla, who was named dictator in 82, with no limit set on the office. But a year later, Sulla resigned as dictator and ran for consul. After two terms as consul, he turned power over to the Senate and retired. Caesar had no intention of following suit. Sulla, he said, did not know his political ABC's.

Caesar did not want to compete with other senators; he wanted to dominate them. He wanted to take power away from the Senate and share it with the common people of Italy and with elites from the provinces—all in order to generate a wide base of support for his rule. Pompey was an egotist, but the senators could tolerate sharing a bit of power with him. Caesar was a titan, and the senators knew that they would either have to destroy him or be destroyed in turn.

Caesar's instinct after Pharsalus was to capture Pompey. Just as Alexander could have scored huge political gains by capturing Darius after Gaugamela, so Caesar could have won big politically by capturing Pompey after Pharsalus. Alive and in Caesar's control, Pompey would be a game changer—and maybe even a willing one. Pompey was a soldier, he was no longer young, and he had no principles. He had supported the Senate because it was good for Pompey, not because he believed in liberty and the republic. If Caesar offered Pompey and his sons a better deal, he might win him over. Together, they would have no trouble defeating the Senate's forces.

And so, after Pharsalus, Caesar hurried on to the chase for Pompey, just as Alexander had hurried on more than one chase for Darius. Each time, the quarry kept one step ahead of the hunter, only to meet an even more dangerous predator.

Pompey went from Pharsalus to the Greek coast, and then by sea to the island of Lesbos, where he picked up his wife, Cornelia, and son, Sextus. He might have gone to North Africa but instead sailed to Egypt, after first recruiting several thousand soldiers in Anatolia and Cyprus. Caesar followed with a small army and navy; he had few ships of his own, and besides, he wanted to travel light in order to catch Pompey.

Fortune, as usual, smiled on Caesar, as an incident along the way shows. He was hurrying across the Hellespont in a ferryboat when he ran into a squadron of Pompey's fleet. With ten warships, they could have easily captured and killed Caesar. Instead, he headed for the flagship and demanded the captain's surrender—and the man gave in without a peep. *"Fortis fortuna adiuvat,"* Caesar might have said, quoting a Roman poet—"Fortune favors the bold."

By going to Egypt, Pompey was taking a leaf from Caesar's book of risk taking. Egypt might allow Pompey to turn the tables on Caesar. It was the richest country in the ancient world, thanks to the amazing agricultural fertility of the Nile Valley. Although the Romans leaned hard on it, Egypt was still an independent state with a major army and navy—the best that money could buy. The king of Egypt, Ptolemy XIII, owed his throne to Pompey, who had saved his father from exile nine years before. Now, Pompey intended to present his bill. He anchored offshore and sent a messenger to Ptolemy, asking that he be allowed to land.

But the Ptolemies were about as hospitable as rattlesnakes. Besides, Ptolemy XIII was engaged in a civil war against his sister. In any case he lacked power—he was only a boy of about thirteen, and in the hands of his advisors. They feared that Pompey would replace them in the boy-king's eyes, so they didn't want him to land. But they didn't want him to leave either, because then he might return one day and take revenge. So, they invited Pompey ashore and promptly had him murdered—in full view of Cornelia and Sextus, who were still aboard ship. Fearing pursuit by the Egyptian fleet, Pompey's ships hurried away, leaving his corpse on the sand. He was fifty-seven years old.

"I cannot but mourn his fate," wrote Cicero of Pompey, "for I knew him as a man of integrity, of spotless and dignified character."

When Caesar arrived in Egypt three days later, he was presented with Pompey's severed head and signet ring. The sources say that Caesar wept. If so, perhaps he cried as much over his failed strategy as over the death of his former son-in-law—now Caesar would have to fight the senators alone. And perhaps it occurred to him that he too was vulnerable to assassination.

Soldiers and Money

It might seem as if Caesar should have hurried to North Africa before his enemies had a chance to regroup. Instead, he spent the next year in the East. This was bad news for Rome's tranquillity, but it had its own logic.

If his first priority was the common good, a Roman patriot would have hoped for a peace agreement between Caesar and the Senate or at least a quick and decisive end to the civil war. A showdown in North Africa might have brought a speedy decision but Caesar was out of money. He needed more ships and men and he had to pay the soldiers he already had. Like Pompey, Caesar looked at Egypt and saw gold. He demanded payment of a debt owed him from a decade earlier by the Egyptian crown—a huge sum, enough to pay a very large army for a year.

The government in Alexandria refused to pay, so Caesar solved the problem with his usual flair for simple solutions—he changed the government. Caesar used his four thousand troops to try to settle the war between Ptolemy and his sister. The woman had a secret weapon—herself. She was smuggled into the palace in Alexandria, wrapped up, as one story has it, in a carpet or blanket, and unrolled in front of Caesar's wide eyes. She was Cleopatra. She was not conventionally pretty—she had a prominent chin, a large mouth, and a rugged nose. But she was clever, cunning, and seductive. She was twenty-one years old and, at fifty-two, Caesar was smitten.

Or so the legend goes, but Caesar had a political reason to prefer Cleopatra to Ptolemy: she was weaker. Ptolemy had strong popular support in the key city of Alexandria; Cleopatra could not win without Rome. Naturally Caesar preferred to have her, a loyal ally, in charge of Egypt. Naturally she would pay him the money he wanted in exchange for the throne.

Realizing that he could not compete with Cleopatra in Caesar's eyes,

Ptolemy had his soldiers besiege the palace. The siege went on all winter (48–47 B.C.). There were moments of drama, including fighting in the harbor, in which Caesar was forced to swim for his life. Once again, Caesar put himself at personal risk.

In the spring, a relief force arrived. Led by Antipater, the Jewish governor of Judaea, it consisted of both Jews and Arabs, with the main strike force consisting of fifteen hundred Jewish heavy infantry. Past history inclined the Jews toward Caesar, because Pompey had entered Jerusalem in 63 B.C. and annexed Jewish territory and desecrated the Temple. Now they won a key battle in the Nile Delta that lifted the siege and freed Caesar. In later years, Caesar treated Judaea and the Jews as allies and friends—they had, after all, saved his life.

But the Jews were only one of dozens of new allies Caesar acquired in the East. Egypt itself was the largest. Before leaving there, Caesar spent two months with Cleopatra and may have fathered her child; she named the baby Ptolemy XV but he was known as Caesarion, or "Little Caesar." From Egypt, Caesar headed eastward, stopping in the great cities of Antioch (Syria) and Tarsus (southern Anatolia) to add them to his supporters. Then he headed to north-central Anatolia to put down a serious revolt by one Pharnaces.

Pharnaces was the son of Mithradates VI of Pontus, the rebel king who had stormed through the Roman east for twenty-five years and nearly destroyed Rome's empire there. From the time Caesar marched into the kingdom of Pontus (in northern Turkey) it took only five days for him to meet Pharnaces and defeat him on August 2 (June 12) 47 B.C. in the battle of Zela. A year later, when Caesar celebrated his triumphs in Rome, he advertised his speedy victory over Pharnaces with a placard in the triumphal procession. It contained one of the greatest slogans in the history of politics: *Veni vidi vici*, a phrase that shines in the English translation or "I came, I saw, I conquered."

Caesar could have used another slogan to describe his activity in the East. It was less catchy but more accurate: *Exegi mutuum sumpsi sustinui*—"I demanded, I borrowed, I supported." Caesar began hitting up the cities of the East for money during his pursuit of Pompey after Pharsalus. He continued demanding funds when he got to Egypt. Then, after defeating Pharnaces, he exacted money from cities, temples, and wealthy private individuals all along the way back to Italy. Where he had a good excuse for taking their wealth—such as a city's having supported Pompey—Caesar called it a "demand." Where he had no excuse, he called it "borrowing"—not that he had any intention of ever paying it back. He had no choice, said Caesar, but to follow a simple arithmetic: states need soldiers, soldiers need support, and support costs money. Caesar understood the infrastructure of war as well as any general.

"My Commander-in-Chief"

The enemy was in North Africa, but now Caesar went straight to Rome. Street violence in the capital between borrowers and lenders had gotten out of hand. Worse still, there was talk of mutiny in the legions billeted outside Rome, and they were some of Caesar's best men, including the crack soldiers of the Tenth Legion. They wanted their back pay and they wanted to be discharged and given land.

When the mutineers marched on Rome, Caesar's friends advised caution. Instead he met the soldiers in their camp. As if that wasn't brave enough, Caesar called their bluff. He needed them, in Africa, but he pretended not to. Since the men said they wanted to be discharged, he discharged them. Instead of calling them "fellow soldiers" (*commilitones*), as was standard Roman practice, he pointedly called them "citizens" (*quirites*). It was audacity at its finest, and it worked. The soldiers loved making war and they had no intention of giving it up. They demanded that Caesar take them back, and so he did. But he didn't forget the mutiny. He is said to have rid himself of the ringleaders later on by giving them the most dangerous assignments in North Africa.

After putting down the mutiny and placing new, more trustworthy politicians in office, Caesar left Rome. He had been there two months, from late September (our July) to late November (mid-September) 47 B.C. He now headed for Africa, using Sicily as his staging ground. Bad weather and organizational slowness held him back. But Caesar had no intention of waiting until all his forces were ready. He departed as soon as the weather broke, on December 25, 47 B.C. (mid-October).

Caesar's "African War," as it was called, was a study in extremes. Careless haste was followed by a patient ability to see the big picture. Rarely was

Caesar more impressive as a field commander; rarely was he less impressive as an organizer, and his generalship more fully eclipsed by his political skill; and never was his dependence on Providence more evident.

Caesar's invasion of Roman Africa was like his invasion of Albania all over again. Both times he took the risk of establishing a bridgehead with a token force and waiting for the big battalions to follow. But the invasion of Africa was infinitely more haphazard. Caesar had assembled in Sicily six legions, two thousand cavalrymen, and many ships' worth of supplies. But strong winds on the crossing scattered the fleet, and the strategic realities prevented Caesar from giving the captains precise instructions about where to put in. The enemy controlled the seas, so the captains would have to find whatever safe harbors they could. Caesar himself landed on the African coast four days later with only three thousand legionaries and 150 cavalrymen. He needed to feed and protect them until the other ships arrived. In the meantime, the enemy struck.

The action took place outside the seaport of Ruspina (modern Monastir, Tunisia). Having left some of his men to garrison other ports, Caesar went on a foraging expedition with a small army of 30 infantry cohorts, perhaps 2,500 men to which he added the only other troops he had—400 cavalry and 150 archers—when he saw the enemy's cloud of dust in the distance. Their commander was Titus Labienus, Caesar's former second-in-command and an excellent tactician.

Labienus had a much larger force than Caesar, consisting of nearly 10,000 cavalrymen—8,000 Numidian and 1,600 Gallic or German—as well as light-armed Numidian infantrymen. The Roman province of Africa (roughly, modern Tunisia) bordered the kingdom of Numidia (roughly, modern Algeria) on its south and west. Pompeians held Roman Africa and King Juba of Numidia was their ally. As in Hannibal's day, Numidia provided quick and deadly light cavalry.

What followed was a thinking-man's battle. Labienus aimed at outflanking Caesar by lining up his cavalry in an unusually long line. Caesar responded by forming his men in an unusual, single-deep line in order not to be outflanked. It worked for a while, but the Numidian cavalry kept attacking again and again, charging and throwing their javelins. They broke up several attempts by Caesar's legionaries to attack Labienus's infantrymen. Eventually Labienus's cavalry surrounded Caesar's forces.

But Caesar proved equal to the challenge. He rearranged his army in two lines, back to back, facing the enemy in two directions. His move bought Caesar breathing space to attack different parts of the enemy line in isolation, which proved very effective. Little by little, Caesar's men were able to force the enemy off a hill that blocked their march, and from there, they limped back to their camp at Ruspina. The battle was a near-run thing but it demonstrated yet again Caesar's cool as a commander, his quickness on his feet, and his inspirational hold on his men.

For several weeks, the Pompeians kept Caesar bottled up in Ruspina. The Pompeians had fourteen legions—ten Roman and four Numidian— plus numerous auxiliaries and 120 elephants. They outnumbered Caesar but they lacked experience. They had nothing to compare with the five veteran legions that Caesar would eventually have, out of a total of ten legions and two thousand cavalrymen. Caesar wouldn't be at full strength for months, but in the meantime, enough reinforcements and supplies arrived for him to break out of Ruspina.

The enemy's generals were a mixed lot. Most of Labienus's colleagues were second-rate, none more so than their commander-in-chief, Metellus Scipio. The Pompeians' alliance with Juba was also a doubtful advantage, since Juba was distracted by an invasion of his kingdom from the west by King Bocchus of Mauretania.

Against them stood Caesar. A small incident sheds light on his political power. The story appears in "The African War," a pamphlet written by an unknown supporter of Caesar. The story is surely exaggerated and might well be invented, but it is brilliant propaganda.

As new Caesarian convoys reached Africa, single ships were scattered by the winds and captured by the enemy. The crew of one such ship, soldiers of the Fourteenth Legion, were taken to see Scipio. He offered them the chance to denounce their "guilt-stained" commander and to join Rome's best in defense of the Republic. Speaking for all of them, an unnamed centurion defiantly refused.

"Should I take a stand in arms against my commander, Caesar?" he asked. He referred to Caesar as *imperatorem meum*, "my commander-in-chief," while pointedly announcing to Scipio that he would not grant him a similar term of respect: "I don't call you commander-in-chief (*imperator*)."

"My *imperator*" is a full-blooded term. Like "my country," it is a phrase that men fought and died for. It suggests the hold that Caesar had over men's minds. It indicates not only why his own soldiers were devoted to him but also why the enemy's soldiers gave up their own cause and deserted to Caesar whenever things began to tip in his favor. It helps explain why Caesar continued to beat the odds both in Africa and elsewhere, in spite of his inferiority in manpower and supplies: men believed in him.

But it did not encourage optimism about the future of free institutions in Rome in 46 B.C. The centurion's language was worthy of a personality cult. The Latin word *imperator* meant "commander-in-chief" but, within a generation, it would come to mean "emperor" as well. When the word *imperator* packed more rhetorical punch than the words *res publica*—"republic"—then the Republic itself was in doubt.

The centurion, by the way, is supposed to have ended his speech by challenging Scipio's men to a fight. An indignant Scipio had him immediately executed. The rest of the captives were either tortured, if they were veterans, or distributed among his legions, if they were new recruits.

Meanwhile, to return to the war, it was around this time that Caesar's men suffered the torrential rainfall mentioned in chapter 1. Nature only added to Caesar's logistical difficulties.

Scipio knew that Caesar would have to keep moving in search of supplies. He planned to use his cavalry in order to whittle Caesar down to pieces. In short, Scipio followed a Fabian strategy. Caesar, in turn, followed Hannibal's strategy—he wanted to fight a pitched battle as soon as his veteran legions arrived. When two more of his legions came, Caesar tried to force Scipio's hand by besieging the city of Uzitta (today's Henchir Makhreba) but Scipio refused to fight a pitched battle.

Caesar's moment came on April 4 (February 4), 46 B.C. By then, his army had reached full strength. Caesar laid siege to the enemy stronghold of Thapsus, a port city about five miles east of today's Teboulba, Tunisia. Scipio came to the city's defense. A pitched battle followed two days later, on April 6 (February 6).

On the landward side of Thapsus, a narrow plain stretched as far as a wide salt lake. In this constricted terrain, Scipio's cavalry could not ride around Caesar's flanks and strangle the enemy as Hannibal's horsemen had done at Cannae. Scipio's ace was his elephants, which he stationed in front of either wing. Caesar posted two of his veteran legions on either wing. To counter the elephants, he added extra punch to the wings by dividing his fifth veteran legion in two and placing the halves in a fourth line on each wing.

But that was the end of military science and discipline. As Caesar's men were taking their final positions, the word went round that the enemy deployment was not going well; in fact, they were clearly in disorder. Caesar's more experienced officers demanded an immediate attack but he insisted on getting all his troops in position. No matter. A trumpeter sounded the advance and other trumpeters followed. The centurions tried to hold the men back but it was too late. Ever the pragmatist, Caesar called out the watchword of the day—*"Felicitas!"* or "Good luck!"—and the battle began.

Caesar's archers and slingers made short work of the elephants, which turned on their own men and trampled them. In a panic, the enemy army simply fell apart. Caesar's men butchered them, even those who tried to surrender. In the end Caesar's forces killed five thousand of the enemy.

For Caesar, Thapsus was a sloppy victory but a great one. Almost all of the enemy's generals in North Africa had been killed or had committed suicide; Labienus was one of the few to escape. But one of the suicides stung.

Caesar left Thapsus for Utica, seaport and capital of the province. The town was under the command of his last great enemy in the Senate still at large, Marcus Porcius Cato. The others were either dead, like Pompey, or recipients of Caesar's pardons, like Cicero. Having Cato accept clemency would be a propaganda coup for Caesar. It would prove that there was no fight left in the party of the Senate.

But Cato said no. He considered Caesar a tyrant and refused to be under obligation to him. Instead, Cato stood his ground and committed suicide. It was not a pretty process. He ripped out his intestines with his sword, only to have his supporters come running and get a doctor to stitch him back up. Cato then tore out the stitches and died.

When Caesar got the news, he is supposed to have said, "O Cato, I begrudge you your death; for you begrudged me the sparing of your life." Caesar knew whereof he spoke. Cato's suicide gave life to the Senate's cause. In military terms, Caesar had won. In political terms, Cato had revenge from beyond the grave. Caesar branded himself as the prince of pardons, but Cato forced the wolf to bare his teeth.

After Utica, Cato belonged to the ages, a martyr for republican liberty.

No wonder a Roman poet would write of Pompey and Caesar, a century later:

> Each for his cause can vouch a judge supreme;
> The victor, heaven: the vanquished, Cato, thee.

"Aren't You Ashamed to Hand Me Over to These Little Boys?"

After cleaning things up in North Africa and after making the by-now-standard fund-raising rounds, Caesar returned to Rome. It was a period of empowerment, reform, and celebration.

Caesar was elected dictator for ten years and censor for three, giving him power over all public officials, including senators. A wealth of public honors also flowed his way.

As early as 49 B.C., Caesar began a wave of reforms in Roman government and society that now continued to roll forward. Government, the economy, citizenship, religion, public buildings, veterans' affairs—all were affected. By far the longest-lasting reform was of the Roman calendar. Caesar gave Rome the solar calendar of 365 days plus leap year that is still in use today by most of the world (with a few adjustments in the 1700s). The new calendar started on January 1, 45 B.C.

And then came celebration. A *triumph* was a spectacular victory march through the city of Rome of a general and his army, culminating in a sacrifice to Jupiter on the Capitoline Hill and a public feast. The Senate gave Caesar permission to celebrate four triumphs in a row—something unheard of. He could not celebrate victory in the civil war, since it was improper to cheer over the death of Roman citizens. So he celebrated his victories over the Gauls—a war that seemed long ago—over the Alexandrians, over Pharnaces, and over King Juba of Numidia (glossing over Juba's Roman allies from Scipio to Cato). For four days in summer 46 B.C., victory parades filled the streets of Rome, followed by six more days of gladiatorial games, feasting, and the dedication of new public buildings. Caesar's soldiers received huge cash bonuses; citizen heads of families got small payments as well.

But celebration was premature, for there was trouble in the West. After conquering Spain in 49 B.C., Caesar made the mistake of appointing a governor who promptly squeezed the locals for money until the Spaniards responded by forcing him out of office, and then welcoming the remains of the Senate's army. The army was led by Pompey's sons, Cnaeus and Sextus, and by Caesar's former second-in-command, Labienus. Spain was the Pompeians' last hope.

Caesar could not leave such a rich and dangerous base in his enemies' hands. So in late 46 B.C., he set out on one more military expedition. His exhausted men were less than enthusiastic. As usual, Caesar made haste, leaving Rome in November and reaching Spain just a month later. The war took place in southern Spain, in the Roman province of Baetica (modern Andalusia).

Caesar had eight legions, including the veterans of the Fifth and Tenth Legions, and eight thousand cavalrymen. The enemy had thirteen legions as well as a large number of cavalrymen and light-armed auxiliaries. Most of the Pompeian forces were of dubious quality, though, so their commanders did not want to risk a battle. That made Caesar's job simple—to force them to fight.

Caesar attacked enemy town after town. At first, the usual supply problems held him back, but after a few weeks he began to make headway. Caesar began to attract enemy supporters and soldiers like a magnet. In order to hold his army together, Cnaeus Pompey had no choice but to fight.

The decisive battle took place outside the hilltown of Munda (near Seville) on March 17, 45 B.C. The Pompeians held the town, while Caesar and his men were camped below it, on the far side of a wide plain. When his scouts reported that the enemy was finally preparing to fight, Caesar flew the battle flag. He arranged his troops with the Tenth Legion on his right and the Third and Fifth Legions on the left, reinforced by the cavalry and the auxiliaries.

Although Caesar was hoping that the enemy would leave the high ground to fight on the plain, the Pompeians refused to give up their advantage. But then they saw Caesar's men hesitate, so they marched down the hill and the fight was on.

The battle of Munda was no second Thapsus, where Caesar's enemies turned and ran practically at the first sight of blood. Munda was harder fought than Pharsalus, where Pompey's legionaries had held their ground as long as they could. In fact, the enemy at Munda put up the stiffest resistance of any foe that Caesar had ever faced.

Pompey's men knew it was the end of the line. For many of them, surrender meant enslavement or execution. They had violated the terms of Caesar's pardon for the war of 49 B.C. and then they had made matters worse by revolting against Caesar's handpicked governor of Spain. On the other side, Caesar's soldiers were fired up by the presence of their commander and bolstered by experience. Besides, they wanted to get the civil war over with once and for all.

For a while, the outcome of the battle was in doubt. Unwilling to leave things to others, Caesar and Cnaeus Pompey themselves entered the fight.

The hardest fighting took place on the two flanks. Caesar's Tenth Legion, reliable as ever, began to push back the enemy's left. In order to shore up his men, Cnaeus Pompey began moving a legion on his right over to support the left. Caesar's cavalry responded by attacking the enemy's now weakened right flank.

Still, the Pompeians held on until a move by Labienus provoked an unexpected panic. Labienus ordered five cohorts—about four thousand men—to shift their position in order to protect their camp from another unit of Caesar's cavalry. To get there, Labienus's men had to cross the battlefield. Veteran soldiers would have understood their move, but to Pompey's inexperienced men, it looked like the beginning of a retreat. The bulk of his army turned and fled.

The result was a rout. Caesar's forces began to slaughter the enemy. When it was all over they killed 33,000 Pompeians, including three thousand Roman knights (very wealthy men)—or so they claimed. Caesar admitted to one thousand dead and five hundred wounded, which are huge casualty figures for him, and signs of how hard the fighting was. Labienus was one of the dead. Caesar gave his old second-in-command a proper funeral.

Various anecdotes circulated afterward about Caesar's low point during the battle. One source had him running to rally his men, who were being pushed back by the enemy. "Aren't you ashamed to hand me over to these little boys?" Caesar supposedly said. Ironic and mocking, it was a far cry from Alexander in his feathered helmet but it stirred the troops all the same.

Caesar is said to have remarked to his friends as he left the battlefield that, at Munda, for the first time ever, his life had been at risk. (Not true, as his life had been at risk before, at Dyrrachium and Alexandria, for example.) Finally, there is the report that Caesar even considered suicide at one moment during the battle, when he thought that all was lost. Perhaps.

At Munda, Caesar's men seemed old and tired but they were more experienced than the enemy and that's what counted in the end. So did Caesar's superiority in cavalry. And last but not least, there was Caesar himself, indefatigable under pressure. The consummate politician, he thought on his feet and said what needed to be said to move his men.

Caesar's campaigns in North Africa and Spain were much sloppier than anything Alexander or Hannibal ever carried out. Unlike them, he was no fancy dancer. The way he parried the cavalry charge at Pharsalus was clever, but Caesar's battle tactics offer nothing to compare with Alexander's combined-arms synergy or Hannibal's guile.

Caesar's logistics were haphazard. It is hard to imagine Alexander, the meticulous planner who crossed the Hydaspes River, tolerating Caesar's disorganized landings on the North African coast. Nor would Hannibal, the master manipulator of Cannae, have stood for the insubordination at Thapsus. And yet, Caesar got the job done, and, neither Alexander nor Hannibal would have had anything to teach him about projecting a winning image to his men.

The battle finished, the town of Munda prepared for a siege. After Caesar's men surrounded it with a ghastly "palisade" of corpses and severed heads on pikes, Munda surrendered. Cnaeus Pompey fled but his enemies caught up with him a few days later. His head too was severed and brought to Caesar.

After settling affairs and raising money, Caesar returned to Rome, which he reached in June 45 B.C. With the end of the Spanish campaign, the civil war was over. Now came the hard part—pacifying the political class of Rome.

ESSENCE OF DECISION

Success at closing the net requires four things: strategy, agility, new infrastructure, and morale management.

A victor's biggest mistake after winning a great battle is to expect success to fall into his lap. On the contrary, since necessity is the mother of invention, the vanquished are likely to be more ingenious than ever, and perhaps even more dangerous. The victor has to judge his next move correctly. He must choose the right strategy. Is it the moment to negotiate or to press home his advantage? If he does attack, what's the right target—the enemy's capital, his army, or his leadership? Assuming that he chooses correctly and attacks successfully, he then needs to decide how he will know when the war is won. Does he require unconditional surrender or will he be willing to allow the defeated enemy to negotiate terms? And if his attack fails and the enemy bounces back, should he consider cutting his losses and pulling out?

To carry out his strategy requires agility. Winning a pitched battle is not the same as carrying out pursuit, taking a city by siege, countering raids and ambushes, or winning over civilian populations.

And it will do no good to plan the next move correctly unless a commander has the resources to carry it out. All three of our commanders needed more money and manpower after their great battlefield victories.

Finally, they had to overcome the frustrations of a long war and maintain support both in their armies and in their political base.

Our commanders faced these challenges with varying success. Note, at the outset, that the quality of the enemies they faced varied greatly. Alexander faced a very able foe in Spitamenes and no mean ones in Bessus and Porus, but none of them could match his resources. Very few people in the Persian empire felt a deep loyalty to the government; not many men were willing to die for Darius or Bessus.

Caesar faced a great tactician in Labienus, but luckily Labienus never held supreme command. But Caesar did have to face the determination of a Cato, the wiliness of a Juba, and the spirit of Pompey's sons. His enemies were awash in money as well. Yet Caesar was fighting a civil war. He was no foreign invader and he pardoned his enemies. Most people found it easy to switch from Pompey's side to his once the wind began blowing Caesar's way.

In Rome, Hannibal faced the greatest republic in the ancient world. Rome came up with and implemented a brilliant counterstrategy to Hannibal—the Fabian strategy. Yes, there were bumps on the road to implementation, but in the end, Rome deployed the strategy forcefully. Support for Rome's government ran very deep among its citizenry. Rome's central-Italian allies were nearly as loyal and patriotic. They hated Hannibal and would never surrender without a fight. The longer the war lasted the greater the chance that Rome's generals would learn from the master and adopt successful battlefield techniques. All the while, they had plenty of money and manpower. Truly, Hannibal had the most difficult enemy to beat.

How well did the three captains each close the net after winning on the battlefield? Caesar followed the best strategy. He correctly concluded that his first target after winning at Pharsalus was the escaped enemy commander Pompey. After Pompey's murder, Caesar turned to his pressing financial need, even though it gave the enemy's army breathing space in North Africa. Likewise, he dealt with a dangerous attack in the East by Pharnaces and a politico-military meltdown in Rome before finally engaging the enemy.

Hannibal chose the worst strategy. His first and biggest mistake was not attacking Rome after Cannae. His second mistake was letting the war drag on after it had become apparent that his plan had failed. Hannibal counted on winning a critical mass of its allies away from Rome. He did not.

Those allies whom Hannibal did persuade turned out to be a burden. He had wanted a strategic lever but instead he got a chain. Hannibal's plan to break Rome's alliance system was his biggest strategic miscalculation. His masterstroke at Cannae had opened a sudden window of opportunity, but he had to jump through it.

Had he been in Hannibal's shoes after Cannae, Caesar would have marched on Rome, since he never had much use for the rulebook. He believed in pushing fortune, not waiting at its knees. So what if he lacked manpower and supplies? As in Epirus or North Africa, Caesar would have planned on improvising. He knew how much the combination of audacity and diplomacy could wring out of a hostile population and he would squeeze everything he could out of the environs of Rome. Then again, Caesar could carry out sieges. Hannibal could not.

Hannibal's post-Cannae Italian strategy was flawed as well, relying too much on cunning and too little on force. And yet, he had no choice, starved as he was of men and money. Carthage certainly made an error in not reinforcing Hannibal and focusing on the war in Italy instead of squandering its resources over too many different military theaters. If he knew Carthaginian politics better, Hannibal might have been able to get what he wanted from the Carthaginian Senate, but he hadn't been in Carthage since he was nine years old.

Alexander showed excellent strategic judgment after Gaugamela in his pursuit first of Darius and then Bessus, but his actions afterward are questionable. Maybe he was right to spill all the blood that he did to defeat Spitamenes, but he might have been better off writing off Sogdiana and saving his resources. India was a magnificent obsession that could have led to an empire like no other—if Alexander could keep it. But that was a highly dubious prospect.

When it comes to agility, Alexander is the standout. He succeeded in the greatest variety of terrains, from the desert to the Himalayas. He excelled equally at pitched battle, at countering desert raiders, at laying siege to rugged fortresses, and at mountain fighting. War elephants were a shock to western soldiers but he turned them into nothing more than a minor inconvenience. After failing the test against the Persian fleet under Memnon, Alexander turned things around and built a navy.

Hannibal was the least agile of the three commanders because of his failure at siegecraft. Nothing else did as much damage to his war effort in Italy. Caesar was agile enough to handle a great variety of terrains, but he didn't take on so many different ways of war as convincingly as Alexander. True, Caesar engaged in urban combat in Alexandria but he almost lost. And he brushed off the elephants at Thapsus, but it is doubtful that the enemy knew how to handle them.

When it came to getting more money, Alexander was the most successful, but he had the easiest target. Had he wintered in Babylon, the Persians might have put up a fight at Persepolis or, worse yet, brought their treasures to safety. But speed and a good, hard push gave Alexander all the money he would ever need.

Caesar had to work harder to fund himself, but he succeeded. Between his limited manpower and nonexistent siege capability, Hannibal was hamstrung in his efforts to get all the money he needed from Italy, and the Carthaginian Senate did little to make things better for him.

None of the three generals had a perfect solution to his manpower needs. Alexander did the best job of raising new troops but they left him sitting on a volcano. Nobody knew whether he could maintain the loyalty of a largely non-Macedonian army, and no one was sure that they could match the fighting skill of the phalanx.

Caesar found new recruits but the deciding factor in pitched battle was having veterans. He managed to hold on to enough of them, but only barely.

Hannibal never filled his manpower needs. Without reinforcements, he was doomed to failure. He lacked the political support at home that Caesar and Alexander each could count on.

But Hannibal did excel in one area: maintaining his army's capability and morale. Alexander and Caesar each suffered multiple mutinies and near mutinies. In fifteen years in Italy, Hannibal faced not one. No one held the loyalty of his men as well as Hannibal did. They were still willing to die for him even when they left Italy for Africa, where they had to fight to keep Carthage safe rather than to line their own purses with the loot of Italy. Small wonder that, in spite of the outcome of his war, Hannibal remains one of the most admired generals in history.

6

KNOWING WHEN TO STOP

IN SUMMER 324 B.C., IN THE CITY OF OPIS (NEAR TODAY'S BAGHDAD), ALEXANDER
invited the cream of his army and his government to an enormous banquet. The sources, unsure of the numbers, record a rumor that nine thousand people were in attendance.

It was a great show—prizewinning political theater—that much is
certain. The purpose was to celebrate victory. Not the successful return
of Alexander and his army from India the winter before but a more dubious success. Just a few days earlier, Alexander had put down a mutiny. The
trouble came after he announced plans to send most of his Macedonian
veterans home to Macedon. They were ten thousand men, a large group. He
would replace them with new recruits from Macedon and Persia. Old and in-
jured, the veterans were also fierce conservatives and hated Alexander's pro-
Persian policies, however limited those policies were. So they rose in protest.

Unlike in India, Alexander refused to budge. He wanted a new army and
he wanted it loyal to him because he had plans for new wars. Alexander had
the ringleaders of the mutiny executed and offered top military commands
to Iranian officers. Within a few days, the Macedonians realized that Alexander was serious about having his own way, so they apologized, and it was
all over.

Having won, Alexander was magnanimous. He gave the leading Macedonians the best seats at the banquet, where they surrounded him in a circle.
The senior Persians sat in a ring around them, surrounded in turn by a
circle of high-ranking representatives of the other peoples of the empire.

Like all ancient Greek or Macedonian meals, the banquet began with a prayer. Ritual called for filling a wine cup and pouring out a few drops in honor of the gods. Alexander gave the Macedonians the honor of ladling their wine from the same huge bowl from which he would drink. Greek and Persian priests began the ceremony, and then Alexander led the prayer. He prayed for "various blessings and especially for unity among Macedonians and Persians as partners in the government."

Remarkable sentiments, but they were just words. The seating plan at the Opis banquet told the real story—Persians would play a role in Alexander's regime but Macedonians (and Greeks) would monopolize the inner circle. But they would be *his* Macedonians and support *his* policy of working with the Persians. They would not be narrow-minded "Macedonia first" types who would challenge the king.

We'll never know if Alexander would have succeeded in his plans, because he barely had a chance to put them into practice. By the next summer, the king was dead.

About 125 years later and about fifteen hundred miles to the west, an even more bittersweet victory party took place. It was summer 205 B.C. outside Croton, Italy. Croton was a small port on the toe of the Italian boot, with a harbor on the Ionian Sea, looking eastward toward Greece. A once great city, famous for its beautiful women and its wealth, Croton was a ghost town after centuries of war and ruin. Only two glories were left—the temple of Hera and Hannibal.

In 205, the area around Croton was all that remained of Hannibal's once vast Italian holdings. It was a grim place, hardly worth keeping, but the Carthaginian government insisted that Hannibal stay. The rulers in Carthage thought he was distracting the Romans, but the Romans had him cornered. Hannibal had his hands full, what with the Roman army nearby, an epidemic, a food shortage, and the bandits who roamed the area. Still, he held his forces together for two more years until the government finally recalled them to Africa, in autumn 203.

Meanwhile, Hannibal made a magnificent gesture. Not far from Croton, on a rocky promontory on the coast, stood the sanctuary of Hera Lacinia. In spite of Croton's decline, this famous and opulent shrine, which contained a solid gold column, had maintained its prestige.

It was here that Hannibal paid tribute to all that he had done. Hannibal placed in the temple a large history of his achievements since leaving Spain, thirteen years earlier, inscribed on a bronze tablet. The text was bilingual, written in Punic and in Greek.

It was a monument in the boondocks. It might have seemed like an empty gesture, but it made Hannibal immortal. It was still standing about fifty years later when the Greek historian Polybius saw it. Polybius took the backbone of his account of Hannibal's war in Italy from the inscription, and Polybius's book is the most trustworthy history of Hannibal that we have. In a real sense, our knowledge of Hannibal in Italy today goes back to the Lacinian inscription.

Hannibal lived for about another twenty-five years. If he ever regretted the long road that led from Cannae to Croton, he shouldn't have. All his men and elephants did less to bring him fame than did one bronze tablet.

One hundred sixty years later and about four hundred miles to the northwest, in October 45 B.C. another victory party took place, this one loud and raucous. Caesar's troops marched through the streets of Rome in triumph—for the fifth time. The previous summer 46, Caesar had stunned Rome by putting on four successive triumphs in just one month: one each for Gaul, Egypt, Pontus, and Africa. Now he celebrated victory in Spain.

Just like the earlier triumphs, the Spanish celebration was splendid. Each event had a theme, as it were—ivory for Africa and silver for Spain—which was used to decorate the floats in the parade. Silver symbolized both Spain's famous mines and Caesar's wealth.

In 46, Caesar tactfully avoided reference to the civil war, since a triumph was supposed to mark a victory over *foreign* armies, but in 45, he showed his true colors. He had fought and beaten fellow Romans in Spain, the sons of Pompey, and he made no bones about it. Caesar didn't care, he had more important things in mind than Roman sensibilities. He was already gearing up for a new war in the East.

But many Romans did care. One of them was Gaius Pontius Aquila, one of the ten tribunes. As Caesar rode past the reviewing stand in his triumphal chariot, nine of the tribunes stood in salute, but Aquila remained seated. The dictator was furious. "Ask me for the Republic back, Tribune Aquila!" Caesar called out. Nor was that the end of it. For days, whenever Caesar promised something in public, he added bitingly, "That is, if Pontius Aquila will let me."

Caesar capped his Spanish triumph with the usual public banquet for the people of Rome. Then, four days later, he feasted them again, which was unprecedented. His motive, he said, was to put on a lavish spread in order to make up for cutting corners in the first meal. Caesar was a politician, though, and perhaps the real reason was that he felt the public's anger and he wanted to make amends.

Five months later, he was dead. Caesar was stabbed twenty-three times by a mob of senators. One of them was Pontius Aquila.

Things did not end well for any of our three commanders. Alexander and Caesar had military glory, at least—although neither one ended his last campaign on a high note. Hannibal did not even have that.

True, Hannibal helped Carthage recover after it had lost to Rome. His postwar statesmanship bought his country two generations of peace and prosperity. But he was paving the road to damnation for Carthage. After Hannibal, Rome would never trust Carthage again and eventually, it avenged Cannae in a way that made that battle's carnage look like a pillow fight.

Neither Alexander nor Caesar bequeathed a legacy of peace. Caesar left Rome one generation of war, Alexander left his empire two generations of war.

Things could have gone differently. Alexander could have come back much sooner from the East and then devoted himself to governing his empire instead of building a new army for more fighting. Hannibal might have left Italy years earlier and protected Carthage and its empire instead of chasing an unreachable victory. Caesar might have negotiated a peace agreement with his Roman opponents years earlier. But that wasn't in their character.

Alexander, Hannibal, and Caesar were conquerors, not statesmen. Conquerors keep on going until they and their men drop from exhaustion or die. Statesmen know when to stop.

They remind us of the wisdom of Winston Churchill, who wrote: "Those who can win a war well can rarely make a good peace, and those who could make a good peace would never have won the war."

ALEXANDER

When Alexander returned from India, he had conquered an empire. The question now was, could he keep it? New empires do not govern themselves. They require enormous attention to the dynasty, the ruling elite, the army, and the administration. While Alexander was not blind to these matters, he was not overly interested in them either.

It was hard to listen to bureaucrats drone on when you still heard the trumpets.

Misgoverning an Empire

Alexander's empire comprised two million square miles from Greece to India—three thousand miles as the crow flies, from end to end. It included dozens of different peoples and languages. How to hold them together?

The first and biggest issue was the new empire's identity. Alexander claimed to be the king of Asia but he acted as if he expected a European elite to hold the upper hand. That was likely to offend everyone. It also conflicted with inconvenient facts of demography. Alexander had veteran Macedonian troops but he distrusted them. He ordered new recruits from Macedon, but Macedon was short of manpower and it needed soldiers to deal with new threats in Greece. The one place where Alexander got plenty of new troops, Iran, was full of people who resented his conquest. Alexander faced a dilemma.

Macedon and the Persian empire offered lessons for governing, both good and bad. Philip of Macedon had done an excellent job of integrating local elites into the ruling class by bringing their sons to his court. He did much the same with their followers by adding them to the Macedonian army. Philip was equally good at winning over foreign states by a combination of threats and bribes. He also founded new cities in territory that he conquered, and they could serve as bases for governing. Otherwise, though, he showed little interest in administration or state infrastructure. He created no bureaucracy and no ladder of offices to tie the middle class to the new regime.

The Persians ruled through a system of provincial governors, royal offi-

cials, military colonies, and constant deals and negotiations with local elites.
Compared with other empires, the Persians governed with a light touch.
There was little attempt to "Persianize" their subjects. While that made the
Persians popular it also left them weak. Revolts were frequent and support
for the empire was thin. When Alexander defeated the Persian army, very
little held the civilian population together. Rome, with its close-knit society
and alliance system, could pull together and bounce back after a defeat like
Cannae. Persia could not rebound from Gaugamela.

Alexander showed leadership in some areas. After neglecting to super-
vise his provincial governors, he caught up. He recognized the severe shortage of Macedonian soldiers and began to build a new army. He took a stab
at integrating a few Iranians into a new, Macedonian-dominated imperial
elite.

But Alexander did not confront the even bigger problems of administering his new empire. Successful empires need large numbers of immigrants
from the home country—soldiers, administrators, businessmen, propagandists, and settlers. They need schools to produce a steady stream of loyal
public servants.

Empires need big garrisons and bases full of willing inhabitants, and not
what Alexander had left behind: a string of vest-pocket-sized "Alexandrias"
whose unhappy inhabitants had been uprooted and forced to live there. Plutarch claimed that Alexander founded seventy cities, but that was a wild exaggeration. The best modern scholarly estimate is that he founded only ten,
of which all but two were on the eastern edge of his empire. It remained for
Alexander's successors to build the great new cities of the East, from Pergamum (in Anatolia) and Antioch (in Syria) to Ai Khanum (in Bactria). In
short, Alexander did not establish the administrative structures his empire
needed to survive.

This isn't surprising. Alexander did not think in such terms. For him,
government wasn't about institutions, much less about citizens. It was about
a great man, his friends, and the army.

Instead of building administrative structures, Alexander did what he
liked doing best—he went back to war.

The provincial governors—satraps—and top officials needed to be
guided by a strong hand from the center. But while Alexander was away in
the East for five years starting in 330 B.C., he paid little or no attention to

the rest of his empire. The result was maladministration, corruption, disloyalty, and rebellion. More than half of the twenty-three provinces of the empire experienced either rebellion or a pretender to the throne.

When Alexander came back to the West, he made an effort to improve things, but it was too little. Opposition was predictable and Alexander ran into plenty of it. If he had fought half as hard against administrative abuse as he fought against Darius, he might have consolidated his rule. Instead, he again turned his attention to the military, where he radically reformed recruitment and began yet another campaign of conquest.

As soon as he reached Iran in December 325, Alexander began cleaning house. In short order he had four provincial governors executed, along with several pretenders to the throne. They were all Iranians, and Alexander replaced them with Macedonians. Earlier, he had kept as many of Darius's governors in place as he could, but now, only four Iranian governors were left. Alexander executed Macedonian officers and troops as well but not Macedonian governors, in spite of their misbehavior.

Alexander wanted cooperation in government between Macedonians (and Greeks) on the one hand, and Persians on the other. But he didn't trust the Persians and the Macedonians didn't see things Alexander's way. They had even less interest than he in governing the former Persian empire. They wanted to loot it.

Alexander backed an ambitious strategy of sharing power with local elites. If he really was the king of Asia, this made perfect sense. He took modest steps forward but even those provoked cries of betrayal and sellout from the Macedonians. For example, they grimaced when, in early 324, Alexander made one hundred of his top officers marry Iranian wives and made ten thousand ordinary soldiers legalize their relationships with the Asian women they had met on campaign. Alexander himself married Stateira, daughter of Darius III, as well possibly as Parysatis, daughter of Artaxerxes III, one of Darius's predecessors on the throne. A polygamist, Alexander had already married Roxane, daughter of a powerful Bactrian noble.

When it came to the degree of compromise needed to govern a state that stretched from the Indian Ocean to the Adriatic Sea, few Macedonians "got it." Some of Alexander's old friends understood. Hephaestion, for example, served as grand vizier, the Persian officer in charge of court ceremonial— and Alexander introduced a great deal of Persian ceremonial. Peucestas, who served as satrap of Persis (modern Fars), the old Persian heartland, learned to speak Persian and wore Persian dress. Seleucus actually loved the Sogdian princess he married, Apama, the daughter of the rebel baron Spitamenes. Ptolemy made wise use of the principle of compromise with native culture when he later became king of Egypt. But these men were the exceptions among Macedonians, not the rule.

Or maybe the Macedonians were realists. When you came right down to it, most Macedonians agreed with Parmenio that Alexander wanted too big an empire. They couldn't say so, of course, because they loved and feared their king. But actions speak louder than words. Many Macedonians behaved as if the empire was ungovernable and would inevitably break down into local units. In Bactria, Egypt, and Macedon itself, local rulers rebuffed Alexander or engaged in outright rebellion. Not that they cared, but they were following time-worn *Persian* precedent.

The default mode of the Persian empire had been devolution—that is, the transfer of power from the central government to local government. When the Great King chose to make an issue of it, devolution became rebellion and it was put down by force. More often, however, the authorities in Persepolis, Susa, and Babylon simply accepted the fact that the governors of Egypt, western Anatolia, Bactria, and Sogdiana—not to mention the more-or-less-lost province of India—would do as they pleased.

Local power was one problem for the Persians and for Alexander. Another was the law of unintended consequences, which reigned in full force in so big an empire. One case in point was the rise of a mercenary problem in Greece because of developments as far off as Afghanistan (Bactria).

Cape Taenarum, in southern Greece near Sparta, became the headquarters of an ancient "Murder Incorporated"—a pirate's nest of mercenaries and brigands looking for trouble. Alexander's conquests caused the problem. Some of the men at Cape Taenarum were political exiles from the regime change in hundreds of cities that Alexander had conquered. Others had been let loose by Alexander in 325, when he ordered all satraps to disband their mercenary armies, which he rightly considered a threat to him—in Bactria, for instance, the mercenaries had rebelled. Still other mercenaries—six thousand, in fact—came to Cape Taenarum along with Harpalus, Alexander's boyhood friend and treasurer, who ran off to Greece in 325 with a small fortune and a private army.

From one point of view, the mercenaries of Cape Taenarum were a cynical gift to Alexander, because they kept the Greek city-states on edge and out of Macedon's hair. From another point of view they threatened Macedon, because it was possible that the Greeks would buy off the mercenaries and use them in a revolt. The upshot was that Alexander had to keep troops in Macedon, which empowered the governor there, Antipater, and denied Alexander valuable military manpower in the Middle East.

The Greek city-states were a problem again by 324, as they had been before 330. Athens was the biggest headache. The Athenians refused entry to Harpalus's mercenaries but they gave asylum to Harpalus himself and to his money. They pocketed the money and shooed Harpalus out. (He was murdered soon afterward.) Meanwhile, Athens ignored an order from Alexander to every state in Greece. Alexander wanted the Greek states to accept political exiles back home, which would have reduced the number of mercenaries but sent many governments teetering. Athens stood to lose its control of the island of Samos, so it kept the exiles out. Once again, a problem of administration and authority loomed for Alexander.

But he much preferred to deal with military matters. Ever since the Macedonians had mutinied in India, he wanted to do something about their power in the army. He made his move in 324. As the story of the mutiny and banquet shows, Alexander succeeded in sending his infirm or older soldiers home to Macedon.

The numbers are telling. About ten thousand Macedonian infantrymen and one thousand five-hundred Macedonian horsemen went home. Alexander was left with thirteen thousand infantrymen and two thousand cavalrymen—a group consisting of both Macedonians and Greek mercenaries. He ordered new recruits from Macedon to replace the men he sent home, but they never arrived. Even if they had, they would have been outnumbered by the new troops from all over Iran who were now pouring into Alexander's army.

Alexander needed a new military force after returning from India, and he got it. In 327 B.C., Alexander had ordered thirty thousand Easterners to be trained as Macedonian infantrymen, and by 324 they were ready. The next year, preparations were under way for a new war, and additional troops had arrived. Alexander's boyhood friend Peucestas, governor of Persis, recruited twenty thousand soldiers from his province. The governors of two provinces in Anatolia sent mercenaries as well. A small number of Iranians had already been enrolled in the elite Companion Cavalry.

Looking ahead, another source of new troops would soon be available— the sons of Alexander's veterans and Asian women. When he sent their fathers home, Alexander kept these boys for training as soldiers.

In short, Alexander was well on his way to creating a new army. If it proved loyal to him, and if it was anywhere near as effective as his old army, it could have put down any revolt in Alexander's empire—or at least in most of it, India being far away and full of hostile armies. The new army might even have carried out Alexander's new conquests. But loyalty and effectiveness were both big ifs.

New Worlds to Conquer

Governing was boring. Alexander wanted to be a conqueror. As a contemporary wrote, "Alexander was always insatiable when it came to conquest, he aimed at being the lord and master of everyone." He had hardly shaken the dust of India off his boots when he was ready for new wars. Audacity, as usual, was his hallmark. The first stage, but only the first stage, was Arabia.

The Arabian peninsula had not been part of the Persian empire, but that didn't stop Alexander from wanting to conquer at least part if not all of it. Arabia was famous for its myrrh and frankincense and the wealth in trade they generated, and it offered naval way stations for the voyage to India. Ancient seafarers avoided the open sea and looked for coastal harbors to break up a journey.

Alexander planned to conquer and settle the Arabian coast of the Persian Gulf. A prime goal was the fertile island of Bahrain and the mainland port opposite it, which was a terminal of the spice trade. But Alexander may have planned to go farther, into what is today Oman and Yemen, to control the areas where spice was produced and to gain ports on the south Arabian coast to use for the trade route to the Red Sea.

As he looked ahead, Alexander gave a much bigger role to warships than in his previous campaigns. In affairs of war, he was gifted with a profound capacity for growth; he was a man of enormous versatility. The success of Nearchus and his fleet, sailing from India to Iran, seems to have inspired Alexander. Now he knew that sea power could project force with little support from land. Sea power multiplied that mobility which the king so prized. Not only the Persian Gulf but other seas could be highways for his armies.

The invasion of Arabia was to be a seaborne expedition, and Alexander would personally sail with the fleet. In preparation for the war, Alexander had a new harbor built at Babylon with room for one thousand warships—a huge number by ancient standards. He sent recruiting agents to Syria and Phoenicia (modern Lebanon) to find sailors. Since timber was scarce near Babylon, he had the ships built in far-off regions, transported and reassembled on the Euphrates and sailed downstream to Babylon. By spring 323 the first ships were practicing drills on the river at Babylon.

Few people thought Alexander's war plans would end with Arabia. It was rumored that he wanted the fleet to continue past Arabia and to sail around Africa to the Pillars of Hercules (Straits of Gibraltar). If so, that would fit in with other reported plans to conquer Carthage and Italy. Ever since Carthage supported Tyre against Alexander in 332, he had had an ax to grind against it. Alexander's uncle had already invaded Italy and achieved considerable success there before being killed by a traitor in 331 B.C. It was only natural for Alexander to pick up the torch.

In spring 323, ambassadors from Carthage, Libya, and various Italian states came to see Alexander in Babylon. One of those states was Rome, which was a rising power in central Italy at the time. After Alexander's death, his papers are supposed to have revealed plans to construct yet another one thousand warships in the eastern Mediterranean and to build a military road across North Africa.

Finally, Alexander was planning another fleet to explore the Caspian Sea and to find what he hoped (in vain) would be a river route to Sogdiana (modern Uzbekistan and part of Tajikistan).

Alexander had already conquered more empire than he was likely to be able to govern. But he wanted more.

"The Great Horn Is Broken"

The last eight months of Alexander's life have the quality of a soap opera as told in a college frat house. The main themes were sex and violence, washed down with gigantic amounts of alcohol.

Since his return from India, Alexander journeyed here and there in

Iran and Mesopotamia, attending to one piece of business after another. He was full of energy but he did not travel light. A huge royal entourage accompanied Alexander. Every trip was expensive and complicated but rarely unpleasant for those at the top, since the locals fell over one another to wine and dine the king and his court.

In autumn 324 the party stopped—Hephaestion died. He was Alexander's closest friend and perhaps once his lover. Hephaestion died in Ecbatana (modern Hamadan) in western Iran. After a week of games and heavy drinking, he came down with a fever. On the seventh day, Hephaestion felt better and began eating and drinking again, against his doctor's advice; he died later that day. Suspecting poison, Alexander had the doctor crucified. Then the king went wild with grief over his lost companion. He went through elaborate mourning rituals, commissioned an enormous monument in Babylon, and had Hephaestion proclaimed a "hero"—that is, a demigod—though the priests whom he consulted balked. Perhaps they figured it would cheapen Alexander's own status as a god if they spread the honor around.

Hephaestion had supported the king in everything. Recently, he had been the mainstay of Alexander's pro-Persian policy. Alexander even had them both marry daughters of Darius III, which made them brothers-in-law; Alexander hoped their children would be cousins. Now, Alexander was on his own.

In winter 324 to 323, Alexander was busy with a campaign against the tribes of the Zagros Mountains in western Iran. The Persians used to pay them protection money for safe passage through the region, but Alexander wanted to break them. He succeeded but only temporarily—a few years later the mountaineers were back to their old business.

In early 323 Alexander and his court went to Babylon. With preparations for the Arabian campaign, embassies from the West, and plans to memorialize Hephaestion, there was plenty to keep him busy. Yet the parties didn't stop. In late May, Alexander celebrated the priests' decision to let Hephaestion be worshiped with a round of celebrations. At one of them, a banquet thrown by a Greek, Alexander came down with a fever. It was May 31, 323 B.C. He never recovered. Eleven days later, on June 10, Alexander died. He was about a month shy of his thirty-third birthday.

"The great horn is broken," says the Book of Daniel, in what is usually taken to be a reference to the death of Alexander. The phrase captures some of the shock the world felt at his sudden and unexpected demise. One minute, he was the all-victorious conqueror and then suddenly, he was gone.

Some people at the time saw the hand of Providence at work. Others turned to rumor, guesswork, and conspiracy theories: Was Alexander poisoned? Did he drink himself to death? Was he lonely and depressed?

The most credible version of what happened is that Alexander contracted a fever. He refused to take it seriously and continued working, even as the fever got worse. Finally, on the ninth day, the fever got so high that he took to his bed and lost the ability to speak. Two days later he fell into a coma and died.

Alexander did not behave prudently when he got sick, but then, he thought he was a god. His body had to bear the brunt of an accumulation of war wounds, including three he had acquired in Bactria, Sogdiana, and India—all unnecessary campaigns. The Indian wounds had been life-threatening. If poison cannot be ruled out as a cause of death, it seems less likely a contributing factor than these wounds.

"The music must always play," says the poet. Alexander too probably felt that way. But suddenly, at the age of thirty-two, the music was over. All that was left was "the unmentionable odor of death."

Unmaking an Empire

On his deathbed Alexander said that his empire should go "to the strongest." He also said that his leading friends would hold "great funeral games" in his honor—those were his last words, in fact—or so men claimed afterward. The fight over the succession had begun.

Alexander's marshals were hard men. They were, nearly all of them, believers in Macedon first. They had no interest in bringing the Persian elite into a big tent—nearly all of them immediately abandoned the Asian wives whom Alexander had forced them to marry—nor did they want to go off and invade new lands, not when they already had such rich territories in their hands. Some of them wanted to hold Alexander's empire together, but most of them were content to grab whatever piece of it they could get. They loved to fight and had no hesitation about going to war to take what they wanted. No one in Alexander's family could stop them.

When Alexander died, he left Heracles, an illegitimate son of his mistress Barsine, widow of Memnon of Rhodes. His wife Roxane was pregnant and eventually gave birth to a son, Alexander IV. Alexander's half brother, Philip Arrhidaeus, was a full-grown man, but he was intellectually disabled.

In principle, Philip Arrhidaeus—now Philip III—and soon the infant Alexander IV were elected co-kings of Macedon. Real power lay in the hands of Alexander the Great's generals.

Alexander did not choose to die young but he did choose not to produce an heir early. If he had followed those who advised him to marry before leaving Macedon in 334, Alexander might have left a ten-year-old legitimate son at the time of his death instead of an incapable brother and an unborn child.

To be sure, producing an heir would not have been without risks. As he grew up, Alexander's son could have become the focus for enemies and rivals of the king—just as young Alexander himself had once been to his father, King Philip. As long as King Alexander was the only adult male member of the Argead royal line, he had no rivals to worry about. Yet his leaving no legitimate heir forced his family to pay the price after Alexander's untimely death. Philip III was murdered in 317 and Alexander IV in 311. Heracles was murdered by 309. It was the end of the glorious dynasty of Philip and Alexander. Macedon would have new kings but they would come from different families.

Alexander's empire did not survive either. Conquering an empire of two million square miles in eleven years was the work of a master. Dismembering it during the next fifty years was the work of a committee. What Alexander built up, his successors tore apart. Sixty years after Alexander invaded the Persian empire, Greeks and Macedonians still ruled most of what he had conquered, but they had ripped it into small pieces.

In fairness, even if Alexander had lived to a ripe old age and left a full-grown heir behind, he would have had trouble maintaining his empire. The Persians had never been able to keep control of India, Thrace, Macedon, or Greece, although they had invaded all of them. They barely held on to the ever-rebellious provinces of Egypt and Anatolia. And they didn't attempt to add Arabia, Carthage, and Italy to their possessions, as Alexander was planning.

Within months of Alexander's death in 323 B.C., Greece rose in revolt.

A year later, in 322, Alexander's generals began fighting one another. The conflict between them, known as the Wars of the Successors, lasted nearly fifty years, until 275 B.C.

Fifty years after Alexander's death, the map of Alexander's empire now looked something like this: Macedon was an independent kingdom, as was Egypt—which also controlled Libya, Israel, Phoenicia, Cyprus, and the Mediterranean coast of Anatolia. Northwest Anatolia was the small but rich kingdom of Pergamum. The heart of the old Persian empire, from Anatolia to Bactria, was still a single kingdom, ruled from Babylon. But India and northeastern Iran had broken away. So had most of the Greek city-states.

Descendants of Alexander's generals ruled the three largest states. The family of Antigonus ruled Macedon, Ptolemy and his children ruled Egypt, and Seleucus and his descendants ruled from Anatolia to Bactria. Pergamum was founded by Alexander's general Lysimachus, but control passed to another family.

Alexander's generals had created the kingdoms of the Hellenistic Era, as historians call the years between 323 and 30 B.C. Alexander had laid the foundation by conquering the Persian empire, but the result looked nothing like what he had planned.

Ironically, the Hellenistic Era bore a certain resemblance to the Persian empire before Alexander. Back then, the Greek peninsula and the Balkans as well as India had maintained their independence, as they did in the Hellenistic period. Egypt and western Anatolia were semi-independent under the Persians and fully independent in the new era. Under the Persians, a great land empire in northwest Asia extended from the Mediterranean to the Hindu Kush, and so it did again under the Seleucid kings. The only difference, of course, was that Persians had ruled the old empire while Greeks and Macedonians ruled the new one.

The saddest irony concerns Macedonia. Alexander's military needs stripped the kingdom of manpower. Few of his soldiers ever came home. Relatively little of the new wealth that he created found its way to Macedon. In fact, Alexander left the Macedonian state weaker than he had found it. Macedonians ruled from vast new realms but the old country suffered.

HANNIBAL

The war in Italy was lost—and Spain and Sicily too. The question before Carthage now was what it could salvage of the situation. The same question confronted Hannibal. But his interests and those of his country were not the same. Now, more than ever, he faced political as well as military challenges.

In a country that crucified failed generals, Hannibal had first of all to survive. Then he had to consider whether his military skills could still help Carthage. Finally, he had to see if he could transform his talents in the field into the skills of statesmanship that might buy Carthage the best peace it could get.

Hannibal's Rival: Scipio

In autumn 203, Hannibal came home. After fifteen years of fighting up and down the Italian boot, he had been recalled to Carthage.

When he landed in Africa in 203 B.C., his countrymen wanted Hannibal to save them. He would have to reach deep into his stock of magic to pull that off.

A little more than a year before, a Roman army had arrived in Africa, led by Publius Cornelius Scipio. In that short period, the army brought Carthage to its knees. Scipio literally burned out one Carthaginian army and defeated another in battle; overthrew Carthage's most important ally, King Syphax of Numidia, and replaced him with a pro-Roman king, Masinissa; and forced Carthage to sue for peace. Scipio imposed terms that deprived Carthage of all its overseas possessions and its navy, and that included a large indemnity.

Harsh terms, but Scipio could have asked for more. If he didn't, it was because time wasn't on his side. Carthage had enormously strong defensive walls, which meant it could withstand a long siege. Scipio's term of office was limited and his political enemies at Rome were sharpening their knives. So he made the best treaty he could and sent it to Rome, where after some grumbling, it was ratified. Unfortunately for Scipio, the Carthaginians had second thoughts. They believed in Hannibal.

They were wrong. If time was unfriendly to Scipio, it was downright hostile to Carthage. The Carthaginians had kept Hannibal in Italy much too long, well past the time when he could win the war there, because they wanted to tie Rome's hands. But it hadn't worked and Rome had invaded Africa, even with Hannibal still in Italy.

Scipio had done so much damage in Africa that by the time Hannibal arrived, he had very little chance of defeating Scipio. Carthage should have accepted its fate and made peace. Instead, hoping for one last hurrah, the city recalled Hannibal and his men from Italy. They believed that Hannibal and the army that returned with him—probably, fifteen thousand men—could form the nucleus of a force that would drive out the Romans. They didn't know when to stop.

Scipio was Rome's greatest general. He came from a fighting family. As mentioned earlier, he had served at the battles of the Ticinus and Cannae, but he made his name in Spain. There, he inherited from his father and uncle a policy of making war on the Carthaginians. They failed but he succeeded.

Scipio wasn't just a great general: he was Hannibal's best student. In fifteen years of fighting in Italy, Hannibal had taught Rome how to wage war. Ironically, he seems not to have had equally apt pupils in Carthage. But it was probably easier to imitate Hannibal from a distance. Great men tend to use up all the air in a room.

From Hannibal, Scipio learned how to be a great and charismatic leader who emphasized mobility and surprise in battle. He trained his men to fight with a professionalism that Rome's citizen militias lacked. Under his inspired leadership, they were the equal of Carthage's armies.

After capturing New Carthage (209 B.C.) and defeating Hannibal's brother Hasdrubal in the battle of Baecula (208 B.C.), Scipio went on to drive the Carthaginians out of Spain altogether. He won his final and greatest Spanish battlefield victory at Ilipa (206 B.C.). Near modern Seville, a large Roman army under Scipio met an even larger Carthaginian army under a general named Hasdrubal Gisgo (no relation to Hannibal or his brother Hasdrubal).

Scipio had drilled his best troops—25,000 Romans and Italian allies— and turned them into an excellent fighting force. Hasdrubal Gisgo's soldiers were not as good. To add to his advantage, Scipio tricked the enemy by putting his best infantrymen on the wings instead of in the center, where the Romans usually placed their best soldiers. He attacked and defeated the Carthaginian flanks, and once they collapsed, the Carthaginian center followed.

Scipio won the battle and the war. Carthage lost its empire in Spain and with it, a major source of its money and manpower. But Scipio wasn't done. He had huge ambition and an audacious vision to sustain it. He wanted to invade Africa. It was a mirror image of Hannibal's invasion of Italy, but Scipio intended to make *his* invasion work.

Scipio knew that Hannibal's strategy in Italy had failed less because of conceptual errors than because of adequate resources. Scipio intended not to repeat that error, but he faced powerful enemies in the Roman senate. Like Hannibal in Carthage, Scipio aroused the jealousy of other politicians in Rome. And he had a powerful enemy in Fabius.

Fabius believed that the war had to be won in Italy, but Scipio had learned from Hannibal that the war would be won by invading the enemy's homeland. Fabius thought that Hannibal would prove even more dangerous back in Africa than he was in Italy. Scipio argued that it was possible to neutralize Hannibal in Africa by stealing Carthage's best ally—the Numidians and their cavalry.

Scipio was elected consul in 205 B.C. but his enemies tried to starve him of troops. In response, Scipio put together an army of his own, an exceptionally good one. At its heart were two legions that the Senate despised. They were the survivors of Cannae and other lost battles. Bitter experience had taught them how to fight, and now they wanted to win back their good names. Scipio raised volunteers as well, and he had allied units at his disposal too. All told, he invaded Africa with about 28,000 men—26,000 infantry (10,000 Roman and 16,000 allied) and 2,200 cavalry (600 Roman, 1,600 allied). Already, when he was in Spain, Scipio had started wooing the Numidians. After landing in Africa in summer 204 B.C., he won them.

The schemes and battles by which Scipio took Numidia deserve a book of their own. A remarkable Carthaginian noblewoman named Sophonisba almost single-handedly saved the Numidian alliance. But Scipio outmaneuvered her and Sophonisba was forced to commit suicide.

To make a long story short, Scipio managed to detach the Numidian prince Masinissa from his alliance with Carthage; to defeat and capture the Numidian king Syphax, who was Carthage's staunch friend; to replace Syphax as king with Masinissa, and to bring Masinissa firmly and finally into Rome's camp. The upshot was that the Numidian light horsemen who had won so many battles for Carthage were now fighting against Carthage.

That change in alliance convinced Carthage to sue for peace. But it wasn't Scipio's first victory in Africa. He had already defeated two Carthaginian-Numidian armies. He beat the first army by fraud rather than force. In a night attack in spring 203 near Utica, northwest of Carthage, he set the mostly wooden structures of their camp on fire and killed large numbers of their soldiers. Scipio was cunning; the enemy was negligent.

The Carthaginian-Numidian alliance put together another army, but Scipio defeated it later that year at the Battle of the Great Plains, about seventy-five miles southwest of Carthage. As at Ilipa, Scipio defeated the enemy on the flanks. After the battle, Masinissa and his horsemen defeated and captured Syphax.

While all this was going on, Hannibal was still in Italy. He sat in the toe of the Italian boot, able to beat off all attacks, but unable to go on the offensive. Mago's landing in northern Italy was the only hopeful sign for Carthage, but his attack soon failed. Carthage wasted its armies in Italy when it should have stood on the defensive in Africa.

In summer 203 the Carthaginian senate sent a delegation to Scipio to sue for peace. They distanced themselves from Hannibal and blamed the war on him and his family. Scipio offered peace on the terms mentioned above. The Carthaginian senate agreed, but many senators, and a large part of the Carthaginian people, were playing for time. They wanted Hannibal back.

Scipio granted a truce for negotiations. Carthage sent ambassadors to Rome who met with the Senate. Once again, Carthage's diplomats blamed the war on Hannibal. The Romans were not impressed but they accepted Scipio's terms on the condition that Hannibal and his brother Mago both leave Italy immediately. Most Carthaginians eagerly agreed.

The Last Battle: Zama

After landing in Africa in autumn 203 B.C., Hannibal spent about a year building up his army. He made his base outside the seaport of Hadrumetum (modern Sousse) about seventy-five miles southeast of Carthage, where his family owned property. At this distance, Hannibal was safe both from

Scipio, who was camped northwest of the city, and from his enemies in the Carthaginian senate.

Hannibal's homecoming did not include a visit to Carthage. In fact, he did not set foot in the capital city until after his final battle with the Romans, a year after his return to Africa.

Hannibal was always fighting two wars, one against the Romans and the other against his enemies in the Carthaginian government. From the time he landed in Africa, the second war loomed ever larger.

His fifteen years in Italy gave Hannibal a bitter education in Carthaginian politics. Everyone knew that the Carthaginian senate had some bad habits—crucifying failed generals, leaving armies in the lurch, making deals behind their generals' backs, even blaming their policies on their generals. Hannibal was attuned to threats—he knew the senators would gladly abandon him.

But Hannibal had his allies in Carthage. Many Carthaginians were pinning their hopes on him when, in spring 202 B.C., they openly violated the truce with Rome. After seizing the cargo of more than one hundred shipwrecked Roman transport ships, they tried to kill Roman diplomats. It was all but a declaration of war. Most of Carthage's politicians had "not small hopes but great hopes that they could win thanks to Hannibal and his men," as Polybius says.

With the hawks ascendant in Carthage and the Romans feeling betrayed, a fight to the finish was inevitable. Hannibal intended to do his part by building an army. It was not a wise decision.

Hannibal should have known, even if his countrymen did not, that he could not pull off a miracle. Great field commander that he was, he did not have enough veteran infantrymen to match Scipio's legionaries, nor did he have Masinissa's cavalry on his side. Yet Hannibal forged ahead. Whether it was hope or wishful thinking or a hedge against crucifixion or a simple error, we do not know.

Hannibal was building an army with the men he had brought with him from Italy. He added Mago's troops, who were mercenaries, and local recruits. He found a rival Numidian prince, an enemy of Masinissa, who supplied two thousand cavalry. Hannibal also bought wheat and horses.

Scipio, meanwhile, contacted Masinissa and asked him to gather his troops and join him immediately. For his part, Scipio attacked the Carthaginian farming communities of the fertile valley of the Bagradas (Medjerda) River. He stormed the towns and sold the population into slavery, making a nice profit while terrorizing the locals.

The Carthaginian government sent a delegation to Hannibal. They urged him to bring the matter to a decisive battle. Hannibal told them to "look after other matters and rest easy about this one: he would choose the right time himself." A few days later, he moved his army inland to the vicinity of Zama, a town about seventy miles southwest of Carthage (the exact site is disputed). Scipio was not far away.

We have to wonder if the Carthaginian senate didn't have a point—if Hannibal had moved more quickly, he might have been able to catch Scipio before Masinissa arrived. Without Masinissa's cavalry, Scipio would have had a difficult time defeating Hannibal. But even if Hannibal had reached Scipio in time, he probably wouldn't have been able to force him into battle.

Three spies sent by Hannibal to scout the enemy's camp were caught by the Romans. But instead of executing them, Scipio gave them a tour of the camp and returned them to Hannibal with an escort and supplies. This suited the Roman's purpose. While Masinissa and his troops hadn't yet arrived, Scipio knew they were near. He wanted Hannibal to know only that they hadn't arrived, because this might tempt him into a trap. By the time Hannibal attacked, Scipio was certain the Numidians would be present. Indeed, they arrived the next day.

Scipio now had his army, consisting of 29,000 infantry (23,000 Romans and 6,000 Numidians) and 6,100 cavalry (1,500 Roman and Italian and 4,600 Numidian). Hannibal had more infantry (36,000) but fewer cavalry (4,000).

But the battle did not begin until Hannibal did a remarkable thing. He requested a conference with Scipio. This wasn't standard procedure in ancient warfare. One ancient writer says that Hannibal was so "amazed" at Scipio's "grandeur of soul and audacity" in returning the three spies that Hannibal "felt an urge" to meet with him. Another says that Hannibal learned of Masinissa's arrival and was so "struck by the enemy's confidence" that he decided it was better to parley with Scipio now, and "seek peace while his army was intact and not defeated."

Neither explanation does justice to the complexity of Hannibal's motives. A man of his depth and experience wouldn't request a meeting without thinking it through. Nor was he ready to surrender. He surely assessed the plusses and minuses of this unusual move before deciding to go ahead.

To request the meeting was an admission of weakness on Hannibal's part. It also gave Masinissa and his men time to familiarize themselves with the Roman army and its battle plan. Yet there were advantages for Hannibal as well. As the older man and a heroic name—Hannibal was forty-five, Scipio, thirty-two—Hannibal probably wanted to intimidate his opponent and gather information firsthand. By getting a read on Scipio, by gauging his style and observing his reactions, Hannibal could better prepare for battle.

But the primary purpose of the meeting was most probably political. It served several agendas. Hannibal knew that he stood a good chance of losing the looming battle, so he made one last try at a peace treaty. Since Carthage had rejected Scipio's terms, Hannibal took a harder line. While offering to abandon all of Carthage's overseas possessions, as Scipio had required, he said nothing about the navy, an indemnity, or grain for Rome's army. No doubt he expected Scipio to reject the offer, but perhaps Hannibal was hoping to bargain. In any case, he might have been playing to the peace party in Carthage. If he lost the battle, at least he could say that he had tried diplomacy. As it turned out, Scipio turned down the terms.

No matter, because Hannibal had another, more personal agenda—he cared what Scipio thought of him. He didn't want Scipio basing his opinion of him on Carthaginian political slander, but wanted him to see the real Hannibal—and to see him now, before the battle, while they were still equals, and not later when Hannibal might have to come to him on bended knee.

The meeting was a private audience. It consisted of just the two men and their interpreters. The mood was intimate and intense.

Meeting with Scipio was a gesture of respect, the equivalent of two boxers touching gloves before the bout. It was a bow to the unwritten code of conduct among fellow warriors. Perhaps it was a reminder too that the politicians did not share their camaraderie.

Hannibal might have guessed that Scipio, like him, had problems with his own government (perhaps his spies had confirmed this). The meeting was a way of hinting to Scipio that he and Hannibal had much in common. They were opponents, not enemies, and they could be useful to each other, come what may. The loser could obtain mercy, while the victor would know someone he respected on the other side.

The meeting was a strategic masterstroke. Hannibal was thinking not only of the field at Zama, but also of the postwar world. He wanted to position himself. Lest he seem merely selfish, consider the lessons of his education in Carthaginian politics. Hannibal was a military man, and yet he had every reason to believe that he could run a wiser, more efficient, and more patriotic republic than the politicians had. That's what two decades of commanding Carthage's armies had taught him.

If Hannibal won the battle, he could exploit a personal relationship with Scipio in the aftermath. Rome would have to decide whether to keep fighting or to accept less generous terms than it had wanted. Hannibal might be able to nudge Scipio in the right direction.

If Hannibal lost the battle, Scipio might help Hannibal avoid the fate of being shipped off to Italy to march in a Roman victory parade that would climax in his execution. By establishing a personal connection with the Roman victor, Hannibal stood to increase his stock in Carthage. By the same token, he could impress on Scipio that he was the one Carthaginian whom Rome could trust if it had to do business with Carthage. Scipio could argue that Hannibal would be more useful to Rome alive and in Carthage, where he could serve as a voice of moderation, chastened as he had been by his war experience.

Finally, there was history. Hannibal knew that if he died in battle and Rome won the war, the enemy would write the history books. When Scipio was interviewed later, Hannibal wanted him to remember the man he had met in a tent before battle.

On the eve of his last pitched battle, Hannibal paid great attention to the postwar world. Neither Alexander before the battle of the Hydaspes nor Caesar before the battle of Munda had done or did anything similar. Hannibal wasn't more intelligent than them but he had experienced a harsher schooling. Ironically, defeat had educated Hannibal.

But there was still a battle to fight, and it took place the very next morning. It was autumn 202 B.C.

Zama pitted Carthage's best general against Rome's best general, neither of whom had ever lost a major battle. The long Second Punic War between Rome and Carthage came down to this one day.

The ancient sources emphasize the drama of the occasion. And yet, Zama lacks the razzle-dazzle of Cannae or Ilipa. There were no flank attacks. Why did Hannibal and Scipio each give up his trademark maneuver? They most probably wanted to keep the other off balance by doing the unexpected. Hannibal displayed particular audacity in his deployments.

Hannibal knew that he stood at a disadvantage against Scipio, who had a better army. He outnumbered Hannibal in cavalry and in experienced, veteran infantrymen. (Hannibal had more infantrymen but most of them were new recruits.) Nonetheless, Hannibal put his ever-fertile mind to the problem and came up with an ingenious solution.

Contrary to his usual practice, he organized his army in three lines. The Romans too arranged their army in three lines, but Hannibal's were different. In the Roman arrangement, the first line consisted of the youngest men, the second line contained the most experienced and mature men, and in the third line were the oldest soldiers—men slightly past their prime. Normally, the first two lines *really* fought a battle; the third line joined only when the going got very rough.

In Hannibal's order of battle, the plan was just the opposite, and everything would come down to the third line. Hannibal's first line consisted of mercenaries; these were the men who had fought in Italy with Hannibal's brother Mago. The second line was made up of recruits drawn from Carthage and the North African countryside. The job of these first two lines was to get the Romans bloody and tired, to blunt the edge of their swords from overuse, and to break up the order of their line. But they were not good enough soldiers to defeat the Romans. That was the job of the third line.

The third line consisted of the men who had come back from Italy with Hannibal. These were a mix of Italians, Celts from the Po Valley, and Spaniards, Numidians, and Africans. In other words, the third line included men who had marched with Hannibal from the very beginning of the war. These were his best troops. Hannibal planned to use them to defeat the Romans after his first two lines had softened them up. They would stand their ground, fresh and firm, and beat back the Romans' attack.

But the bigger problem was Scipio's superiority in cavalry. With his combination of Italian cavalry and Numidia's magnificent horsemen, Scipio could take Hannibal's army in the flanks and the rear the way Hannibal had taken the Roman army at Cannae. Hannibal knew that he needed to stop that from happening, and so he employed two strategies—elephants and decoys.

Hannibal had more than eighty elephants with him at Zama. Like Porus at the Hydaspes River, Hannibal deployed them in front of his first line, hoping to use them to break up the enemy's well-ordered formation. As terrifying as the charge of eighty elephants was, it didn't work. Some of the elephants panicked at the sound of the trumpets and turned and trampled some of Hannibal's cavalry units. Others simply stampeded off the battlefield. A third group of elephants charged the Romans and killed some light-armed troops but otherwise did little damage. Like Alexander before him, Scipio was prepared. He had arranged alley-like gaps between his legionary formations, and his men funneled the attacking beasts down them.

Hannibal's elephants failed; now came the turn of Scipio's cavalry. He placed it, as usual, on his flanks, with the Romans and Italians on his right and the Numidians on his left. Scipio ordered them to charge the much-outnumbered cavalry on Hannibal's flanks. In response, Hannibal's horsemen turned and fled, with the enemy in hot pursuit. For a long time, there simply were no cavalry on the battlefield. It is possible that Hannibal planned things this way, hoping to win the infantry battle before the enemy horses returned. Once they did, he could form his men in squares to ward them off.

It all came down to the infantry. Things went according to Hannibal's plan. His first two lines—the mercenaries and the North Africans—got in some good blows before the Romans savaged them and drove them off the field. They left so many corpses and discarded weapons on the battlefield after the first phase of the fighting that the Romans had a hard time wading through them without slipping on the bloodstained ground in order to reach Hannibal's third line—his veterans.

It was a moment of the highest drama. Veterans of Cannae stood on both sides. For the Romans, it was a grudge fight; for the Carthaginians, a final chance to save everything. Evenly matched, the two lines fought for a long while, but eventually Scipio's cavalry returned. They made a decisive attack on the rear of Hannibal's line and slaughtered them. It was Cannae in reverse.

Ancient battles sometimes ended on unequal terms. When an enemy was trapped, without hope of surrender or flight, the result was slaughter, at relatively little cost to the victor. The result was a lopsided but credible set of casualty counts. And so, at Zama, the Carthaginians had about twenty thousand dead and almost as many taken prisoner. The Romans had only about one thousand five hundred dead. Scipio had won a crushing victory. Hannibal had suffered his first defeat in a pitched battle.

Hannibal has been criticized for not using his third line to attack Scipio's flanks at Zama. The critics also blame him for not regrouping his elephants or the survivors of his first two lines to screen off the rear and flanks of his third line. No doubt Hannibal thought of these moves but concluded that his men lacked either the numbers or experience to pull them off. Polybius says that Hannibal was admirable at Zama: he did everything in the battle that a good general with a great deal of practical experience could possibly have done.

After the defeat, Hannibal galloped back to the coast at Hadrumetum, over 120 miles away, abandoning what was left of his army. Shortly afterward, the Carthaginian senate sent an embassy to Scipio to sue for peace.

Scipio's terms weren't much harsher than the ones that Carthage had earlier accepted and then rejected. Carthage had to abandon all its overseas possessions; it had to pay an indemnity and supply grain for Scipio's troops. But the indemnity was doubled from five thousand to ten thousand talents and Carthage lost its navy and its elephants. It could not make war outside Africa and needed Roman approval before making war in Africa. The peace terms also licensed Masinissa to harass Carthage by making the open-ended demand that it "restore" his ancestral possessions.

In Carthage, the Senate debated the treaty. In spite of everything, there remained war hawks, but they had to deal with Hannibal. For the first time in thirty-five years, he returned to the city of his birth.

Hannibal took part in the debate. He literally dragged an opponent of the treaty from the speaker's platform. The senators were aghast and Hannibal apologized for the rough behavior that he had learned in the field. But he had made his point. After Zama, he said, all was lost, hopelessly lost. There was nothing left for the Carthaginians except to bow to Scipio's terms. And so they did.

In the following year, 201 B.C., the peace terms formally went into effect. After seventeen years, the Second Punic War was over.

The Lion in Winter

We might have expected the Romans to bring Hannibal back to Italy as a prisoner. Instead, they let him stay in Carthage. It is tempting to give Scipio credit for this. Hannibal continued to serve as general through 200 B.C. He used his troops as a kind of police force in Libya, where Carthage's authority had lapsed, and as a civilian conservation corps closer to home, where they planted olive trees to make up for the devastation left by the Roman army.

Then Hannibal stepped down from office. For the next three years he watched Carthage struggle with the Roman indemnity and political corruption on a massive scale. The Barca faction was out of power, and so people turned to Hannibal. In 197 B.C. he ran for office as *suffete*, Carthage's chief magistrate—the equivalent of a Roman consul. He held a one-year term in 196.

After losing the war with Rome, after costing Carthage its empire in Spain, territory in North Africa, and much blood and treasure, Hannibal went on to a new political career at home. As chief magistrate, Hannibal streamlined the Carthaginian government and made it more democratic. He put a series of financial reforms into effect that ended a corrupt taxation system that had funneled tax revenue into the hands of the old boys' club. Hannibal's new system made it possible for Carthage to pay back the tribute imposed by Rome without raising new taxes.

It is the rare man who serves his country both as a commander in the field in wartime and as a political reformer at home in peacetime. It is even rarer to find someone who fails as a general but succeeds as a politician, but Hannibal had this distinction. Unfortunately, the combination of political success and military failure can be toxic. Success breeds jealousy.

Six years after accepting defeat, Carthage was booming and prosperous. The Roman government took note. The Romans hadn't expected the great general to prove an equally great administrator, but they had learned the hard way not to underestimate Hannibal's skill. A man in his midfifties, he was still vigorous, and this made them worry about where his strong hand might lead Carthage next.

Scipio said to leave Hannibal alone but the Roman senate rejected his advice. So, in 195 B.C., Rome demanded that Carthage hand him over. Hannibal fled to the East, first to Tyre, Carthage's Phoenician mother city, and then to Anatolia and the kingdom of Antiochus III, another enemy of Rome.

Hannibal failed in his attempt to guide Antiochus to victory against Rome. Once again, he was forced to flee. This time, he ended up in the kingdom of Bithynia (in northwestern Turkey). In 183 B.C., the Romans cornered Hannibal in the port of Libyssa (near Istanbul). Rather than face humiliation as a prisoner, Hannibal took poison that he is supposed to have carried in his ring. He left behind a letter bitterly accusing the Romans of being too impatient to wait for an old man to die.

But the Romans knew what they were doing. Although in his midsixties, Hannibal still breathed fire. The military advisor to the Bithynian king, he had just won a naval victory over a Roman ally.

Carthage lived on in the afterglow of Hannibal's success. Thanks to Hannibal's statesmanship, Carthage was more prosperous than ever within fifty years of losing the Second Punic War. This was more than the Romans could stand.

In 149 the Romans gave the people of Carthage an ultimatum: either they surrender their city and move ten miles inland or face war. The Carthaginians chose to fight. They held out for three years. Finally, in spring 146, the Romans took the city by storm. A large part of the population died by starvation or the sword; the rest were sold into slavery. A great fire destroyed most of the city.

If Hannibal hadn't set it on so sound a footing, Carthage might not have become prosperous enough to frighten Rome. Then again, if Hannibal hadn't invaded Italy in the first place, Rome would surely not have feared Carthaginian prosperity.

That's not the final irony, though. A century after Carthage was destroyed it was reborn. In 46 B.C. it was decided that the city was now to be a Roman colony and to be populated by immigrants from Italy. The new founder of Carthage was none other than Julius Caesar!

CAESAR

After Munda, Caesar had no more military enemies. Politics was another matter. All Romans admitted Caesar's preeminence on the battlefield but few were willing to grant him supremacy at home. Rome was still a republic and liberty remained an ideal. Most people were willing to give up some of their privileges for the sake of peace, but just how many privileges and under what terms had to be negotiated.

To bring peace at home, Caesar had to shift from commanding Romans to courting them.

The Man Who Would Not Be King

It all depended, of course, on what Caesar wanted. But precisely what was that?

We have a rough idea but we can't be certain. Caesar wrote no manifesto. He had less then two years left to live when he celebrated his four triumphs in 46 B.C., and that wasn't long enough to change Rome thoroughly. But Caesar got a lot done during those two years, and he made some telling comments over the course of his last decade, so we're not completely in the dark.

Caesar wanted to dominate Rome; that much is clear. He once said, upon passing through a village in the Alps, that he would rather be the first man there than the second man in Rome. Though admittedly self-centered, he was also a patriot and a reformer. At the same time, he was not willing to pin himself down to a specific constitution—and maybe that showed wisdom. When men propose big change, details become targets.

When Caesar crossed the Rubicon in 49 B.C. and started the civil war, he cited two motives. He said that he was defending the power of the tribunes—the representatives of the common people. He also said that he was defending his own rank and honor. Then, in a letter of 48 B.C. to Metellus Scipio, who was fighting for Pompey, Caesar spoke of three priorities: "the tranquility of Italy, the peace of the provinces, and the well-being of the empire."

What's interesting is what Caesar *doesn't* mention, and that is the Roman senate. To Caesar's opponents, the Senate was the crowning glory of the Roman system. The Senate, they thought, made Rome wise and free. A council of elders made up of experienced former magistrates, the Senate guided the ship of state. The Senate also guaranteed liberty, because it alone allowed free and unfettered debate. So its defenders argued.

Caesar was unimpressed. "The Republic," he once said, "is nothing, just a name without form or substance." His behavior between 46 and 44 B.C. demonstrated that he meant what he said.

Caesar believed that the Senate had kept Rome from making essential reforms, both in Italy and in the empire. He considered the senators narrow-minded and self-interested. And they were—and proud and prickly as well. Caesar insulted them in multiple ways, by acts of omission and commission—by neglecting to stand when they entered the room, for example, or by making them wait to see him. The Senate joined the chorus of Romans offering Caesar unprecedented honors, so many that they came close to worshiping him as a god—but not quite. The old aristocracy hated themselves for it, and they hated Caesar.

Caesar considered himself to be beyond such pettiness. He believed that only a man of supreme wisdom and talent could bring change. Caesar was that man—at least as he saw it. Many of his countrymen were willing to concede his greatness. At least, they were willing to grant him semi-divine status. But supreme political authority was another matter.

Caesar wanted to have the power of a king but without the title. In Rome, "king" was a dirty word. The Roman republic was founded in 509 B.C. (to use the traditional date) in a rebellion against a king. In Roman eyes, "monarchy" spelled corrupt and arbitrary rule—tyranny, in short.

Caesar flirted with the trappings of monarchy. He claimed to be descended from Rome's first kings (and from the gods) and wore the special boots that they were supposed to have worn. He installed his mistress, Queen Cleopatra of Egypt, in a house across the Tiber, which seemed suspect to republican tastes. She brought her son, Caesarion, whom she claimed was Caesar's child.

A few of his supporters dared to call Caesar king in public, but he rejected the term. Perhaps they were floating trial balloons for him, but Rome wasn't ready for a king. Instead, Caesar had himself declared *dictator perpetuo*—dictator for life—in February 44 B.C. This was just an extension of three shorter dictatorships that he had already been voted since crossing the Rubicon.

A dictator for life was as unconstitutional in Rome as it would be in any modern state. Caesar believed that he deserved the title and that the country would accept it rather than risk a return to civil war. What he failed to understand was that even many of his own supporters wanted him to show respect for the Senate and its ways and for the Roman constitution, but he was disrespectful of both. When, for example, one of the consuls of 45 B.C. died on the last day of the year, Caesar appointed one of his allies as consul—for less than one day.

Caesar believed that his dictatorship served the public good, and he did bring Rome temporary tranquility—and a heaping program of reforms to boot.

Caesar didn't really care about the tribunes, but he did care about the ordinary people of Rome and Italy. He passed a series of laws to their benefit. The city of Rome was teeming with unemployment, violence, and corruption. Caesar cracked down on political gangs. He offered jobs through public works projects—a new forum and new temples—as well as entertainment and food through games and spectacles. He encouraged doctors and teachers to immigrate to Rome and he provided for the city's public library.

At the same time, he cleaned up Rome's crowded and dangerous streets. He used the carrot and the stick to move poor people out of town. On the one hand, he cracked down on noncitizens who had been getting free grain, which was a welfare benefit for Roman citizens. On the other hand, he set up new colonies for citizens. Eighty thousand Roman citizens, most of them poor, were chosen to emigrate to Anatolia, Greece, or North Africa. Meanwhile, he gave his veterans land in Italy, Spain, and Gaul.

The provinces too benefited from Caesar's reforms. Before Caesar, all Italians were Roman citizens except for those living north of the Po River or in Sicily. Caesar enfranchised Italians north of the Po and gave Sicilians "Latin rights," a limited form of Roman citizenship. Meanwhile, he brought relief to the province of Asia (western Turkey), where Roman tax collectors were notorious for abuses. Caesar ended that.

He reformed the Senate too, increasing its size from six hundred to nine hundred members and naming many new senators. They were loyal to him, of course, and they included men who were sneered at by the old senators: junior officers, army contractors, and Celts from northern Italy. But they brought new blood and talent where it was needed.

Meanwhile, in the midst of all this energetic reform, Caesar made plans to leave Rome. He was voted the authority to make war on the Parthian empire. An Iranian state founded in a revolt against Alexander's successors, the Parthian empire stretched from Iraq to Afghanistan.

Caesar had two reasons to make war on Parthia; honor and security. In

53 B.C. the Parthians had demolished a Roman army at the battle of Carrhae (today in Turkey) and humiliated the legions by capturing their standards. In 46 B.C., the Parthians threw their support behind a revolt in Syria. Caesar wanted to put down the rebellion and avenge the defeat.

He planned a massive undertaking. The Senate voted him the largest army that he had ever commanded. It consisted of sixteen legions (on paper, about eighty thousand men) and ten thousand cavalry. The campaign was slated to begin in spring 44 B.C. After mustering across the Adriatic Sea, the punitive expedition would move against King Burebista of Dacia (modern Romania) whose armies had been raiding the Roman province of Macedonia—and who had supported Pompey. Then Caesar would cross into Asia.

Caesar planned to invade the Parthian empire through Armenia, a border state. He insisted on taking his time in order to study the Parthians and their fighting methods before attacking. They were fierce foes and especially well-known cavalrymen.

Whether Caesar had a new territorial conquest in mind or whether he just wanted to defeat the Parthian army is unclear. Rumor said that he wanted to conquer southern Russia on the way back and then fight his way to Gaul, but that strains belief. What is certain, though, is that Caesar projected a long campaign. He expected to be away from Rome for three years.

What about the Roman government while he was gone? Caesar appointed officeholders in advance to cover that period. They could help maintain his system, but they couldn't rule with Caesar's authority. Rome would never be as stable with Caesar away as it was with him present.

Perhaps that was the point. Maybe Caesar wanted the Romans to get a taste of life without his strong, guiding hand. When he returned, he would offer not only his authority but, as he hoped, new wealth and honors won for Rome, and won against a foreign enemy, not in another civil war. Caesar thought that the Roman people might welcome his dictatorship with sighs of relief.

Or so we might suppose. Maybe the real attraction of the Parthian War was escape. Better to take up arms against the Parthians on the field of honor, Caesar might have thought, than to trade words with Rome's stubborn and treacherous grandees.

Caesar was scheduled to leave Rome on March 18, 44 B.C. At fifty-four years of age, he was no longer young. Caesar knew that when he left Rome for the front, he might have been looking at the city for the last time. He might not have minded.

The Ides of March

Caesar never left Rome, of course. He was assassinated three days before his scheduled departure. A conspiracy of sixty senators attacked him at a meeting of the Senate on March 15—the Ides of March, as the day was known on the Roman calendar. Brutus and Cassius, Cinna and Casca—the names of the leading conspirators are familiar to any reader of Shakespeare. They had been mulling over the plan for months and knew that this was their last chance to act.

The Senate was not meeting in the Senate House that day, as the building was under renovation. Instead, they met in a recent public works project of Caesar's rival—the Portico of Pompey. Caesar died at the foot of a statue of Pompey.

The assassins wielded daggers and wounded Caesar twenty-three times. Hundreds of senators watched in helpless shock. The *imperator* struggled and fought back. He cried out in indignation and stabbed one attacker with his pen. The story goes that he gave up only when he saw Marcus Brutus attack him.

Brutus was the son of Caesar's former mistress, Servilia. Rumor made Caesar the father but that is unlikely. Still, it adds poignancy to the wounded man's comment. Looking at Brutus, Caesar is supposed to have said, in Greek, "You too, my son?" (He did not say, *"et tu, Brute."*) And then he fell, never to get up.

It was one of the most famous assassinations in history. It is also a gigantic crack in the edifice of Caesar's achievements—a huge fault line that cuts to the heart of his character. At first, it looks like a simple security blunder. Look deeper, though, and you can see the problem that underlaid everything that Caesar did in Rome. The great general had all that it took to be a great statesman as well—all except the realism. In the end, Caesar, the hard-bitten veteran of fifty pitched battles in which he claimed to have killed 1,192,000 people, was a romantic. He cared what the Roman people thought of him. That was his biggest mistake.

If Caesar had simply been a dictator, he would have surrounded himself with a bodyguard and stained the streets of Rome with the corpses of his enemies. But he would have nothing to do with the bloodshed and murders that marked the dictatorship of Sulla a generation earlier. Instead, Caesar continued his famous policy of clemency.

After returning to Rome in 46 B.C., he pardoned yet more of his enemies and allowed them to come back to Italy. He appointed many former supporters of Pompey to high office. He did nothing to stop Romans from publishing pamphlets in praise of his archenemy, Cato, who was now a martyr to freedom.

It would have been easy for Caesar to protect himself. All he needed was a bodyguard, which would have made it virtually impossible to assassinate him. As a general, he had had a bodyguard, like any Roman commander. Usually a troupe of Spanish auxiliaries protected him, but in early 44 B.C. he dismissed them. The Senate, it is true, had sworn an oath of loyalty and granted Caesar permission to form a new bodyguard of senators and knights, but Caesar was in no hurry to establish it.

Having a bodyguard would have meant admitting that he had to live in fear, and Caesar didn't want that. Perhaps there was another factor as well. Caesar continued to think of himself as a member of Rome's elite of nobility and culture. He did things like going to dinner parties at Cicero's villa and discussing literature. When Brutus and Cicero each published books in praise of Cato as the ideal Roman, Caesar ordered his literary assistant to write a reply—and then, as soon as time permitted, Caesar wrote his own *Anticato*. But the man who had indirectly caused the deaths of Cato, Pompey, Metellus Scipio, Domitius Ahenobarbus, and so many other champions of the Roman aristocracy could not easily claim his place in it.

Caesar was done in by a combination of arrogance and neediness. He wanted Rome's aristocrats to acknowledge his supremacy while accepting him as a member of their club. He really couldn't have both. If he wanted his fellow aristocrats to pat him on the back, he couldn't force them to kneel before him. If he insisted that they knuckle under, then he should have been ready for their knives. As wise as he was, Caesar was blind to this truth.

Caesar may have made the additional mistake of thinking that he was untouchable. Perhaps he really did believe that he was protected by the *Fortuna Caesaris*—"the good fortune of Caesar." Perhaps his calculations were strictly secular, but in that case they were arrogant. Caesar's sense of his own genius and his exaggerated estimate of his own superiority made it seem like treason even to imagine that any of the lesser men whom he had beaten could possibly harm him.

Half of Rome, he thought, loved him, and the other half feared him. It was irrational, he reasoned, for anyone merely to hate him. But he forgot the importance of *dignitas*, or rank—a strange omission indeed for a man who justified his decision to cross the Rubicon by saying that his *dignitas* was dearer to him than life itself.

Alexander the Great gave up on trying to have the Macedonians kiss the ground in his presence. Caesar never tried anything so obvious with Rome's proud aristocrats, but what he did offended them just as much. He made a mockery of the honors that meant so much to them. He flirted with being called king. And, worst of all, he forgave his enemies.

The assassins of 44 B.C. would never forgive Caesar for pardoning them. Caesar aroused their jealousy and their fear. His achievements dwarfed theirs. His demagoguery threatened to siphon off their wealth to the common people. His reforms offended innate Roman conservatism. But worst of all, his arrogance humiliated them. The very clemency that Caesar was so proud of was the nub of his enemies' case against him. As Cato is supposed to have said, Caesar had no right to lord it over people by exonerating them.

And so, the conspirators gathered, now squawking like geese, now sharpening their knives like soldiers.

The Men Who Would Be Caesar

Rome's senators were narrow-minded and self-defeating. They were stingy to Rome's soldiers and unwelcoming to the elite of northern Italy and Gaul. In return, both of those groups supported Caesar. So did the ordinary people of Italy—the main target of the senators' exploitation. And yet, these same selfish senators were the most stubborn and magnificent defenders of political liberty that the world has ever seen.

It was liberty for a very few but it was liberty nonetheless. Nothing would make them surrender the right to do and say what they pleased. Caesar would have to kill all of them to make them submit. He was too much of an old Roman aristocrat himself to do any such thing. Caesar couldn't kill the likes of Brutus and Cassius because he cared too much about what they thought. But after they killed him, the rules changed.

The men who came after Caesar didn't mind killing most of Rome's nobility if that's what it would take to keep them securely in power. So they did.

That was the tragedy of the Ides of March. Rather than restore the Republic, it brought back the civil war, and with a vengeance. Caesar's civil war lasted five years; the new outbreak lasted fourteen. Caesar had steadfastly steered clear of what the Romans called "proscription," that is, posting lists of enemies whose lives and property were both forfeit. The new war brought it back.

The list included two thousand three hundred of the wealthiest and most prominent members of the Roman elite. Many of them escaped with their lives but not their property. But even that wasn't enough to satisfy the desire for loot, so eighteen of the richest cities in Italy, with their lands, were given to the soldiers who still supported Caesar by their commanders.

Among those who did not survive was Cicero. The orator's hands and tongue were brought as gruesome trophies to the man who ordered his murder, Mark Antony. Caesar's former lieutenant emerged after the Ides of March as one of the two most important leaders of Caesar's troops. The other was Caesar's nineteen-year-old grandnephew.

Gaius Octavius, the grandson of Caesar's sister, was Caesar's legal heir. Caesar had traveled back from Spain with young Octavius in 46 B.C. and was impressed by him. Octavius was sharp, cunning, and ambitious. Having no living, legitimate children of his own, Caesar adopted Octavius posthumously, which was not an unusual procedure in Rome. When Caesar's will was read, Octavius became Gaius Julius Caesar Octavianus—often called Octavian today.

Unlike Alexander, Caesar had an adult heir. But like Alexander, Caesar left a succession struggle behind him. Mark Antony had no intention of giving way to Octavian. Antony was a grown man of about forty and a great soldier. Octavian was no solider, but he had more important qualities. Octavian had not only Caesar's name he also had Caesar's political talent, and then some. He began outmaneuvering Antony from the start.

The two of them fought in Italy and Octavian's troops won the upper hand. Then they joined forces against the army of Brutus and Cassius, which they defeated at the battle of Philippi, in Macedonia, in 42 B.C. Antony and Octavian then divided up the Roman world. Octavian got Italy and the West, while Antony got the East—and Cleopatra.

Caesar's former mistress now hitched her wagon to Antony's star. Together, the two of them planned to build a new Eastern empire and then defeat Octavian. But Antony went down to defeat against Parthia, where he tried and failed to carry out the invasion that Caesar had planned.

Octavian, meanwhile, gathered his own forces. He defeated the last remaining son of Pompey, Sextus Pompeius, in a naval war off Sicily. He solidified his support in Italy and the West while caricaturing Antony as the love slave of an Eastern queen.

Octavian's propaganda proved more successful than Antony's heroics. In 32 B.C., the Senate declared war on Antony and Cleopatra. The conflict was decided in the naval battle at Actium in 31 B.C., a victory for Octavian.

In 30 B.C., Antony and Cleopatra each committed suicide. Caesarion was killed on Octavian's orders. Octavian was now the sole master of the Roman world. Known by the title Augustus ("Majestic") from 27 B.C. on, he would rule Rome as its first emperor. Between the two of them, Caesar and Augustus established a succession of emperors that lasted in Rome for five hundred years.

By 30 B.C., there was nobody left in Rome who remembered what the old Republic had been like. Years of war and proscription had swept them all away. The field was clear for Augustus to finish what Caesar had started. But, in turning Rome from a republic to a monarchy, Augustus learned from Caesar's example.

Augustus would take no title such as "dictator for life." He merely called himself *princeps*, that is, "first among equals." Nor did he display disrespect for the Senate. On the contrary, Augustus claimed that he was restoring the Republic. He pretended to follow all the old rules of the political game.

But no one was fooled. All Rome understood that Augustus had established a new regime, one that brought law and order at the price of liberty. But law and order were better than war.

THE ESSENCE OF DECISION

None of our three commanders ended his war well. None managed to combine military victory with statesmanship. And yet, each failed in a different way.

Hannibal's conflict ended in disaster. When he left for Italy in 218 B.C., he launched what he might have expected to be a relatively short war. When it became clear that it would be a long war, he proved to be unable to acquire the resources—the manpower and money—needed to win. He did not adapt well to changing circumstances. He demonstrated neither good judgment nor sound strategy.

When he invaded Italy, Hannibal was the essence of audacity. When it came to leaving Italy, he seemed to be stuck. After Hasdrubal's defeat at the Metaurus in 207, the failure of Hannibal's Italian expedition should have been obvious. And yet he stayed in Italy for four more years.

If the choice to stay was his, then it demonstrates stubbornness and illusion on his part. If the Carthaginian government was forcing him to stay, then Hannibal showed a lack of leadership by not persuading them otherwise.

When he finally was recalled to Africa in 203, Hannibal probably behaved about as well as any general could under the circumstances. But by then it was too late. It is an open question whether he should have refused to continue fighting at all.

Alexander avoided disaster, but he stretched his empire to the limit. The last years of the war, from Sogdiana to India, had been of limited strategic value or none at all. Spitamenes did not pose enough threat to justify Alexander's campaigns. India offered great wealth, but it was nearly impossible to hold.

Caesar ended his war most successfully. Neither North Africa nor Spain will go down as his most smoothly run campaign, and each offered moments of great danger. But he handled them in the proper order and kept returning to Rome to manage political affairs. His strategy was sound.

Things look different if we turn to each man's peacemaking skills. Alexander showed a lack of interest in organizing the infrastructure needed to make his claim to be "king of Asia" into a reality. He paid insufficient attention to the new governing class, beginning with his own dynasty. At the age of thirty-two, and after more than a dozen years on the throne, he was just getting around to producing a legitimate heir. He demonstrated leadership in promoting mixed marriages, but he left open the question of whether the children of these unions would be able to govern the empire. He had a new army but its effectiveness was untested.

The Persians had barely held their empire together, and Alexander's realm was even larger. Rebellions were a foregone conclusion, but cohesion was not. Alexander did little to tighten his grip on his "spear-won" land. On the contrary, he set off on a new war in Arabia, with other expeditions in the works. The warrior had insufficient interest in becoming a statesman.

Caesar did better, at least to an extent. A politician before he became a general, Caesar took internal issues much more seriously than Alexander did. But Caesar displayed only limited patience with the process of reform. He proved unable to manage the old Roman aristocracy who stood in his way, and he paid for it with his life. But even had he been more diplomatic he would not have been more focused on the task at hand. Like Alexander, he hardly ended one war before he began the next.

In an irony of history, Alexander and Caesar each died as he was about to start a vast new war. Neither man could stand life in the capital when the camp beckoned.

Alexander did not succeed in creating a great new empire or dynasty, but he did succeed in destroying an old empire—the Persian empire. And he did lay the groundwork for a series of successor states under a new Greek and Macedonian ruling class. In that sense, he was a successful statesman.

Caesar failed in his attempt to lead a long life as a dictator. But he began the process of reforming Rome that, under his chosen successor, Augustus, turned it from the Roman republic into the Roman empire. Caesar's statesmanship, although flawed, seems far greater than Alexander's.

Each man also left a brand behind. From Alexander's successors to Pyrrhus to Hannibal to Caesar and beyond, to Trajan and Julian the Apostate, would-be conquerors looked to Alexander as their model. Caesar had such an impact as a conqueror that not only did every Roman emperor take his name, but so did the rulers of such far-off states as Germany, Austria, and Russia, whose kaisers and tsars are just variations of "caesar."

But Hannibal's is the most ironic case of all. At the very moment that his military dreams died, his political skills came alive. By establishing a relationship with Scipio, he probably did the single most important thing he could to save himself from exile or execution. He then proceeded to reinvent himself as a statesman and reformer, doing for Carthage what Caesar did for Rome—and then some. It might seem selfish if Hannibal considered himself indispensable, but it was probably true. Could anyone other than Hannibal have saved Carthage? No one else combined the magical name with his audacity and leadership, and with a good judgment that had been honed in adversity,

Tragically, Hannibal was not permitted to stay in Carthage to enjoy the fruits of his success. Even worse, Carthage found that its very prosperity brought ruin at the hands of a vengeful Rome. But thanks to Hannibal, the last generations of the great north African metropolis were among its most peaceful and well-governed.

Few could have expected that from the man who once looked at Italy from the heights of the Alps with murder in his eyes.

CONCLUSION

In spring 322 B.C., the crowds gathered everywhere along the ancient roads from Babylon to Syria. What they saw passing by, heading westward, was a procession like no other. First came the engineers and road-repair crew to smooth the way, then the military guard, then a team of sixty-four mules and—finally—the object that the beasts were pulling, a funeral cart. It was so grand and magnificent that the cart had taken two years to construct. It was decorated with sculpture and paintings and covered with enough gold and jewelry to make it gleam in the sun. Inside the covered cart, hidden from view, buried under a gold-embroidered purple robe and a hammered-gold coffin with a golden lid, lay the body itself, embalmed and surrounded by spices. It was all that was mortal of Alexander the Great, dead nearly two years now.

Since his death, Alexander's marshals had jockeyed not only over his empire but his corpse. The body conveyed prestige and, if you believed the soothsayers, the favor of the gods. Some wanted to bring it to the traditional burial place of Macedonian kings at Aegae in Macedon. Others wanted it in the Shrine of Ammon, at an oasis in Libya, where Alexander had once been welcomed as the son of Zeus. The governor of Egypt, Ptolemy son of Lagus, had the last word. Accompanied by an army, he met the funeral procession in Syria and brought it to Egypt. Ptolemy had no intention of shipping the body off to the desert; instead, he gave it a place of honor in his capital city, Alexandria.

There Alexander's Tomb invited visits by kings and emperors for the next seven hundred years, until it was finally sacked.

Nearly three hundred years after Alexander's funeral procession, a funeral took place in the Roman Forum. It was March 18, 44 B.C., three days after the Ides and the most famous assassination in the history of the Western world. There might not have been a funeral at all if the assassins—the

Liberators, as they called themselves—had followed their original plan. They intended to dump the corpse of Julius Caesar in the Tiber River. But they panicked and left the body where they had killed it, which allowed it to be brought to Caesar's home. Then, instead of insisting on a private burial, they agreed to a public funeral in the Forum with full honors. It was a mistake.

And so, the scene was set for Shakespeare's famous "Friends, Romans, countrymen!" speech. Although Shakespeare's version is fiction, the speech is based on fact. When Caesar's body was brought to the Forum for a public funeral, Mark Antony really did give the funeral oration. It was a short speech and lacked the three famous words, but it was powerful. Antony mixed his sorrow with anger at the killers. When he was finished, Antony held up Caesar's bloodstained robe and pointed out the wounds.

The crowd responded by rioting. The ordinary people of Rome had supported Caesar when he was alive. Now they missed him, especially when they heard that Caesar's will left a cash gift to every citizen and a new public park to the city. Antony's words and gestures set their passion ablaze. The crowd burst into nearby buildings, hauled out wooden benches and stands, and built a pyre. Although the plan had been to carry Caesar's body to his daughter's tomb across town and cremate it there, the people would have none of it. They cremated Caesar on the spot. Then they streamed out of the Forum with torches and attacked the houses of the men who had killed him. Caesar himself could not have turned the tables more dramatically.

The third funeral—actually, a memorial service—took place two thousand years later, in 1934. The site was a hill outside the industrial city of Gebze, thirty miles east of Istanbul. The spot looks over the Gulf of Izmit, the ancient Astacus Gulf, toward the rugged hills of the far shore. None other than the president of the Turkish republic, Mustafa Kemal Atatürk, delivered the eulogy. One of history's most successful generals and statesmen, Atatürk had come to honor another general who had reached a dead end here. He had ended his life on the coast, below the very hill where Atatürk stood, about 2,115 years before. He was Hannibal. It was here, in ancient Libyssa in 183 B.C., that Hannibal took poison rather than let the Romans take him alive.

Atatürk genuinely admired Hannibal, but he had an ulterior motive for the memorial. In 1934 Benito Mussolini, dictator of Italy, was trying to pressure Turkey. Atatürk responded by honoring Hannibal, one of the greatest enemies Italy had ever had. He ordered a monument to be put up at the traditional but unconfirmed site of Hannibal's tomb. It took nearly fifty years, until 1981, for the monument finally to be built.

"The brave have the whole earth for their sepulcher," said the Athenian general and statesman Pericles. Alexander's tomb in Alexandria is long gone. Caesar's temple in the Roman Forum lies in ruins. How ironic it is that Hannibal, who failed against Rome and died a suicide, has a modern monument to his passing.

We've come, at last, to bury Caesar—and Alexander and Hannibal too. It's worth asking what good, if any, lives after them. What lessons are to be learned from the stories of the ancient world's three greatest generals?

Their military reputation is secure. They rank among history's greatest commanders. They got more out of small armies than most generals are able to accomplish with a horde. They were inspired leaders. They triumphed on the battlefield against enemies who vastly outnumbered them in manpower and money. They led devoted armies over vast distances, collectively fighting from Spain to India. Although they did not shrink from terror when needed, they appealed to the masses by branding themselves as populists and as favorites of the gods.

Ambitious and audacious, they aimed at nothing less than the greatest deeds. Hannibal failed as a military strategist but he succeeded as a combat commander. Alexander and Caesar triumphed in both arenas. Not that they didn't falter—they did. Some of their decisions might have proved fatal, but these two captains had the support of Divine Providence.

There are permanent lessons here for students of war, especially because the three cases look so similar on the surface. All three of our commanders illustrate certain things in common:

Shock and awe is the beginning of a military campaign but not the end of it. Even successful attacks invariably run into obstacles. The history of war is the history of mistakes, and the mark of a good general is less knowing how to avoid errors than being able to recover from them. He must also know how to maneuver for the best position. The side with a better army should do everything it can to draw the enemy into pitched battle, because the alternative is a war of attrition, and that plays to the other side's strengths.

So far, so similar, but Hannibal parted company from Alexander and Caesar when it came to the next step. Winning a pitched battle is a great thing, but wars are not won by battle alone. You have to know how to use victory. A great commander goes on to close the net and does so in a timely and cost-effective way. This stage is the most challenging and difficult part of waging war, and all too easy to be forgotten amidst the glamour of a famous victory. Hannibal fell short, for instance, despite a stunning effort at Cannae.

Alexander and Caesar succeeded in closing the net, but only at a steep price. Their wars dragged on too long and took so high a toll in blood and money that they undercut the possibility of winning a lasting peace. And they turned the supreme commander into a war addict who would rather go off to find new dragons to slay than build a stable society at home.

When it came to translating military victory into political capital, Alexander and Caesar each faltered. Neither of them achieved lasting success, and yet they paved the way for others to succeed.

As politicians, they were great destroyers and, in an indirect way, great builders. Alexander destroyed the Persian empire, Hannibal destroyed his own empire, and Caesar destroyed the government of the Roman republic. Alexander made the Hellenistic kingdoms possible, Hannibal spurred Rome to expand across the Mediterranean, and Caesar was, in effect, the first of the Roman emperors. They cast a giant cultural shadow as well. Thanks to Alexander, Greek civilization spread on a vast scale. Thanks to Hannibal, Rome began to think like an empire. Thanks to Caesar, Romans began to feel like subjects of an emperor.

If we had to sum up the three commanders' political achievement in a single word, that word would be: *one.* Before Alexander, Greece, Rome, and Carthage were small, independent states. After Caesar, they were one empire. What Alexander dreamed—universal kingship—Caesar and Augustus carried out. Hannibal tried to stop the process but in the end he only hurried it along.

Government by one man—monarchy—was efficient and orderly. After a long period of war, monarchy made the world more peaceful. But it also slowly smothered political liberty. The world wasn't big enough for citizens and great captains.

As I wrote this book, a colleague asked me what I was working on. I told him that I was writing about Alexander, Hannibal, and Caesar. "Ah," he said, "tyrants." No, I protested, pointing out the complexities, but eventually I had to admit that he was right. Alexander and Caesar were tyrants. Hannibal was not, although some in Carthage feared that he wanted to be.

Alexander promoted democracy here and there while Caesar forgave his opponents, but those were tactical moves. Neither man intended to share power. Alexander executed his own generals; Caesar made war on his fellow Romans. Alexander was a king who leaned toward absolutism; Caesar was a dictator for life who leaned toward monarchy.

With the possible exception of Hannibal, none of our three captains stood for modest, restrained constitutional government. They wanted to dominate the state by the allure of their achievements. They were self-promoters who branded and marketed themselves to the maximum. They all appealed, and perhaps still appeal to those who like charisma in their leaders. But none of them promoted celebrity as successfully as Alexander did.

Alexander the Great, Hannibal, and Julius Caesar are models and warnings. We ignore them at our peril, but we should imitate them only with caution. War will always be a sad fact of life, and they were too good at war for us not to learn from them. But a good society never lets war be guided by anything other than the public interest. What guided Alexander, Hannibal, and Caesar was their selves.

ALEXANDER

Alexander overwhelms us. He burst on the world already a phenomenon, a conquering cavalry commander even before he became king at age twenty, and he kept the attention of three continents until the day of his passing—and well beyond it. Charm won him a lot of what he wanted, and the rest he took by force. The story is told that one of his subordinates trembled when he saw a statue of Alexander, years after his death. I think that would have pleased Alexander.

Rarely has there been a leader whose virtues match his vices so closely.

As the crown prince of Macedon, he grew up in a royal court that combined privilege and paranoia. His ambition launched him and undid him. He wanted to be nothing less than king of Asia, but he never determined what that would mean. His gift for making war gained him an empire but the actual administration of it bored him. His talent for leadership won his Macedonians' love but left them with the fury of a jilted suitor when he moved on. His breadth of vision let him glide smoothly into the new role of king of Asia but then his role as king of Macedon seemed narrow and parochial, so he neglected it. His belief in his own destiny made him take huge risks in battle, which won military success, but at the cost of seven wounds to his own body. Perhaps it was the wounds that left him vulnerable to a virus that killed him in his thirty-third year. Hannibal and Caesar took risks in battle but not to the same degree. They were wounded less often and less seriously.

Providence favored Alexander. Gifted with courage and intelligence, he received an ideal education. He quarreled with his father, King Philip of Macedon, but Philip was assassinated when Alexander was twenty, leaving his son with a martial legacy: a plan to conquer the Persian empire and the tools to do so. Alexander's Persian enemy had a great general who could have stopped his invasion before it succeeded—Memnon of Rhodes. But Memnon died suddenly, leaving only lesser men to stand up to Alexander. They failed to do so.

Alexander was a combat commander for all seasons. His was an amazingly versatile military talent. He displayed equal mastery of pitched battle and sieges, and he was as much at home against elephants and desert raiders as against an enemy phalanx. At heart he was a cavalryman, with a cavalryman's speed, mobility, and agility. In pitched battle, he orchestrated the interplay of infantry and cavalry with a skill that was as elegant as it was deadly. His ability to size up an enemy or a battlefield and come up with a quick and effective answer made him the embodiment of strategic intuition. Darius III of Persia was no mean general, but Alexander outclassed him.

Alexander excelled as a leader of men. He led by example. He shared the men's hardships on campaign and their dangers in battle. He had great insight into what it felt like to be an ordinary soldier. Alexander did his best to keep Macedonian casualties low and rewards high, from pay to loot. He also went the extra mile to take care of soldiers' widows and orphans.

Alexander was audacious, but he took greater chances on the tactical level than the strategic level. Although he risked his body in battle, he engaged the enemy on a step-by-step basis. For instance, he did not head farther eastward before he took care of business in Anatolia. Winning battles was only the start of things for Alexander: he also raised money, won political support among the local population, and neutralized the Persian fleet.

On that last point, Alexander faltered. He didn't appreciate sea power enough to come up with a proper response to Memnon's naval offensive. Divine Providence stepped in and saved Alexander.

Throughout his long march eastward, Alexander rarely neglected his infrastructure. In a lightning campaign after his battlefield victory at Gaugamela, he made a beeline for Persia's treasuries at Susa and Persepolis, and they solved his financial problems for good. He maintained close enough control of his home government that he got additional soldiers from Macedon when he asked for them. He proved extremely creative and adaptable when it came to finding new and foreign sources of manpower as well.

Alexander displayed excellent judgment in domestic politics. Much as he may have wanted to get rid of the older generation of commanders, especially Parmenio and his family, Alexander knew that he needed them. They knew more of war than he did and they had strong support in the army. But after he defeated Darius, Alexander decided to settle scores.

He inspired many with the ideals of democracy, divine intervention, and military glory. Yet terrorism and simple murder were parts of his character as well. He destroyed the great Greek city of Thebes and massacred or enslaved its inhabitants. A similar fate awaited tens of thousands of civilians in Sogdiana and India. He had his rivals and opponents in the Macedonian court killed before they could kill him.

Alexander was never more impressive than in the aftermath of his two greatest battle victories, Issus and Gaugamela. In both cases, he showed his understanding of the stages of war. After Issus, he might have headed inland or directly to Egypt, but he stopped to conquer Tyre instead. He recognized that he could not close the net in the West as long as the Persian fleet retained a base like Tyre. After Gaugamela, he appreciated the need to close the net by capturing Darius's treasuries—and Darius himself. Battlefield victory is not enough. Alexander demonstrated his wise understanding of this rule.

Unfortunately, his strategy grew less measured as he went farther east.

Alexander's priority should have been an empire that was big but manageable, and one in which Greeks, Macedonians, and Asians could work out a new administrative arrangement, guided by Alexander and his sons. That would have meant ending the war as soon as was practical. Instead, Alexander's priority was conquest, glory, and surpassing his Persian predecessors.

The result was unnecessary wars in Sogdiana and India, wars of such cost that eventually his men mutinied and forced his return. But he never went back to Macedon. Babylon was his capital now, and he planned gigantic new wars from there, beginning with a seaborne invasion of Arabia and continuing with expeditions to the Caspian Sea, Carthage, and Italy. At the end of his career, Alexander finally appreciated the value of sea power.

The most striking thing about Alexander's final years was the disconnect between the breadth of his vision and the narrowness of his interest in administration. He was a visionary, not a manager. He showed great flexibility in adopting some of the dress of Persian royalty and the protocol of the Persian court. He laid the foundations of a new army, rooted in Asia. It was never tested in battle, but the very audacity of this post-Macedonian military was remarkable. He integrated the Macedonian and Persian elites through intermarriage.

None of this amounted to the idea of universal brotherhood that has sometimes been attributed to Alexander. He fully intended Greeks and Macedonians to be on top in his new empire. He merely recognized the need to make the Persians partners in governance if the new regime was going to have a chance to succeed. Alexander was not a bigot, but he was more of a pragmatist than a believer in pluralism.

Yet Alexander showed little interest in basic questions of his new empire. What roles would Greeks and Macedonians play in administering it? Would they emigrate eastward and, if so, where would they live? What new institutions would support the new regime? How would it be governed?

Instead of grappling with these fundamental questions, Alexander preferred to make war again. But war is a young man's game, and Alexander was the avatar of youth, just like his idol and supposed ancestor, Achilles.

Another idol of Alexander's was Cyrus the Great, the king who founded the Persian empire, and on whose throne Alexander now sat. Cyrus was no administrator either—he was a warrior-king.

All three commanders claimed divine support, but only Alexander insisted that he was the son of a god—Zeus, the king of the Greek gods—and only Alexander demanded to be worshiped during his own lifetime. All expected deference, but only Alexander had his subjects, at least his Eastern subjects, bow and scrape in his presence.

Alexander offended ancient notions of constitutional government in another big way, by promoting youth. Ancient republics and democracies believed that good government requires maturity, which began around age thirty. Anyone younger seemed too inexperienced and emotional. Hannibal was nearly thirty when he invaded Italy and Caesar was fifty, but Alexander was only twenty-two when he invaded the Persian empire. Yet, far from hiding his age, he proclaimed it in sculpture and on coins. That hardly reassured ancient lovers of liberty. They considered rule by the young to be the enemy of free and constitutional government.

The sad truth about Alexander was never more apparent than in his alleged last words. When asked to whom he wanted to leave his empire, he replied, "To the strongest." This is sometimes cited as a sign that, in his death spiral, the king was no longer thinking things through. I believe the opposite is true. Alexander had not won his empire through justice or piety or wisdom but through his strength as a warlord. How better to choose a successor?

HANNIBAL

Hannibal was an outstanding wartime commander, both in battle and on campaign, and both as manager and as tactician.

Polybius revered Hannibal's "leadership, bravery, and ability in the field." He marveled at Hannibal's success in keeping his army together in Italy— that is, in enemy territory—for fifteen years of constant fighting. We may add more than two years of war in Spain (221–219 B.C.) and another year of war in North Africa (203–202). It was an army of different races, different nationalities, and different languages, Polybius says, but Hannibal made them "hearken to a single command and obey a single will." All three commanders were great leaders of men, but Hannibal takes the prize. His soldiers never mutinied, unlike Alexander's men or Caesar's. Hannibal held them together "like a good ship's captain."

His battles were masterpieces of combined-arms work that only an army united under "a single will" could have carried out. He rivaled Alexander's skill at coordinating infantry and cavalry and perfected his favorite tactic of envelopment. And Hannibal added a dimension of cunning and surprise that was generally lacking in Alexander's battles. From the concealed Carthaginian soldiers at the Trebia to the third-line veterans at Zama, Hannibal was the master of military tricks.

This is not to say that Hannibal was perfect as a combat commander. He won all his pitched battles until his last one—Zama. He rarely achieved much through siegecraft, a key tool of the art of war of his day. He paid a high price for his bold crossing of the Apennines in 217 and an even higher one for traversing the Alps in the snow the year before, when he could have chosen a milder season to cross. Indeed, his first campaign in the war against Rome, the long march from Spain to Italy, was arguably his worst, because it cost him more than half his army.

But a great captain has to be more than a combat commander, and that's where Hannibal falls down. When it came to politics and strategy, he was simply out of his depth. Certainly, he did a fine job of branding himself as a liberator, a populist, and a strong man—a new Hercules. But public relations skill wasn't enough to win the war against Rome.

Hannibal did not succeed as a strategist. He displayed a complete lack of understanding of the stages of war. He simply had not given enough thought to how to transfer success on the battlefield into closing the net around the enemy. Unlike Caesar, he failed to think ahead.

The heart of Hannibal's plan—invading Italy—was not new. Pyrrhus had paved the way. What was new about Hannibal's strategy was marching overland to Italy from Spain. It was audacious, it caught the Romans unprepared, and it forced them to give up their planned invasion of North Africa. But it cost Hannibal half his army. It played the opening notes of Hannibal's funeral march, a piece whose theme was *manpower.*

Manpower—Hannibal had too little and the Romans had it in abundance. That leads to his deeper strategic failure, the underestimation of the enemy. Hannibal expected Rome's confederacy to crack after battlefield defeat and he thought Rome would sue for peace shortly afterward. But he didn't understand Rome's strengths.

Rome's republican constitution bred solidarity and patriotism—and it did so on the grand scale, because of a shrewd policy of sharing Roman citizenship with local elites. By the time Hannibal invaded Italy, there were nearly one million Roman citizens all over Italy, a huge number by ancient standards.

In a long war, Rome's manpower resources gave it a big advantage. Once Fabius put the policy of attrition into place—and once he made it stick— Rome got in the way of Hannibal's plans. That's why Hannibal needed to win a quick victory. His moment came after Cannae. He should have followed Maharbal's advice and sent his cavalry dashing off to Rome. His bruised and battered army could have lumbered after it.

While Hannibal was in no position to storm the city, much less to take it by siege, his shock attack might have scared a traitor into opening a gate. It might have shaken loose one or more of Rome's central-Italian allies. It might have impressed the Carthaginian government enough to send adequate reinforcements. It might have done any number of things to bring a better outcome than Hannibal got.

At the moment that called for the height of audacity, Hannibal shrank back. It was his biggest mistake and it greatly reduced his chances of victory.

In the years following Cannae, Carthage opened a second front in Sicily and tried, without success, to open another in Sardinia. It reinforced its army in Spain, where Rome had opened a second front of its own. This took the focus off the Italian campaign, to disastrous effect. During the entire Second Punic War, Carthage sent about eighty thousand troops to Sardinia, Sicily, and Spain, and only four thousand to Hannibal. He might very well have won the war with those additional troops.

Much of the fault for Hannibal's ultimate failure lies with Carthage's government, which had priorities outside Italy. But Hannibal himself was not blameless. He too looked outside Italy for victory. After the Carthaginian government refused to send him the reinforcements he requested in 215 B.C., perhaps he decided to bow to political reality. He had huge influence in other theaters of war through his brothers' commands in Spain and his connections to important men in Sicily. And he negotiated an alliance with Philip V of Macedon.

None of it worked. Neither Carthage's admirals nor its generals were up to the task. Carthage had no other Hannibals.

But Rome had the capacity to come up with Scipio Africanus. He copied Hannibal's best qualities but added political and strategic skill to them. The result, after a long struggle, was total victory for Rome.

No one could say that Divine Providence favored Hannibal in the Second Punic War, but it did allow him to achieve something in failure that neither Alexander nor Caesar achieved in success. Providence made Hannibal a greater statesman than he was a general.

Various anecdotes circulated about Hannibal in exile. It's dangerous to set too much store by them. But if they are true, they suggest that Hannibal retained his intelligence and his charm even as he grew increasingly bitter.

One story says that Scipio came to Ephesus, a city in Anatolia, on an embassy to Antiochus and met Hannibal. Scipio asked Hannibal who the greatest general of all time was. Alexander, said Hannibal, because he achieved so much with such a small army and because he traveled such vast distances. Second came Pyrrhus because of his talent for choosing the right battleground and deploying his men well, and because of his skill at winning the support of Italians for him, a foreigner. Hannibal ranked himself third.

Then Scipio asked what Hannibal would have said if Hannibal had defeated him. Without missing a beat, the story goes, Hannibal replied that, in that case, he would consider himself the greatest general of all.

It was a graceful compliment and shrewd—"Punic wit," as Livy says. But Hannibal did not give it up easily. He was too politically astute to make an enemy of Scipio, but Hannibal proved less polite when he wasn't facing Rome's greatest general.

The story goes that his hosts in Ephesus invited Hannibal to a lecture by the renowned philosopher Phormio. He spoke on generalship and wowed everyone except Hannibal. Excusing himself first as a Phoenician speaker whose Greek was imperfect, he then stuck in the knife. Hannibal "said that he had seen many doddering old men but he had never seen anyone more senile than Phormio."

If the tale is true, it reveals a man of wit who used diplomacy only to soften up the audience for bluntness. He was angry too and maybe sensitive to his own age, since he was in his midfifties at the time, an age that his two heroes, Alexander and Pyrrhus, never reached.

CAESAR

Caesar was mature. That's one of the main reasons for his success. Unlike Alexander or Hannibal, each of whom was a supreme commander in his twenties, Caesar did not hold supreme command until his early forties. That was in Gaul; he was fifty when he crossed the Rubicon and began the civil war.

Caesar had other advantages as well compared with Alexander and Hannibal. He came last of the three, and so he could learn from his predecessors' mistakes. When he began the civil war, he had the experience, the self-confidence, and the veterans of one of the most successful military campaigns in history, the conquest of Gaul.

Gaul made up for what might have been a disadvantage for Caesar—he was more or less a self-made man. Caesar was neither a king nor the son of a famous warrior father. True, he came from an aristocratic family with important connections, but he had to rise on his own talent. That, as much as his family's tradition, may explain the rapport with the common man that Caesar always had, and that earned him so much political capital.

But it was his status as a mature adult that really set Caesar apart from the other two commanders. He had seen enough of life to be surprised by very little of it. He had nothing to prove in battle; he would just as soon win the war by bribery and payoffs. "To know all is to forgive all," as the saying goes, and Caesar had known a great deal by the age of fifty. That may help explain his policy of clemency.

Perhaps his age also contributed to Caesar's famous speed. He was an old man in a hurry. Caesar conquered the Roman empire and won the civil war in just a little more than four years. It took Alexander nine years to conquer the Persian empire, and an advance force of Philip's army had been softening up the Persians for two years before Alexander began. Hannibal's war with Rome lasted seventeen years.

Caesar's long life also let him show the extraordinary range of his talent. Unlike the other two commanders, he was a successful domestic politician before he became a general. He knew how to use all the levers of power. He was also an outstanding public speaker. Alexander and Hannibal were literate men, but only Caesar wrote books—brilliant books. Even two thousand years later, his *Commentaries* are classic works of military narrative and political propaganda.

These talents helped Caesar greatly but they also entailed costs. On the one hand, he had mastered the art of outdoing his rivals or making an end run around them. And he raised communication to an art form. On the other hand, he identified too closely with the class from which he had risen. In spite of his populist tendencies, he was every inch a Roman aristocrat. Caesar still wanted the admiration and respect of the noble peers over whom he eventually towered. He was no longer one of them but he couldn't accept the fact.

And yet, unlike Alexander or Hannibal, Caesar had learned that there was more to life than battlefield triumphs. He knew how satisfying it was to enact laws that made his country better. So, after winning the civil war, he enacted many new laws.

Caesar failed to solve the political problems of the Roman republic that caused the civil war in the first place. Yet he showed more interest in governing than Alexander did even if, in the end, Caesar followed Alexander by opting out. Both men preferred new wars abroad to the messy and frustrating business of governing at home. Still, some of Caesar's reforms had consequences that lasted for centuries—and, in the case of his calendar, for thousands of years. He came as close to combining military and political success as any of the three commanders did.

Like Hannibal, Caesar took moderate risks in battle. He proved immensely cautious on the strategic level, though. He didn't make a big move without thinking ahead two, three, even five or ten moves. For instance, after winning control of Italy in 49 B.C., he didn't turn eastward before first conquering Spain. On the operational level, by contrast, Caesar was a daredevil. From his late autumn crossing of the Adriatic in 49 B.C. to his leap into battle in Alexandria in 48 to his scattershot crossing from Sicily to Africa in 46, Caesar took big chances. He had every reason to fail but, again and again, he succeeded. He attributed his success to the good fortune of Caesar, but we may look for the hand of Divine Providence.

Caesar's battle tactics had nothing of the elegance of Alexander's or Hannibal's, but the Romans rarely were elegant in war. Cavalry was never a Roman strong suit, and their infantry was powerful and flexible but rarely balletic. Fortunately for Caesar, most of his enemies were Romans too. He had considerable advantages over them. A large number of his men were veterans and they were buoyed by their success in Gaul.

As a commander, Caesar was a great improviser, whether against Pompey's cavalry at Pharsalus or his own men's near-mutinous behavior at the start of Thapsus. He never lost his nerve, whether in the face of deadly Numidian cavalrymen at Ruspina or the sudden specter of defeat at Munda.

And he was a great leader of men. Caesar's soldiers loved him. Few generals could have kept their army together through the near-starvation conditions of Dyrrachium or the long march that followed defeat there. Only a commander with political instincts as sharp—and as cold-blooded—as Caesar's would then have rewarded them by granting permission for them to sack a city. To turn to another occasion, only Caesar had the oratorical skill to end a mutiny with a single word.

Logistics was not Caesar's strong suit, as shown both by Dyrrachium and the North African campaign. He should have paid more attention to infrastructure. But he certainly knew the importance of money, as shown by his actions everywhere, especially in Egypt and the Near East. And organizational skill will take a general only so far. Pompey was a great organizer but he lacked Caesar's killer instinct. Pompey was too cautious, for example, to take the risk of trying to finish off Caesar after getting him on the run at Dyrrachium. Caesar would never have held back.

Caesar won the civil war by audacity, talent, and sheer will. He lost the peace through frustration and arrogance. Political bickering in the Roman Forum was a huge comedown from smart salutes in a military camp. Caesar must surely have been relieved in March 44 B.C. as he readied to leave Rome for three years of war in the East.

And then, there was the problem of his arrogance. Caesar refused to understand how insulted the other Romans were by his "clemency" or, if he understood it, he refused to believe that anyone would have the guts to touch him. So he dismissed his bodyguard and died on the Ides of March.

A leader must listen not only to his heart and his head; he must have his finger on the pulse of the body politic. In the end, Caesar communed only with himself and with the gods whom he thought were on his side. Like Alexander, he fell prey to delusions of grandeur and omnipotence.

FAIREST OF THEM ALL?

Three great commanders, but which of them was the greatest? When it comes to ambition and audacity, we are spoiled for choice. All three unleashed terror on civilians. All three were guided by the hand of Divine Providence. And yet, certain differences stand out.

Hannibal was probably the greatest commander, both in combat and in the field. He carried out one of the most elegant and destructive examples of victory by envelopment in the annals of military history—Cannae. If Philip and Alexander began the art of battlefield mobility, Hannibal brought it to perfection. Then too, Hannibal held his army together for fifteen years in Italy without a mutiny. That was true leadership.

Hannibal was also the worst strategist. Caesar was probably the best. Not only did he conquer the Roman empire quickly, in little more than four years, he did so methodically and by design. His good judgment was all but unfailing. Alexander was a great strategist as well but he made a major blunder against Memnon and the Persian fleet. Only the intervention of Divine Providence saved him. Nor did Alexander know when or how to end the war. He continued fighting far too long.

Both Alexander and Caesar showed deep insight into the stages of war, but Caesar wins this prize. He indulged in nothing as unnecessary and draining as Alexander's wars in Sogdiana and India. Hannibal did not understand the stages of war.

Alexander was nearly as good a field commander as Hannibal and nearly as good a strategist as Caesar. When it came to military operations, he was the most adaptable and agile. He was also the most successful manager of logistics and infrastructure. He started out broke and ended up the richest man in the world. He always had plenty of manpower.

Alexander was without peer when it came to branding. Caesar's name is unforgettable and his success is stamped on every page of his *Commentaries*. But Alexander was selling youth and charisma—literal charisma, in its original sense of divine grace. Neither the wit of *Veni Vidi Vici* nor the force of Hannibal as Hercules can compare with that.

Conquerors rarely make good peacemakers and they are even worse as administrators. Hannibal did succeed as an administrator but not as a conqueror. Alexander showed remarkable grandeur of vision for his new empire, but he paid so little attention to the practical details that it collapsed on his death. He changed the world by ending the Persian empire and laying the foundation for the Hellenistic kingdoms, but they went their own way rather than following his stamp.

Caesar closed the door on the Roman republic and its limited liberty. He was Rome's first post-republican king, even if he avoided the term. Caesar left an heir, Octavian, the later Augustus, to complete the project that he began. Finally, however flawed and arrogant his policy of clemency was, he pardoned his enemies rather than execute them. He deserves credit for that.

All in all, Caesar was the greatest of antiquity's great commanders. Hannibal is the hero of lost causes and perfect battles. Alexander has an unmatched star quality. Caesar, for all his flaws, came closest to statesmanship.

ACKNOWLEDGMENTS

Michael Fronda and Jacob Nabel read through the manuscript and made valuable comments. Adrienne Mayor, Josiah Ober, Jan Parker, Matthew Sears, David Teegarden, and Kevin Weddle did the same for individual chapters. Thanks to C. R. Zwolinski for developmental and line editing and for coaching my writing.

I benefited greatly from conversations with and comments by Andrew Amato, Hans Beck, David Blome, Max Boot, Flaminia Cervesi, Judith Dupre, Robert Faulkner, Michael Fontaine, Richard Fontaine, Charlie Goldberg, Victor Davis Hanson, Jayne Hanlin, Chris Harper, Bart Howard, Bettany Hughes, Isabel Hull, John Hyland, Ann E. Killebrew, Stephen Kling, Damien Lazar, Christopher Lynch, Sturt Manning, Luciana Mariotti, Kim McKnight, Katherine Milne, Ian Morris, Waller R. Newell, Brandon Olson, Marissa Valle Pittaluga, Richard Polenberg, Hunter Rawlings, Joseph Roisman, Jeffrey Rusten, Philip Sabin, Walter Scheidel, J. R. Son, Rob Tempio, Viviana Valenti, and Theodora Zemek.

Serhan Güngör provided friendship and expert guidance along the path of Alexander in Turkey. The American School of Classical Studies at Athens first set me on Alexander's footsteps in Greece long ago. Jim Zurer supplied professional travel advice about Italy. Susan Dixon does a great job with my Web site. Suzanne Lang provides invaluable secretarial and logistical assistance.

It is a pleasure to thank the faculty, students, and staff of the departments of history and classics at Cornell, as well as the staff of the John M. Olin Library there.

My agent, Cathy Hemming, gave sage advice every step of the way, from first idea to finished manuscript. My editor, Bob Bender, gave the manuscript his wise and careful touch, aided by his assistant, Johanna Li.

My wife, Marcia, offered me more wisdom and support than anyone has the right to ask for. But she earned special merit by tromping around the battlefield of Cannae with me in hundred-plus-degree heat. Our children, Sylvie and Mike, wisely stayed at home.

Finally, this book would never have been written without the influence of three commanders of the classroom, the late Alvin Bernstein, Donald Kagan, and Walter LaFeber. I dedicate this book to them, with gratitude.

A NOTE ON SOURCES

I include the main works in English, with a few essential, foreign-language texts, that I used to write this study and as a guide to further reading.

Students of classics and ancient history should have *The Oxford Classical Dictionary*, 3rd edition (Oxford: Oxford University Press, 1999) by their side. Excellent maps of the ancient world can be found in Richard J. A. Talbert, ed., *The Barrington Atlas of the Ancient Greco-Roman World*. (Princeton: Princeton University Press, 2000).

ALEXANDER

None of our three commanders has generated as many scholarly books and articles as Alexander. What follows is just a taste.

A good place to begin is Philip Freeman's recent *Alexander the Great* (New York, Simon & Schuster, 2011), which offers a knowledgeable and readable overview. The most thorough and scholarly introduction to Alexander is A. B. Bosworth, *Conquest and Empire* (Cambridge: Cambridge University Press, 1988), but it is not an easy read. Robin Lane Fox's *Alexander the Great* (London: Penguin Books, 1973) is a powerful narrative and just as well grounded in the scholarship—and the author wears his learning lightly. Peter Green's *Alexander of Macedon: A Historical Biography, 356–323 BC* (Berkeley: University of California Press, 1991, originally published 1974) is also good but not as good on military matters. Green and Bosworth are harsher on Alexander than are Freeman and Lane Fox. J. R. Hamilton's *Alexander the Great* (London: Hutchinson University Library, 1973) is very concise.

Other good, recent introductions to Alexander include Paul Cartledge, *Alexander the Great: The Hunt for a New Past* (Woodstock & New York:

Overlook Press, 2004); Waldemar Heckel, *The Conquests of Alexander the Great* (Cambridge: Cambridge University Press, 2008); Guy MacLean Rogers, *Alexander: The Ambiguity of Greatness* (New York: Random House, 2004), and Joseph Roisman, ed., *Brill's Companion to Alexander the Great* (Leiden and Boston: Brill, 2003).

For introductions to the history of Macedonia and Philip II, see Eugene N. Borza, *In the Shadow of Olympus: The Emergence of Macedon* (Princeton: Princeton University Press, 1990); Joseph Roisman and Ian Worthington, eds., *A Companion to Ancient Macedonia* (Malden, MA: Wiley-Blackwell, 2010), and Ian Worthington, *Philip II of Macedonia* (New Haven: Yale University Press, 2008).

Scholars strive for balance. Still, Alexander has a way of bringing out extremes and some of the best historians of Alexander tend to fall among his admirers or detractors. The dean of the admirers is W. W. Tarn, *Alexander the Great*, 2 vols. (Cambridge, England: Cambridge University Press 1948), who wrote a classic and influential account offering an idealistic portrait of Alexander as a proponent of universal brotherhood. A year later, in 1949, Fritz Schachermeyr described Alexander as a terrifying and dangerous genius in a magisterial work, revised in 1973 as *Alexander der Grosse: Das Problem seiner Persönlichkeit und seines Wirkens* (Vienna: Österreichische Akademie der Wissenschaften; Philosophisch-Historische Klasse; Sitzungsberichte, 1973). In English the leading skeptic of the late twentieth century was Ernst Badian, who sketched an image of Alexander as opportunistic, fallible, and anything but idealistic in a series of influential essays. Among the best are "Alexander the Great and the Unity of Mankind," *Historia* 7 (1958): 424–44; "Alexander the Great and the Loneliness of Power," *AUMLA* 17 (1962): 80–91, reprinted in Badian, *Studies in Greek and Roman History* (New York: Barnes & Noble, 1964), 192–205; "Alexander the Great and the Greeks of Asia," in E. Badian, ed., *Ancient Society and Institutions: Studies Presented to Victor Ehrenberg on his 75th Birthday* (Oxford, England: Blackwell, 1966), 37–69; "Agis III," *Hermes* 95.2 (1967): 170–92; "Alexander the Great, 1948–1961," *Classical World* 65 (1971) 37–56, 77–83; "Alexander in Iran," in I. Gershovitch, ed., *The Cambridge History of Iran*, vol. II (Cambridge, England: Cambridge University Press, 1985), 420–501; "Darius III," *Harvard Studies in Classical Philology* 100 (2000): 241–68. Badian also wrote a series of short but sharp encyclopedia entries on Alexander topics for *En-*

cyclopedia Iranica, http://www.iranica.com/, and *Brill's New Pauly: encyclopaedia of the ancient world* (Leiden, Brill: 2007).

A. B. Bosworth is the most important skeptic writing about Alexander today. In addition to his *Conquest and Empire* (above), see his *Alexander and the East: The Tragedy of Triumph* (Oxford: Clarendon Press, 1996). For a stimulating if overdrawn argument for Alexander as strategic failure, see J. D. Grainger, *Alexander the Great Failure* (London: Continuum Books, 2007).

Frank L. Holt has written several important books about Alexander's campaigns in Bactria and Sogdiana, among them the intriguing *Alexander the Great and the Mystery of the Elephant Medallions* (Berkeley: University of California Press, 2003) and the provocative *Into the Land of Bones: Alexander the Great in Afghanistan* (Berkeley: University of California Press, 2005). Pierre Briant emphasizes Alexander's debt to the Persians in *Alexander the Great and His Empire: A Short Introduction*, translated by Amélie Kuhrt (Princeton: Princeton University Press, 2010).

Most of the ancient sources are available in paperback. The reader should begin with Arrian, *The Campaigns of Alexander* (Harmondsworth, England, & Baltimore, MD: Penguin Books, 1976), and then continue with Quintus Curtius Rufus, *The History of Alexander* (Harmondsworth, England: Penguin Books, 2004). Next comes Plutarch's "Life of Alexander," which is conveniently found in Plutarch, *The Age of Alexander: Nine Greek Lives*, translated and annotated by Ian Scott-Kilvert (Harmondsworth, England, 1973). Another important source, Diodorus Siculus, is best read in the Loeb Classical Library edition: C. Bradford Welles, translator; Diodorus Siculus, *Library of History*, Volume VIII, Books 16.66–17 (Cambridge, MA: Harvard University Press, 1963). A minor ancient source, Justin's Epitome of the *Philippic History*, of Pompeius Trogus, can be found in translation at http://www.forumromanum.org/literature/justin/english/index.html.

On the Macedonian way of war, F. E. Adcock's *The Greek and Macedonian Art of War* (Berkeley: University of California Press, 1962) is still a good introduction. J. R. Ashley, *The Macedonian Empire: The Era of Warfare Under Philip II and Alexander the Great, 359–323 B.C.* (Jefferson, NC, & London: McFarland, 1998), is insightful although not always accurate.

On Alexander as commander, a good place to begin is the perceptive sketch by John Keegan in his *The Mask of Command* (New York: Penguin Books, 1988). The great military theorist J.F.C. Fuller offers an incisive analysis in *The Generalship of Alexander the Great* (New Brunswick, NJ: Rutgers University Press, 1960), if not one always backed up by later scholarship. N.G.L. Hammond, *Alexander the Great: King, Commander, and Statesman* (Park Ridge, NJ: Noyes Press, 1980), is scholarly and perceptive if sometimes worshipful; A. B. Lloyd, "Philip II and Alexander the Great: The Moulding of Macedon's Army," in A. B. Lloyd, ed., *Battle in Antiquity* (London: Duckworth, in association with the Classical Press of Wales, 1996), 169–98; Nick Sekunda, *The Army of Alexander the Great* (Oxford: Osprey Publishing, 1984); Idem, *The Persian Army 560–330 BC* (London: Osprey Publishing, 1992).

On Alexander's pitched battles, see the following studies, in addition to the books above: *Granicus*—E. Badian, "The Battle of the Granicus, A New Look," *Ancient Macedonia II* (Thessaloniki: 1977): 271–93; Clive Foss, "The Battle of the Granicus: A New Look," *ibid.*: 495–502; N.G.L. Hammond, "The Battle of the Granicus River," *Journal of Hellenic Studies* 100, Centenary Issue (1980): 73–88; Devine, A. M. "Demythologizing the Battle of the Granicus," *Phoenix* 40 (1986): 265–78; Nikos Th. Nikolitsis, *The Battle of the Granicus* (Stockholm: [Svenska Institutet i Athen], 1974); M. Thompson, *Granicus 334 BC: Alexander's first Persian victory* (Oxford: Osprey Publishing, 2007). *Issus*—A. M. Devine, "The Location of the Battlefield of Issus," *Liverpool Classical Monthly* 5.1 (1985): 3–10; Idem, "The Strategies of Alexander the Great and Darius III in the Issus Campaign (333 B.C.)," *Ancient World* 12 (1985): 25–37; Idem, "Grand Tactics at the Battle of Issus," *Ancient World* 12 (1985): 39–59. *Gaugamela*—E. W. Marsden, *The Campaign of Gaugamela* (Liverpool: Liverpool University Press, 1964); A. M. Devine, "Grand tactics at Gaugamela," *Phoenix* 29 (1975): 374–85; Idem, "Gaugamela, a Tactical and Source-Critical Study," *Ancient World* (1986) 13: 87–16. *Hydaspes*—A. M. Devine, "The Battle of Hydaspes, a Tactical and Source-Critical Study," *Ancient World* (1987) 16: 91–113.

I have benefited from the following studies on specific subjects: Ada Cohen, *The Alexander Mosaic: Stories of Victory and Defeat* (Cambridge: Cambridge University Press, 1997); Due, B. (1993), "Alexander's Inspiration and Ideas," in Jesper Carlsen, ed., *Alexander the Great: Reality and Myth* (Rome: L'Erma di Bretschneider, 2002) 53–60; R. Edwards, "Two Horns, Three Religions. How Alexander the Great ended up in the Quran," *American Philological Association, 133rd Annual Meeting Program (Philadelphia, 5 January 2002) 36*, under *Reception of Classical Literature, No. 5.*; D. W. Engels,

Alexander the Great and the Logistics of the Macedonian Army (Berkeley: University of California Press, 1978); E. A. Fredricksmeyer (1982), "On the Final Aims of Philip II," in W. Lindsay Adams and Eugene N. Borza, eds., *Philip II, Alexander the Great, and the Macedonian Heritage* (Washington, DC: University Press of America, 1982): 85–98; E. A. Fredricksmeyer, "Alexander the Great and the Kingship of Asia," in A. B. Bosworth, ed., *Alexander the Great in Fact and Fiction* (New York: Oxford University Press, 2000), 136–66; A. Pasinli, *The Book of Alexander Sarcophagus* (Istanbul: A Turizm Yayinlari, 1997); E. M. Anson, "The Persian Fleet in 334," *Classical Philology* 84 (1989): 44–89.

On Alexander's route, see the classic studies by Freya Stark, *Alexander's Path from Caria to Cilicia* (London: J. Murray, 1958) and "Alexander's March from Miletus to Phrygia," *Journal of Hellenic Studies* 78 (1958): 102–20; and the irresistible book and television documentary by Michael Wood, *In the Footsteps of Alexander the Great: A Journey from Greece to Asia* (Berkeley: University of California Press, 1997), and *In the Footsteps of Alexander the Great* (London: BBC Worldwide, 2010). See also Doganer, S. (2007), "Alexander the Great: Warrior King as Geographer," [in Turkish] *Türk Cografya Dergisi* 48: 19–58.

Two very different books about Alexander as a strategist, each offbeat and each worth reading, are Partha Bose, *Alexander the Great's Art of Strategy* (New York: Penguin, 2003), and David J. Lonsdale, *Alexander the Great, Lessons in Strategy* (London and New York: Routledge, 2007).

Mary Renault's two fine novels about Alexander now seem a little dated: *Fire from Heaven* (New York: Vintage, 2002, originally published 1969) and *The Persian Boy* (New York: Vintage, 1988, originally published 1972). For insightful, imaginative, and exciting re-creations of Alexander's battles, see two novels by Stephen Pressfield, *The Virtues of War: A Novel of Alexander the Great* (New York: Bantam, 2005) and *The Afghan Campaign: A Novel* (New York: Broadway, 2007). Valerio Massimo Manfredi has a trilogy about Alexander: *Alexander: Child of a Dream* (New York: Washington Square Press, 2001), *Alexander: The Sands of Ammon* (New York: Washington Square Press, 2002), and *Alexander: To the Ends of the Earth* (New York: Washington Square Press, 2002). My favorite is *The Sands of Ammon* because of its dramatic portrayal of Memnon of Rhodes and its evocation of the Anatolian landscape.

HANNIBAL

Lost causes have a special appeal and Hannibal is no exception. He brings out something endearing for writers although readers should be aware that older books, especially those before 1945, often purvey a certain amount of nonsense about the "Semitic character."

There is no such problem in an excellent, recent, and short introductory book by an outstanding scholar of the Punic Wars, Dexter Hoyos, *Hannibal: Rome's Greatest Enemy* (Exeter, UK: Bristol Phoenix, 2008). An introductory article by Hoyos is also enlightening, "Hannibal: What Kind of Genius?" *Greece and Rome*, 2nd series 30.2 (1983): 171–80. Three older, idiosyncratic, and usually charming introductions to Hannibal are G. P. Baker, *Hannibal* (New York: Cooper Square Press, 1999, originally published 1929); Leonard Cottrell, *Hannibal Enemy of Rome* (New York: Da Capo Press, 1992, originally published 1960); Ernle Bradford, *Hannibal* (New York: Dorset Press, 1981). The best and most reliable scholarly volume in English is Serge Lancel, *Hannibal*, translated by Antonia Nevill (Oxford: Blackwell, 1998). Jakob Seibert wrote a magisterial biography in *Hannibal* (Darmstadt: Wissenschaftliche Buchgesellschaft, 1993), but it has not been translated from German to English. Dexter Hoyos offers an excellent analysis of Hannibal and his family in *Hannibal's Dynasty: Power and Politics in the Western Mediterranean, 247–183 BC* (London & New York: Routledge, 2003).

The best introduction to the Punic Wars is Adrian Goldsworthy, *The Punic Wars* (London: Cassell, 2000). See now the essays in Dexter Hoyos, ed., *A Companion to the Punic Wars* (Malden, MA: Wiley-Blackwell, 2011). For an insightful analysis, see Brian Caven, *The Punic Wars* (New York, St. Martin's Press, 1992). See also R. M. Errington, *The Dawn of Empire: Rome's Rise to World Power* (Ithaca, NY: Cornell University Press, 1972); N. Bagnall, *The Punic Wars: Rome, Carthage, and the Struggle for the Mediterranean* (London: Pimlico, 1999). T. A. Dorey and D. R. Dudley, *Rome Against Carthage* (Garden City, NJ: Doubleday & Company, Inc., 1972), is short and sound.

The single best military history of the Second Punic War is J. F. Lazenby, *Hannibal's War* (Norman: University of Oklahoma Press, 1978). John Peddie, *Hannibal's War* (Thrupp, Stroud, Gloucestershire, England: Sutton

Publishing, 1997), is insightful and often unconventional in its judgments. There is much of value in the essays in Tim Cornell, Boris Rankov, and Philip Sabin, eds., *The Second Punic War: a reappraisal* (London: Institute of Classical Studies, School of Advanced Study, University of London, 1996). Terence Wise and M. Healy, *Hannibal's War with Rome* (Oxford: Osprey Publishing, 2002), is a fine source of illustrations.

Richard Miles offers an excellent introduction to Carthage, with special insight into Hannibal's use of communications and a sober discussion of child sacrifice, in *Carthage Must Be Destroyed: The Rise and Fall of an Ancient Civilization* (London: Allen Lane, 2010). A gorgeous collection of photos of art objects and archaeological finds from Carthage and the Carthaginian empire can be found in *Hannibal ad Portas: Macht und Reichtum Karthagos/ herausgegeben von Badesischen Landesmuseum Karlsruhe* (Stuttgart: Theiss, 2004); the text of this museum catalog is in German.

For an introduction to Rome in the era of the Second Punic War, see Michael H. Crawford, *The Roman Republic*, second edition (Cambridge, MA: Harvard University Press, 1993). See also H. H. Scullard, *A History of the Roman World from 753 to 146 B.C.* (London: Methuen & Co, 1970).

For the Roman army, see below under "Caesar."

On the man who beat Hannibal, see B. H. Liddell Hart, *Scipio Africanus, Greater than Napoleon* (Cambridge, MA: Da Capo Press, 2004, originally published 1926) and H. H. Scullard, *Scipio Africanus: Soldier and Politician* (Ithaca: Cornell University Press, 1970).

On the origins of the Second Punic War, Donald Kagan, *On the Origins of War and the Preservation of Peace* (New York: Anchor Books, 1996), offers a chapter of astute and concise analysis. For a detailed account, see Dexter Hoyos, *Unplanned Wars: The Origins of the First and Second Punic Wars* (Berlin & New York: Walter de Gruyter, 1998). On Polybius and Hannibal's decision to go to war against Rome, see A. M. Eckstein, "Hannibal at New Carthage: Polybius 3.15 and the Power of Irrationality," *Classical Philology* 84.1 (1989): 1–15.

Some other valuable studies of topics in the Second Punic War include: *On Hannibal and Rome's Italian allies*, see Michael P. Fronda, *Between Rome and Carthage* (Cambridge: Cambridge University Press, 2010). *On Fabius's strategy*, P. Erdkamp, "Polybius, Livy, and the Fabian Strategy," *Ancient Society* 23 (1992): 127–47. *On Hannibal and religion*, see T. W. Africa, "The

One-Eyed Man against Rome," *Historia* 19.5 (1970): 528–38; B. Corinne, "Melqart," in Lindsay Jones, editor in chief, *The Encyclopedia of Religion* (Detroit: Macmillan Reference USA, 2005), vol. 9: 5,846–849.

On the battle of Cannae, start with Robert O'Connell, *The Ghosts of Cannae: Hannibal and the Darkest Hour of the Roman Republic* (New York: Random House, 2010), or Adrian Goldsworthy, *Cannae: Hannibal's Greatest Victory* (London: Cassell Military, 2001); see also Mark Daly, *Cannae: The Experience of Battle in the Second Punic War* (London & New York: Routledge, 2002); Martin Samuels, "The Reality of Cannae," *Militärgeschichtliche Mitteilungen* 47 (1990): 7–29. On the aftermath of the battle, see J. F. Shean, "Hannibal's Mules: The Logistical Limitations of Hannibal's Army and the Battle of Cannae, 216 B.C.," *Historia* 45.2 (1996): 159–87.

The two most important ancient sources are available in English translation in paperback: Polybius, *The Rise of the Roman Empire*, translated by Ian Scott-Kilvert, selected with an introduction by F. W. Walbank (Harmondsworth, New York: Penguin, 1979), and Livy, *The war with Hannibal; books XXI–XXX of The History of Rome from its foundation*, translated by Aubrey de Sélincourt, edited with an introduction by Betty Radice (Harmondsworth: Penguin, 1965). Plutarch's Lives of Fabius Maximus and Marcellus, two important Roman commanders of the Second Punic War, can be found in Plutarch, *Makers of Rome*, translated with an Introduction by Ian Scott-Kilvert (Harmondsworth: Penguin, 1965). Appian's uneven account is available in Horace White, translator, *Appian's Roman History*, vol. 1 (Cambridge, MA: Harvard University Press, 1930). For Cornelius Nepos's short biographies of Hamilcar and Hannibal, see *Epitome of Roman History / Lucius Annaeus Florus* [with an English translation by Edward Seymour Forster]. *Cornelius Nepos* [with an English translation by John C. Rolfe], (Cambridge, MA: Harvard University Press, 1929). For a translation of the fragments (that is, surviving passages) of Diodorus Siculus, *Library of History*, Books 26 and 29, on Hannibal, see http://penelope.uchicago.edu/Thayer/E/Roman/Texts/Diodorus_Siculus/26*.html, and http://penelope.uchicago.edu/Thayer/E/Roman/Texts/Diodorus_Siculus/29*.html, and Book 25, on Hamilcar Barca, see http://penelope.uchicago.edu/Thayer/E/Roman/Texts/Diodorus_Siculus/25*.html.

David Anthony Durham, *Pride of Carthage: a Novel of Hannibal* (New York: Anchor, 2006), is a stirring and readable account of the Second Punic

War. Ross Leckie, *Hannibal* (Washington, DC: Regnery, 1996), vivid and powerful, is a novel written in the form of a memoir. Gustave Flaubert's classic historical novel *Salammbo* is set in Carthage shortly after the First Punic War, during the mercenary revolt or Truceless War (ca.240 B.C.). For a historical account, see Dexter Hoyos, *Truceless War: Carthage's Fight for Survival* (Leiden & Boston: Brill, 2007).

CAESAR

There are many good books about Caesar. For the man in a nutshell, it would be hard to beat J.P.V.D. Balsdon's excellent little volume *Julius Caesar* (New York: Atheneum, 1967). An outstanding recent biography is Adrian Goldsworthy, *Caesar: Life of a Colossus* (New Haven: Yale University Press, 2008). Philip Freeman, *Julius Caesar* (New York: Simon & Schuster, 2008), is astute and concise. A classic of good judgment and good scholarship is Matthias Gelzer, *Caesar: Politician and Statesman*, transl. by Peter Needham (Oxford: Blackwell, 1969). Christian Meier, *Caesar*, transl. by David McLintock (New York: Basic Books/Harper Collins, 1995) is a great book, scholarly and gripping, but sometimes idiosyncratic. *On Caesar as communicator*, see Zvi Yavetz, *Julius Caesar and His Public Image* (Ithaca, NY: Cornell University Press, 1983). *On Caesar's appeal to the poor and noncitizens*, see Luciano Canfora, *Julius Caesar: The Life and Times of the People's Dictator*, transl. by Marian Hill and Kevin Windle (Berkeley & Los Angeles: University of California Press, 2007).

For an introduction to the turbulent era of the late Roman republic, see Tom Holland, *Rubicon* (New York: Doubleday, 2003), or Mary Beard and Michael Crawford, *Rome in the Late Republic* (London: Duckworth, 2009). For a detailed account, see Erich Gruen, *The Last Generation of the Roman Republic*, second edition (Berkeley: University of California Press, 1995).

On Caesar as military commander, see J.F.C. Fuller, *Julius Caesar: Man, Soldier and Tyrant* (New Brunswick, NJ: Da Capo, 1965); Kimberly Kagan, *The Eye of Command* (Ann Arbor: University of Michigan Press, 2006).

On Caesar as a writer and historical source, see F. E. Adcock, *Caesar as Man of Letters* (Cambridge: Cambridge University Press, 1956); the essays in Kathryn Welch and Anton Powell, eds., *Julius Caesar as Artful Reporter:*

The War Commentaries as Political Instruments (London, Duckworth, Swansea: Classical Press of Wales, 1998); J. E. Lendon, "The Rhetoric of Combat: Greek Military Theory and Roman Culture in Julius Caesar's Battle Descriptions," *Classical Antiquity* 18 (1999): 273–329; L. F. Raditsa, "Julius Caesar and His Writings," in H. Temporini, ed., *Aufstieg und Niedergang der römischen Welt; Geschichte und Kultur Roms im Spiegel der neueren Forschung, Joseph Vogt zu seinem 75. Geburtstag gewidmet, I: Von den Anfängen Roms bis zum Ausgang der Republik,* vol. I.3 (Berlin, New York: De Gruyter, 1973): 417–56.

On Pompey, see Peter Greenhalgh, *Pompey, the Republican Prince* (Columbia: University of Missouri Press, 1982), and Robin Seager, *Pompey the Great, A Political Biography,* second edition (Malden, MA: Blackwell, 2002); Patricia Southern, *Pompey* (Stroud: Tempus, 2002). See also Kurt von Fritz, "Pompey's Policy Before and After the Outbreak of the Civil War of 49 B.C.," *Transactions of the American Philological Association* 74 (1942): 145–80; John Leach, *Pompey the Great* (London: Croom Helm, 1978).

On the battle of Pharsalus, see W. Gwatkin, "Some Reflections on the Battle of Pharsalus," *Transactions and Proceedings of the American Philological Association* 87 (1956): 109–24; C. B. R. Pelling, "Pharsalus," *Historia* 22 (1973): 249–59; Matthew Leigh, *Lucan: Spectacle and Engagement* (Oxford: Clarendon Press, 1973), 77–157; J. D. Morgan, "Palaepharsalus—the Battle and the Town," *American Journal of Archaeology* 87 (1983): 23–54; Graham Wylie, "The Road to Pharsalus," *Latomus* 51 (1992): 557–65.

On the Roman way of war, see the old but still good F. E. Adcock, *The Roman Art of War under the Republic* (Cambridge, MA: Harvard University Press, 1940). For a more recent overview see either Adrian Goldsworthy, *Roman Warfare* (New York: Smithsonian Books/Collins, 2005), or Jonathan P. Roth, *Roman Warfare* (Cambridge: Cambridge University Press, 2009). For a more detailed introduction, see Adrian Goldsworthy, *The Complete Roman Army* (New York: Thames & Hudson, 2003); C. M. Gilliver, *The Roman Art of War* (Charleston, SC: Tempus, 1999), offers thoughtful analysis. See also Kate Gilliver, Adrian Goldsworthy, and Michael Whitby, *Rome at War* (Oxford: Osprey Publishing, 2005), and the relevant essays in Paul Erdkamp, ed., *A Companion to the Roman Army* (Oxford: Blackwell, 2007). L. J. F. Keppie, *The Making of the Roman Army: From Republic to Empire* (Norman: University of Oklahoma Press, 1984), offers a detailed analysis of the evolution of the Roman army in the Republic, and John Peddie, *The Roman War Machine* (Conshohocken, Penn.: Combined Publishing, 1996), is good on generalship. *On logistics*, see Paul Erdkamp, *Hunger and the Sword: Warfare and Food Supply in Roman Republican Wars (264–30 B.C.)*, (Amsterdam: J. C. Gieben, 1998), and Jonathan P. Roth, *The Logistics of the Roman Army at War (264 B.C.–A.D. 235)*, (Leiden and Boston: Brill, 1999).

A valuable selection of the sources, with commentary and bibliography, can be found in Matthew Dillon and Lynda Garland, eds., *Ancient Rome: From the Early Republic to the Assassination of Julius Caesar* (London and New York: Routledge, 2005). Julius Caesar, *The Civil War, with the anonymous Alexandrian, African, and Spanish Wars*, translated with an Introduction and Notes by J. M. Carter (Oxford: Oxford University Press, 1997); Appian, *The Civil Wars*, translated with an Introduction by J. M. Carter (London; New York: Penguin Books, 1996). For Dio Cassius's history of Rome, Books 41–44, consult the Loeb Classical Library edition, Dio Cassius, *Roman History*, volume 4: Books 41–44 trans. Earnest [sic] Cary and Herbert Baldwin Foster (Cambridge, MA: Harvard University Press, 1916); the English translation is available online at http://penelope.uchicago.edu/Thayer/E/Roman/Texts/Cassius_Dio/home.html. Plutarch's lives of Pompey and Caesar can be found in Plutarch, *Fall of the Roman Republic*, revised edition, translated with Introduction and Notes by Rex Warner, revised with translations of comparisons and a Preface by Robin Seager, with series Preface by Christopher Pelling (Harmondsworth: Penguin, 2005); Plutarch's lives of Brutus and Mark Antony can be found in Plutarch, *Makers of Rome*, translated with an Introduction by Ian Scott-Kilvert (Harmondsworth: Penguin, 1965); Suetonius's life of Caesar is available in Gaius Suetonius Tranquillus, *The Twelve Caesars*, transl. by Robert Graves, revised with an introduction by Michael Grant (London, New York: Penguin, 2003).

On Cleopatra, see Stacy Schiff, *Cleopatra: A Life* (New York: Little, Brown 2010); Duane Roller, *Cleopatra: A Biography* (Oxford: Oxford University Press, 2010); Diana E. E. Kleiner, *Cleopatra and Rome* (Cambridge, MA: Belknap Press of Harvard University Press, 2005).

Studies of specific subjects include: J.V.P.D. Balsdon, "The Ides of March," *Historia* 7 (1958): 80–94; Elmore, J., "Caesar on the Causes of Mutiny," *Classical Journal* 20 (1925): 430–32; Peter Green, "Caesar and Alexander: Aemulatio, Imitatio, Comparatio," *American Journal of Ancient History* (1979) 3: 1–26.

Colleen McCullough, *Caesar: A Novel* (New York: William Morrow, 1997), is popular and faithful to the historical sources; Steven Saylor, *The Judgment of Caesar: A Novel of Ancient Rome* (New York: St. Martin's Minotaur Books, 2004) and Steven Saylor, *The Triumph of Caesar: A Novel of Ancient Rome* (New York: St. Martin's Minotaur Books, 2008) are engaging detective stories. Conn Iggulden's *Emperor: The Gods of War* (New York: Delacorte Press, 2006) paints a picture of the civil war in broad strokes. Thornton Wilder's *The Ides of March* (New York: Harper Perennial, 2003, originally published 1948) is a subtle delight.

ANCIENT WARFARE

There is no textbook, but for something close to it, see John Gibson Warry, *Warfare in the Classical World: an illustrated encyclopedia of weapons, warriors and warfare in the ancient civilisations of Greece and Rome* (Norman: University of Oklahoma Press, 1995), and Simon Anglim et al., *Fighting techniques of the ancient world 3,000 BC–500 AD: equipment, combat skills, and tactics* (New York: Thomas Dunne Books: St. Martin's Press, 2002). Harry Sidebottom offers a thematic approach in *Ancient Warfare: A Very Short Introduction*, (Oxford and New York: Oxford University Press, 2005). Peter Connolly, *Greece and Rome at War.* (London: Greenhill Books, 2006), offers superb illustrations and sound history.

On strategy in ancient warfare, see the essays in Victor Davis Hanson, ed., *Makers of Ancient Strategy* (Princeton: Princeton University Press, 2010). *On psychology in ancient battles*, see J. E. Lendon, *Soldiers and Ghosts: A History of Battle in Classical Antiquity* (New Haven: Yale University Press, 2006).

Giovanni Brizzi offers an overview of ancient warfare, with an especially good analysis of Hannibal's tactics, in *Il guerriero, l'oplita, il legionario. Gli eserciti nel mondo classico* (Bologna, Italy: Il Mulino, 2002), in Italian.

Philip Sabin, *Lost Battles: Reconstructing the Great Clashes of the Ancient World* (London: Hambledon Continuum, 2008), combines war-gaming and scholarship to reconstruct the ancient battlefield.

On cavalry, see Philip Sidnell, *Warhorse: Cavalry in Ancient Warfare.* (London, Hambledon Continuum, 2006).

GREAT COMMANDERS

One begins with Theodore Ayrault Dodge, *Great captains: a course of six lectures showing the influence on the art of war of the campaigns of Alexander, Hannibal, Caesar, Gustavus Adolphus, Frederick, and Napoleon* (Boston: Houghton, Mifflin, 1892, copyright 1889). Dodge also published detailed, individual volumes on each of these six commanders.

Richard A. Gabriel offers astute analysis and a series of case studies, including Hannibal and Scipio Africanus in *Great Captains of Antiquity*, forewords by Mordechai Gihon and David Jablonsky (Westport, CT: Greenwood, 2001).

Insightful studies of later commanders who might be called "great captains," from the medieval period to the twentieth century, include Sir Basil Henry Liddell Hart, *Great Captains Unveiled* (Freeport, NY: Books for Libraries Press, 1967); Martin Blumemson and James L. Stokesbury, *Masters of the Art of Command* (Boston: Houghton Mifflin, 1975); Martin van Creveld, *Command in War* (Cambridge, MA: Harvard University Press, 1987); Eliot Cohen, *Supreme Command: Soldiers, Statesmen, and Leadership in Wartime* (New York: Free Press, 2002); John Keegan, *The Mask of Command* (New York: Penguin Books, 1988).

For an introduction to modern social science and its scholarship on leadership, see Bernard M. Bass with Ruth Bass, *The Bass Handbook of Leadership*, fourth edition (New York: Free Press, 2008), and various entries in George R. Goethals, Georgia J. Sorenson, James MacGregor Burns, ed., *Encylopedia of Leadership* (Thousand Oaks, CA: Sage Publications, 2004).

On elephants in ancient warfare, see H. H. Scullard, *The Elephant in the Greek and Roman World* (Ithaca, NY: Cornell University Press, 1974).

On strategic intuition, see William R. Duggan, *Coup d'oeil: strategic intuition in Army planning* (Carlisle Barracks, PA: Strategic Studies Institute, U. S. Army War College, 2005) and Idem, *Strategic Intuition: The Creative Spark in Human Achievement* (New York: Columbia Business School Pub., 2007).

I found a great deal of wisdom in two recent books on great leaders by political philosophers: Robert Faulkner, *The Case for Greatness: Honorable Ambition and Its Critics* (New Haven: Yale University Press, 2007), and Walter Randy Newell, *The Soul of a Leader: Character, Conviction, and Ten Lessons in Political Greatness* (New York: Harper Collins, 2009). I also benefitted greatly from Winston S. Churchill, *Great Contemporaries* (Chicago: University of Chicago Press, 1973, originally published 1937).

NOTES

1: TEN QUALITIES OF SUCCESSFUL COMMANDERS

2 wearing a mail breastplate: the details of Hannibal's armor are based on a likely reconstruction.

2 bright and fiery look: Livy, *History of Rome* 21.4

6 *Book of Daniel*: 8:1–8, 15–22, 11:2–4.

6 "tribe of the eagle": Abraham Lincoln, "Address to the Young Men's Lyceum of Springfield, Illinois, January 27, 1838" in *Speeches and Writings 1832–1858*. Library of America: New York, 1989, 34.

8 "I didn't follow the cause. I followed the man—and he was my friend": paraphrase of Gaius Matius in his letter to Cicero of 44 B.C.: "*neque enim Caesarem in dissensione civili sum secutus sed amicum,*" Cicero, *Letters to Friends* 11.28.2.

8 The sight of Hannibal in his army cloak: Livy, *History of Rome* 21.4.

9 "Because he loved honor, he loved danger": Plutarch, *Caesar* 17.2.

10 Only the need for sleep and sex: Plutarch, *Life of Alexander* 22.6.

12 "And young man," he said: Plutarch, *Life of Caesar* 35.11.

13 he killed a million people: Plutarch, *Life of Caesar* 15.5.

13 Or so the Romans claimed: Livy, *History of Rome* 31.20.6.

19 "spear-won" land: Diodorus Siculus 17.17.2.

19 No man has ever outdone Alexander's feat: Genghis Khan conquered a much larger empire but he took twenty years to do so and lived to be sixty-five.

2: ATTACK

22 "the splendor of the great prize": Polybius, *Histories* 3.6.12, Loeb translation, http://penelope.uchicago.edu/Thayer/E/Roman/Texts/Polybius/3*.html.

23 "He was by his very nature truly a marvelous man": Polybius, *Histories* 9.22.6.

26 "young, full of martial ardor": Polybius, *Histories* 3.15.6, Loeb translation, http://penelope.uchicago.edu/Thayer/E/Roman/Texts/Polybius/3*.html.

28 first man in Rome: Plutarch, *Life of Caesar* 11.3–4.

28 "The Republic is not the question at issue": Cicero, *Letters to Atticus* 10.7.1.

29 "reputation and rank": Caesar, *Civil War* 1.7.

29 "the rank of the republic": Caesar, *Civil War* 1.9.

29 "a benefit granted to me [Caesar]": Caesar, *Civil War* 1.9.

29 "He [Caesar] says he is doing everything": Cicero, *Letters to Atticus* 7.11.1.

31 "The enemy would have won": Plutarch, *Life of Caesar* 39.8.

35 "had been trained in actual warfare constantly": Polybius, *Histories* 3.89.5–6, Loeb translation, http://penelope.uchicago.edu/Thayer/E/Roman/Texts/Polybius/3*.html.

37 "honor and empire": Livy, *History of Rome* 22.58.3.

37 "wholly under the influence": Polybius, *Histories* 3.15.9.

46 "It is not the big armies": Martin Blumenson and James Stokesbury, *Masters of the Art of Command* (Cambridge, MA: Da Capo Press, 1990), p. 146.

49 "famous for his good judgment as a general": Diodorus Siculus 17.18.2.

50 "advocated a policy": Diodorus Siculus 17.18.2.

52 shoving: Arrian, *Anabasis of Alexander* 1.15.2.

52 "horses fighting entangled with horses": Arrian, *Anabasis of Alexander* 1.15.4.

55 "For his men had not only suffered terribly": Polybius, *Histories* 3.60.3, Loeb translation, http://penelope.uchicago.edu/Thayer/E/Roman/Texts/Polybius/3*.html.

59 "more essential to a general than the knowledge of his opponent's principles": Polybius, *Histories* 3.81.1, Loeb translation, http://penelope.uchicago.edu/Thayer/E/Roman/Texts/Polybius/3*.html.

59 the weak spots: Polybius, *Histories* 3.81.3.

60 "he had come above all": Polybius, *Histories* 3.77.3–7, trans. Penguin.

60 "He thought surprise": Plutarch, *Life of Caesar* 32.2.

60 "used to depend on the surprise": Appian, *Civil Wars* 2.34 [136], trans. Matthew Dillon and Lynda Garland, *Ancient Rome from the Early Republic to the Assassination of Julius Caesar* (New York: Routledge, 2005), p. 643.

63 "This he did": Caesar, *Civil War* 1.23.

63 "Let this be": (Caesar in [Cicero] *Letters to Atticus* 9.7c (ca. 5 March 49).

64 "insidious clemency": Cicero, *Letters to Atticus*, 8.16.

65 "Men are apt to think": Thucydides, 7.69.2.

3: RESISTANCE

69 "do not envision the consequences": Polybius, *Histories* 11.2.4–6.

69 "The challenge of education": cited in Craig Mullaney, *The Unforgiving Minute: A Soldier's Education* (New York: Penguin, 2009), p. 365.

69 Aristotle had taught him: Aristotle, *Politics* 4.1296a.

72 "soft underbelly": Richard M. Langworth, *The Definitive Wit of Winston Churchill* (New York: Public Affairs, 2009), p. 109.

78 The roar echoed: Curtius 3.10.1–2; Diodorus Siculus 17.33.4.

81 "in three battles": Curtius 4.1.35.

82 "I would accept": Plutarch, *Life of Alexander* 29.8.

85 land made for ambushes: Livy, *History of Rome* 22.4.1.

86 The sources hint at a debate in the Carthaginian high command: Dexter Hoyos, "Maharbal's Bon Mot: Authenticity and Survival," *Classical Quarterly* n.s. 50.2 (2000): 610–14.

87 "that his army could not drive or carry it all off": Polybius, *Histories* 3.86.10, Loeb translation, http://penelope.uchicago.edu/Thayer/E/Roman/Texts/Polybius/3*.html.

87 "in a country abounding in all kinds of produce": Polybius, *Histories* 3.87.1, Loeb translation, http://penelope.uchicago.edu/Thayer/E/Roman/Texts/Polybius/3*.html.

87 "inexhaustible supplies of provisions and men": Polybius, *Histories* 3.89.9. Loeb translation, http://penelope.uchicago.edu/Thayer/E/Roman/Texts/Polybius/3*.html.

88 "to send aid to their allies" Plutarch, *Fabius* 2.5., Loeb translation, (vol. 3, 1916), http://penelope.uchicago.edu/Thayer/E/Roman/Texts/Plutarch/Lives/Fabius_Maximus*.html.

88 "He therefore made up his mind": Plutarch, *Fabius* 5.3, Loeb translation, (vol. 3, 1916), http://penelope.uchicago.edu/Thayer/E/Roman/Texts/Plutarch/Lives/Fabius_Maximus*.html.

88 "Hannibal's manservant": literally, "Hannibal's *paedagogus*," a Greek slave who served as a young Roman noble's attendant.

89 "art of Punic fraud": Florus, *Epitome* 1.22.13.

93 best stratagems: Plutarch, *Life of Pompey* 63.1.

93 "wars are not won by evacuations": Winston Churchill, Speech to the House of Commons, June 4, 1940, http://www.churchill-society-london.org.uk/Dunkirk.html.

94 going against an army without a leader: Suetonius, *Julius Caesar* 34.2.

97 "not through lenience": Suetonius, *Julius Caesar* 69.

98 *"et devotissimi . . . et fortissimi"*: Suetonius, *Julius Caesar* 68.1.

98 "the most potent thing in war is the unexpected": Appian, *Civil Wars* 53.

99 "There can be no peace for us until Caesar's head is brought in": Caesar, *Civil War* 3.19.

100 "Caesar's good fortune": Appian, *Civil Wars* 2.57.

101 animals and not men: Appian, *Civil Wars* 2.61.

101 wrote to his famous father-in-law: Cicero, *Letters to Friends* 9.9.2–3.

102 "fortune . . . produces great changes": Caesar, *Civil War* 3.68.

102 *"Imperator!"*: Caesar, *Civil War* 3.71.

103 "Today the enemy would have won": Plutarch, *Caesar* 39; cf. Appian, *Civil Wars* 2.62. Translated by Rex Warner: Plutarch, *Fall of the Roman Republic*, rev. edn. Trans. Rex

270

Notes

Warner, rev. Robin Seager, preface by Christopher Pelling, London: Penguin Books, 2005, p. 294.

103 In private: Appian, *Civil Wars* 2.64.

103 In public: Caesar, *Civil War* 3.73.

103 faith in its father—himself: Dio Cassius, *Roman History* 41.27.

104 "War is a harsh teacher": Thucydides 3.82.2.

4: CLASH

117 "For a short time the battle became a hand-to-hand fight": Arrian, *Anabasis of Alexander* 3.14.3.

117 "the air . . . with the groans of the fallen": Diodorus Siculus 17.60.4.

118 There was none of the usual spear throwing: Arrian, *Anabasis of Alexander* 3.15.2.

125 "a strange and terrifying appearance": Polybius, *Histories* 3.114.

126 might as well have handed themselves over to his men in chains: Livy, *History of Rome* 22.49.3.

128 "slaughter rather than battle": Livy, *History of Rome* 22.48.6.

128 so many Roman dead: the most credible ancient casualty figures are found in Livy, *History of Rome* 22.49.13–18, but they don't quite jibe with the total number of Roman soldiers in the usually reliable Polybius, *Histories* 3.113.

132 Caesar's drunken and bloated men: Appian, *Civil Wars* 2.64.

132 "disciplined and desperate men": Appian, *Civil Wars* 2.64, trans. Loeb, http://www .perseus.tufts.edu/hopper/text?doc=Perseus%3Atext%3A1999.01.0232%3Abook%3D 2%3Achapter%3D10%3Asection%3D66.

132 "the most prudent calculation": Appian, *Civil Wars* 2.64, trans. Loeb, http://www .perseus.tufts.edu/hopper/text?doc=Perseus%3Atext%3A1999.01.0232%3Abook%3D2 %3Achapter%3D10%3Asection%3D66.

133 "more reserved": Tacitus, *Histories* 2.38.

133 At last, Pompey gave in: Caesar, *Civil War* 3.86; Appian, *Civil Wars* 2.10.67; Plutarch, *Life of Pompey* 67.4–5; Polyaenus, *Stratagems of War* 8.23.14.

133 like a ship's captain surrendering the rudder: Lucan, *Pharsalia*, 7.126–128.

133 they had to keep moving: Caesar, *Civil War* 3.85.

134 "Hope": Thucydides 5.102.

134 The battle probably took place: the exact location of the battle is uncertain. Here, I follow the arguments of C.B.R. Pelling, "Pharsalus," *Historia* 22 (1973), 249–59, and John D. Morgan, "Palaepharsalus—the Battle and the Town," *American Journal of Archaeology* 87 (1983), 23–54.

135 One source reports that Caesar told his soldiers: Plutarch, *Life of Pompey* 68.4.

135 "Let us be ready in our hearts": Caesar, *Civil War* 3.85.

135 "the crisis of the chiefs": Lucan, *Pharsalia* 7.242–43.

138 included the weight of groans: Lucan, *Pharsalia* 7.571–73.

138 "its wings deployed across the entire plain": Lucan, *Pharsalia* 7.506.

138 Archers and slingers: Cassius Dio 41.60.1–2.

138 melting in the heat: Lucan, *Pharsalia* 7.511–13.

138 "No circumstance contributed more": Frontinus, *Stratagems* 2.22.

139 "They wanted this": Asinius Pollio as cited by Suetonius, *Julius Caesar* 30.4.

140 The results of Pharsalus: Caesar, *Civil War* 3.99; Appian, *Civil Wars* 2.82, who cites the
     now lost history of Asinius Pollio, an eyewitness who fought at Pharsalus for Caesar.

5: CLOSING THE NET

151 he didn't want Darius's corpse: Justin 3.3.

152 a speech that touched on three themes: Plutarch, *Life of Alexander* 47.1–3, claims to be
     paraphrasing a letter to Antipater in which Alexander describes what he actually said.

152 he grossly underestimated the distance: Quintus Curtius 6.3.16.

164 Mago: Livy, *History of Rome* 28.46.7, 14; 29.4–5; 30.18–20. Mago had dreamed of
     glory, but today his only share of immortality may come via an egg sauce. The city
     of Mahón on Minorca claims to be the place where mayonnaise began—and Mahon
     also prides itself on being named after Mago. But the city's etymology is debated, and
     other places too insist that they invented mayonnaise.

164 "of that sort worn only by Knights, and only by the first among them": Livy, *History of
     Rome* 23.12.2.

168 "Now I understand the fate of Carthage!": Livy, *History of Rome* 27.51.12.

168 "for themselves and their native soil": Polybius, *Histories* 3.118.5.

169 "Truly the gods have not given": Livy, *History of Rome* 22.51.4.

169 "It is widely believed that the day's delay": Livy, *History of Rome* 22.51.4.

169 all the way back to men who lived through the Second Punic War: Michael P. Fronda,
     Between Rome and Carthage: Southern Italy during the Second Punic War (Cambridge,
     England: Cambridge University Press, 2010), p. 42, n. 106, citing Hans Beck and
     U. Walter, eds. *Die frühen römischen Historiker*, vol. 1. (Darmstadt, Germany: Wissen-
     schaftliche Buchgesellschaft, 2001), 4 F13–14.

172 "neither the Carthaginians nor their enemies": Livy, *History of Rome* 21.12.1.

176 Sulla, he said, did not know his political ABC's: Suetonius, *Julius Caesar* 77.

177 *"Fortis fortuna adiuvat"*: Terence, *Phormio* 203.

178 "I cannot but mourn his fate,": Cicero, *Letters to Atticus* 11.6.5.

179 "I demanded, I borrowed": Cassius Dio, *Roman History* 42.49–50.

180 simple arithmetic: Cassius Dio, *Roman History* 42.49.

180 "citizens": Suetonius, *Julius Caesar* 70; Plutarch, *Life of Caesar* 51.2; Appian, *Civil Wars*
     2.13.92–94; Cassius Dio, *Roman History* 52–54.

180 He is said to have rid himself of the ringleaders: Cassius Dio, *Roman History* 42.55.2.

182 "guilt-stained": *The African War* 44.

182 "Should I take a stand in arms": *The African War* 45.

182 "I don't call you commander-in-chief": *The African War* 45.

184 He considered Caesar a tyrant: Plutarch, *Cato the Younger* 72.2, may have invented Cato's speech, but it rings true.

184 "O Cato, I begrudge you": Plutarch, *Cato the Younger* 72.2.

185 "Each for his cause can vouch a judge supreme": Lucan, *Pharsalia* 1.127–28, translated by Sir Edward Ridley. *Pharsalia. M. Annaeus Lucanus.* (London: Longmans, Green, and Co., 1905), http://www.perseus.tufts.edu/hopper/text?doc=Perseus%3Atext%3A 1999.02.0134%3Abook%3D1%3Acard%3D33.

187 "Aren't you ashamed to hand me over to these little boys?": Plutarch, *Life of Caesar* 56.2.

6: KNOWING WHEN TO STOP

194 "various blessings and especially": Arrian, *Anabasis* 7.11.8.9, modified from the translation by P. A. Brunt, *Arrian, Anabasis of Alexander, Books V–VII* (Cambridge, MA: Harvard University Press), 1983, p. 241.

196 "Those who can win a war well can rarely make a good peace": Winston Churchill, *My Early Life: A Roving Commission* (New York: Charles Scribner's Sons, 1987), p. 331.

202 "Alexander was always insatiable": Aristoboulos as cited in Arrian, *Anabasis of Alexander* 7.19.6, and Strabo, *Geography* 16.1.11, cf. Arrian *Indica* 9.11.

204 "The great horn is broken": Book of Daniel 8:8.

205 "The music must always play": W. H. Auden, "September 1, 1939."

205 "the unmentionable odor of death": W. H. Auden, "September 1, 1939."

205 "to the strongest": Arrian, *Anabasis* 7.26.3, Diodorus Siculus 17.117.4, cf. 18.1.4; Quintus Curtius 10.5.5, Justin 12.15.8.

205 "great funeral games": Diodorus Siculus 17.117.4.

212 "not small hopes but great hopes": Polybius, *Histories* 15.2.3.

213 "look after other matters": Polybius, *Histories* 15.5.2.

213 "amazed" . . . "felt an urge": Polybius, *Histories* 15.5.8.

213 "struck by the enemy's confidence": Livy, *History of Rome* 30.29.4.

213 "seek peace while his army was intact": Livy, *History of Rome* 30.29.5.

218 Polybius says that Hannibal was admirable at Zama: Polybius, *Histories* 15.15.3.

221 rather be the first man there: Plutarch, *Life of Caesar* 11.3–4.

221 "the tranquility of Italy": Caesar, *Civil War* 3.57.

222 "The Republic," he once said, "is nothing": Suetonius, *Julius Caesar* 77.1.

225 "You too, my son?": Suetonius, *Julius Caesar* 82.2.

225 fifty pitched battles in which he claimed to have killed 1,192,000 people: Pliny the Elder, *Natural History* 7.91–92.

227 Caesar had no right to lord it over people: Plutarch, *Life of Cato the Younger* 66.2.

CONCLUSION

235 "The brave have the whole earth for their sepulcher": Thucydides, *The Peloponnesian War* 2.43.3.

237 one of his subordinates trembled: the reference is to Cassander, Plutarch, *Life of Alexander* 74.6.

241 Hannibal's "leadership, bravery, and ability in the field:" Polybius, *Histories* 11.19, the source of all citations in this paragraph. All translations in this paragraph are modified versions of W. R. Paton, Loeb Classical Library translation, http://penelope.uchicago.edu/Thayer/E/Roman/Texts/Cassius_Dio/42*.html.

244 Scipio came to Ephesus: Livy, *History of Rome* 35.14.5–11; Plutarch, *Life of Flaminius* 21.3.

244 "Punic wit": Livy, *History of Rome* 35.14.11.

244 "said that he had seen many doddering old men": Cicero, *On the Orator* 2.75.

INDEX

More from historian
BARRY STRAUSS

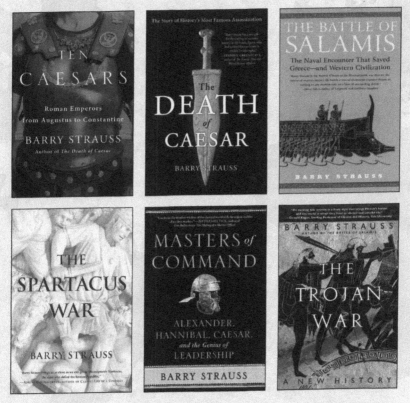

Pick up or download your copies today!

BarryStrauss.com